Reinventing Brantford

Reinventing Brantford
A UNIVERSITY COMES DOWNTOWN

| Leo Groarke |

Foreword by William Humber

NATURAL HERITAGE BOOKS
A MEMBER OF THE DUNDURN GROUP
TORONTO

Published by Natural Heritage Books, A Member of The Dundurn Group

Library and Archives Canada Cataloguing in Publication

Groarke, Leo
        Reinventing Brantford : a university comes downtown / Leo Groarke.

Includes bibliographical references and index.
ISBN 978-1-55488-459-9

        1. Urban renewal--Ontario--Brantford--History. 2. Central business districts--Ontario--Brantford--History. 3. Wilfrid Laurier University--History. 4. Central business districts--Conservation and restoration-- Ontario--Brantford. 5. Brantford (Ont.)--History. I. Title.

FC3099.B743G76 2009   971.3'47   C2009-902998-7

1   2   3   4   5   13   12   11   10   09

Front Cover: (Top) The Brantford Carnegie Library, 1906. *Courtesy of the Brant Museum and Archives, cat. no. 200727032.* (Bottom) The Brantford Carnegie Library, the first building of the Brantford campus of Laurier University, 2006. *Photo by Darragh Christie. Courtesy of the author.*
Back Cover (Top) The Brantford Bicycle Club, 1897. *Courtesy of Brant Museum and Archives, cat. no.ch 937101.* (Bottom) The former Wilkes House. *Courtesy of JG Group of Companies.*

Project Editor: Jane Gibson
Text design by Erin Mallory
Copyedited by Allison Hirst
Printed and bound in Canada by Transcontinental

Care has been taken to trace the ownership of copyright material used in this book. The author and the publisher welcome any information enabling them to rectify any references or credits in subsequent editions.
J. Kirk Howard, President

We acknowledge the support of the Canada Council for the Arts and the Ontario Arts Council for our publishing program. We also acknowledge the financial support of the Government of Canada through the Book Publishing Industry Development Program and The Association for the Export of Canadian Books and the Government of Canada through the Ontario Book Publishers Tax Credit Program and the Ontario Media Development Corporation.

Dundurn Press
3 Church Street, Suite 500
Toronto, Ontario, Canada
M5E 1M2

Gazelle Book Services Limited
White Cross Mills
High Town, Lancaster,
England
LA1 4XS

Dundurn Press
2250 Military Road
Tonawanda, NY
U.S.A. 14150

This book is dedicated to the people of Brantford and Brant County — past, present, and future. I want, in particular, to acknowledge those whose commitment to Brantford's downtown did not waver in the midst of its most troubled times. It is easy to believe in something in the good times; it takes faith and courage to remain committed in the bad.

CONTENTS

| ACKNOWLEDGEMENTS |

In assembling the story of Laurier Brantford and the rebirth of downtown Brantford, I have benefited from the thoughts of many colleagues. While I am reluctant to single out a few individuals, I would like to acknowledge a special indebtedness to a handful of people who have, over an extended period, discussed the history of the Brantford campus with me: in particular, Gary Warrick, Tracy Arabski, David Prang, Holly Cox, and Sherri Bocchini. Outside the university, Wayne Hunter, Vyrt Sisson, John Starkey, Colleen Miller, Chris Friel, Mike Hancock, Mary Stedman, and others welcomed discussions of Brantford's past, present, and future. Cindy McDonald-Krueger and the Brant Museum and Archives were always willing to help with research, and my good friends Arlene Mahood and Lynn Osborne-Way provided me with extensive comments on the finished manuscript. Lynn's knowledge of local history, architecture, and Brant County, and her advice on how to tell a story were invaluable guides in finishing the present project. Bill Humber immediately understood the reasons why I thought it important to tell the story of the rebirth of downtown Brantford.

I am indebted to Barry Penhale and Jane Gibson for their interest in this book and their help in preparing it for publication. Their enormous contribution to the preservation of local history in Canada is something I am pleased to be a part of. Last but not least, I am grateful to Wilfrid Laurier University and the Brant Museum and Archives for permission to use many of the photos included in this book, and to Kevin Klein for helping me to assemble them.

| FOREWORD |

by William Humber, Seneca College

We all cherish well-loved places, be they scenic vistas, an apple orchard on the edge of town, a character-filled old building, or a favourite fishing hole. Then one day they're gone and we sigh and reflect that this must be the price paid for that dreaded, non-contestable phenomenon called progress. It is amazing how accepting we are of such actions that seem so devastating.

One person who noticed and decided to write about it was Storm Cunningham, one of the world's leading advocates of restoration. He is an avid scuba diver, but realized that his visits to some of the pristine waters of the world were too often a hollow reminder of how things had only got worse with time, including decaying coral reefs, loss of diverse fisheries, and the disappearance of quaint local lifestyles associated with such places. Then about ten years ago he noticed a startling change, at least in some places. Plans and actions were actually contributing to an improved world.

He originally set out to write a book on how that grand but illusive theme of sustainability must be the reason for this more hopeful world. But in investigating its practice he made a stunning discovery. Too often sustainability proved to be no more than a stop-gap measure by which preserving a little piece of property here, a green building there, or temporarily protecting a tiny living thing in the path of a freeway, were simply small thumbs in the dyke of irreversible damage — smokescreens for greater devastation rationalized by the "greening" of some built or natural feature, but achieved by depleting or eliminating another.

He recognized that an environmentally acclaimed new community built on a former wetland, or an accredited green building on a rural, agricultural site reachable by any reasonable measure only by car, were problematic and ultimately unacceptable responses to the loss of biodiversity, climate change, and the degradation of once-loved places. As a result, Storm's first book, *The Restoration Economy*, told a far different story than he originally intended. It began with a significant history lesson. "For some five thousand years," he wrote, "much of humankind, especially Western civilization in the past five centuries, has been in a pioneer mode of development that sustains economic growth by developing raw land and extracting virgin resources. New lands and virgin resources, however, are rapidly becoming myths from a bygone era."[1]

He then described the second phase of the three-stage growth cycle as being that of maintenance and conservation, in which humans tackle challenges of breakdown in their built and natural environments through increasingly patchwork strategies — for instance, preserving small wooded areas disconnected from the necessary routes living things need to move from one place to another, or refurbishing older buildings without attention to the economic catastrophe surrounding them.

Today he argues we are confronting three crises as a result of this development style. These include contamination, in which a majority of soil around the world is degraded and oceans are increasingly acidified and filled with toxic waste such as carelessly disposed-of pharmaceuticals and plastic detritus; corrosion, in which much we currently build is virtually garbage the first day it is occupied; and constraint, in which we suddenly find that our magical gift for generating new solutions for resource depletion is running up against a world challenged by peak oil, the loss of biodiversity, and potential food shortages.

We are left with little choice but to enter into the third stage of development, namely restoration. It is a comprehensive and integrated approach to restoring the integrity and interconnectedness of built and natural environments. We do so despite living in a world still engaged in pioneer modes of development. In the process we continue to deplete limited resources, overwhelm ecosystems, destroy downtowns, and empty countryside locations that have provided comfort to their inhabitants but less apparent value to their despoilers.

Dams are still being built, landscapes flooded and tar sands mined, though in the case of the latter, the cost reflected in cleaner energy used for this purpose and fresh water expanded might, if ecosystem services were properly calculated, challenge the economic merit of such a project. So while there has been a great human shift from nomadic to settled existence, we still live as if we are nomads, damaging the places we live and moving on. Except that now there is nowhere to move. The carbon-based economy, which allows us to off-shore cheaper production to China, haunts all of us.

Restoration on the other hand is premised on bringing places back to life, creating new value and employment opportunities, and enticing investment, which asks only what way the market is going and spends its dollars accordingly. Its magic lies in the way it includes market-based integration with a deliberate uplift of the soul. A philosopher such as Leo Groarke might call this a "metaphysics of restoration." It is predicated on leaving places better than we found them, an approach taking us far beyond new development models equating economic growth with conquering new lands and extracting virgin resources. Restorative development is an economically resilient model that understands, for instance, that the eventual cleanup of a gold mine or nuclear facility should include the site's necessary restoration to have a true picture not only of the project's complete cost but also its opportunity.

It reflects a shift from artificial and simple static mechanical models to complex dynamic living ones. It recognizes the messiness of reality and the challenge of finding tools to begin modelling it. It celebrates an ability to differentiate, select, and amplify multiple options.

It acknowledges that what briefly benefits a few now may poison everyone's children for a long time. All restorable human-made assets were, of course, originally created by what Cunningham calls "dewealth" activities, which failed to recognize the value of perpetual ecosystem services, such as air, water, and wildlife. Nor did they account for nature's regenerative powers characterized by its ability to break down harmful compounds and sequester harmful elements. For most of human history this approach was manageable and even acceptable though we now know that civilizations have disappeared because of their failure to appreciate their resource limitations.

In our advanced western societies this harmful decoupling of the economy from its resources dates back to Adam Smith. Neoclassical economists following in Smith's path have argued that as a resource becomes scarce its price will increase, providing incentives to develop substitutes. But when we depend on non-market-based ecosystem services, which have no price (such as climate, clean water, and waste absorption) and these become increasingly scarce, there has been no market incentive to produce or restore them — until now, that is.

Increasingly, our success stories will have to combine economic and environmental initiatives in community revitalization such as infrastructure improvements, a hierarchy of energy and water demand and supply side strategies, and neighbourhood revitalization for greater mixed use, heritage re-use, and mobility options; along with natural resources restoration, such as reclaiming waterfronts, reintroducing riverbeds, or upgrading groundwater sources. These not only allow for maximum utility of limited resources but, by the integrating multiple elements of the built and natural environment, enhance financial advantage for a long-term return on initial investment.

Ultimately, such an approach could provide Ontario with leading edge expertise in successfully addressing issues of water management and community decline within the cross-border Great Lakes Region. It also has global application by its potential to create a knowledge base of professionals who demonstrate that Ontario is a place for leadership in revitalization, akin to that of Silicon Valley for the information technology industry.

This compelling restoration story involving the City of Brantford and Laurier Brantford makes explicit what is already being practised in so many places, but it is only now entering the broader public conversation. Until now, environmentalism, greening, and sustainability have been the common reference points for this discussion, but each of these has in its own way become part of the silo thinking that reduces their use to that of special interests and "nice to haves." They have been critiqued as being essential to most people's lives only when they have reached a certain degree of personal comfort. Environmentalism has become, and perhaps always was, a lifestyle movement within advanced western industrial countries, with little relevance to depressed parts of the world.

Restoration, and its complement of *re* words including *re*vitalization, *re*generation, *re*newal, and *re*development, on the other hand, link, indeed embed, environmental imperatives within an economic development context, and therefore more robustly recognize the real potential for a more mature understanding of the relationship between what have been seen as contradictory ideas — improving the environmental character of the world while making money.

Restoration, Cunningham says, is the "sweet spot" of sustainability where we can actually measure the enhancement of our built and natural resources, rather than the depletion of one in service of another. The challenge is moving this insight from the level of storytelling to that of real, on the ground proposals for improvement consistent with revitalization. Increasingly jurisdictions from municipalities to regions and national governments are beginning to understand the need for resiliency in their public policies, particularly as the reality of climate change, global economic competition, and loss of local biodiversity impinge daily on their former "business as usual" responses. Ontario's Places to Grow strategy, based on maintaining and enhancing the character of its rural and countryside locations for the purposes of agriculture, watershed protection, and scenic amenity, is aligned with the goal of intensifying growth and population in existing urban areas.

A restorative development strategy clearly benefits both of these goals. On the one hand it supports measures for agricultural transformation to higher-end commodities that are healthier, more value-laden, and, in the bargain, taste better and can be delivered locally, while responding to climate change through reforestation of damaged lands. Such a strategy supports watershed enhancement through restorative measures that improve the quality and access to drinking water while revitalizing fisheries and ultimately the health and long-term sustainability of the Great Lakes. It maintains and enhances the scenic, and with it the tourist potential inherent in features such as the Oak Ridges Moraine and the Niagara Escarpment.

From an urban perspective the value of restoration is even more pronounced. Yet many of our urban places are dispiriting in quality either because of their low density, single use, automobile-dependent, disconnected street character, or because those in inner cities and their surrounding post-war suburbs have experienced several generations of out migration, becoming in the process places of last resort either for long-time citizens at the bottom of the economic scale or new immigrants looking for a toehold in the Canadian economy. The revitalization challenge for the latter places has been recognized by agencies as diverse as the United Way and the Canadian Urban Institute. They have supported or engaged in a more deliberate policy and practice of neighbourhood-based intervention in everything from community support resources such as jobs and shopping places, to transit and place-making improvements such as heritage recognition. The commonly used term of regeneration as practised in the United Kingdom provides a model for such activity.

Just as problematic, however, are the single-use, low-density, car-dependent places generally at some remove from the places people work, play, and shop. This broader realm of interaction has become the existential terrain of people's lives. The mortgage fiasco in the United States, the often short-term life expectancy of contemporary constructed projects, and the galloping cost of fuel and its likely peak oil character are creating a perfect storm of almost invisible catastrophe for such places within what is acknowledged to be the broader "megapolitan" modern city reality (Toronto, for instance, has effectively become an area defined at minimum by Orillia in the north, Peterborough and Belleville in the East,

Waterloo in the West, Brantford in the southwest, and St. Catharines around the lake). Revitalization of such places has become an urgent public priority.

Cunningham's recipe, spelled out in greater detail in his latest book *reWealth*[2] indicates that a restorative strategy must account for the integration of four elements of the built environment — heritage, infrastructure, brownfields, and places harmed by catastrophe, along with four elements of the natural — fisheries, agriculture, ecosystems and watersheds, and finally with the socio-economic elements of schooling, services such as public safety, culture, and commerce. Their successful integration works best within a non-partisan renewal coalition standing outside normal electoral cycles, and it should be managed by creative partnerships between public and private interests.

Above all, restoration requires hard examples that can inspire and provide a foundation for manufacturing new opportunities. The Brantford experiment is one of the best in southern Ontario. Its frustrations included a lack of provincial support, changing local administrations, and hard choices faced by university decision-makers conscious of their primary mission to deliver education. Town heritage advocates have had to recognize that preservation might not always be feasible but the values of past models such as streetscape integration, human scale models, and architectural detailing could be replicated in the new with careful planning. Wilfrid Laurier University's triumphant visionary approach in restoring the heritage built environment of Brantford, and in so doing revitalizing a downtown that a former mayor had once called the worst in Canada, are exemplary.

New investment has followed Wilfrid Laurier into the downtown, the vibrant presence of students has rejuvenated a once sad place, and a wider audience of citizens and public authorities have been instilled with a sense that good things can happen with the right vision. These benefits have followed the University's bold commitment to what Leo Groarke calls "a new kind of economy." It is one no longer dependent on sprawl and short-term retail big-box models either outside of the old town or in its downtown.

Brantford has become a poster child for the magic of restorative development.

William Humber

Leader of Seneca College's outreach in urban sustainability and regional renewal
Toronto, Canada.

| INTRODUCTION |

On June 7, 2008, the City of Brantford celebrated the death of its downtown. The funeral featured brightly coloured carriages, bicycles, and costumes. It proceeded down Colborne South, the city's original main street, and came to a stop at a new public square that was christened Harmony Square. In the funeral that followed, representatives of the city, a new university campus, the arts community, and downtown churches blessed, eulogized, and toasted the old downtown. In a daring move the health authorities had not approved, the toast featured untreated water taken from the Grand River two blocks away. A fifteen-piece New Orleans jazz band provided music for the event.

The funeral celebrated the death, but also the rebirth, of downtown Brantford. It was organized and orchestrated by the Brantford Arts Block, a not-for-profit arts organization dedicated to the role of culture in the new downtown. Its executive director, Josh Bean, one of the founders of a nationally recognized music venue called The Ford Plant, served as chair of the city's Downtown Business Improvement Association. "If celebrating a rebirth," he told the press, "then there should also be a funeral."[1]

To anyone who lived in Brantford, the funeral symbolized the end of a downtown mired at the bottom of a downward spiral. Over the course of thirty years, an ailing economy, the flight of residents to the suburbs, and failed attempts at urban renewal had reduced a once-grand city centre to a bleak caricature of its former self. In an article in the *Toronto Star*, Brantford's mayor, Chris Friel, described the downtown core as "the worst downtown in Canada." No one liked the article but no one disagreed. At a time when the downtown included block after block of squalid boarded-up buildings, it was difficult to argue with this description. Scattered among them one could find once-grand edifices that had fallen on hard times. Like the ruins of some former civilization, their forlorn demeanor gave locals little to look forward to and even less to celebrate.

A decade is a short span in the life of a city. Ten years might seem of little consequence to a city that owes its existence to the American Revolution but it only took a decade for Brantford's collapsed downtown to take the steps that allowed the city to celebrate its death and its rebirth. The crux of the story was a new presence in an old city. The new arrival was a campus of Wilfrid Laurier University. This

Artists set to bury bad old downtown

A "funeral" to celebrate the demise of Brantford's old downtown was celebrated in June 2008. Here Tim Southern paints the coffin for the old downtown above a headline from The Expositor. *Photo by Heather King.*

book recounts how, in the face of many odds, the campus developed, and what impact this had on the city that embraced it. Building on a rich heritage, the city and the university found a way to negotiate the adverse elements of a derelict city core, the collapse of Brantford's once-booming industrial economy, limited public funding, political debate, skepticism, and apathy. In doing so, they midwifed the new campus into being and created the tonic that Brantford needed to produce a more confident, reinvigorated downtown.

The main events in the founding of Laurier Brantford, and the re-emergence of the downtown the campus embraced, incorporate two stories within one. The first tells of the founding of a new university campus and the way in which it managed, after a shaky and uncertain start, to find a way to thrive, prosper, and sustain itself. The second tells of the rise and fall of downtown Brantford and the way in which an experiment in higher education is bringing a city back to life. The one story feeds the other.

The protagonists and antagonists in this history are many and varied. They include a struggling city, a once proud but then derelict heritage downtown, and a small university with entrepreneurial administrators. Both the university and the city could already claim impressive histories, a myriad of leaders and would-be leaders, and critics and supporters. Mayors, city councillors, heritage advocates, journalists, community leaders, supporters and skeptics, professors, deans, students, vice-presidents, and presidents all played a decisive role in the developments, which were characterized by many false starts, outspoken differences of opinion that were

manifest in politics in the city and the university, and frequent conflict and debate. However it may appear in hindsight, the path forward was never simple or straightforward.

The Brantford story is a new strand in the histories of both Brantford and Laurier. But it has a broader significance. For the changes in downtown Brantford have taken place at a time when countless North American downtowns — from Savannah to Vancouver, from Calgary to Dayton — are struggling with the same issues. As Pierre Filion, Heidi Hoernig, Trudi Bunting, and Gary Sands have written in a study of small cities, "Everywhere in North America, suburbanization has caused a relative and, in many cases, absolute decline of downtown areas. The effect on the downtowns of small metropolitan regions (small-metro downtowns) has been particularly severe …"[2] Across North America, downtowns that were historically important centres of civic and public life have faltered, declined, and been deserted during the second half of the twentieth century. The families that resided downtown have moved to suburbia, retail businesses have moved to suburban shopping malls, and industries and warehouses have been closed or moved to major highways on the edge of town (or, further afield, to countries like Mexico and China).

What happened in Brantford is a case study that illustrates these trends. As a city, it emerged as an internationally important centre of manufacturing at the end of the nineteenth century, boasting a proud history of invention and innovation. Most famously, that history incorporated Alexander Graham Bell's invention of the telephone. At the centre of "The Telephone City" was a bustling downtown that featured mercantile businesses, factories, banks, parks, theatres, courts, social clubs and fraternal societies, monuments, public buildings, and churches. Brantford's wealth and significance was evident in superior examples of the best that Victorian architecture and design had to offer.

The collapse of Brantford's city centre is but one instance of the decline of downtowns across Canada and the United States, a decline that has been decried by many commentators troubled by the fate of their own downtowns. "A case in point is Tampa, whose central business district has thus far resisted every effort at revitalization. Speaking in 1992, a year after Maas Brothers, downtown Tampa's last department store, closed its doors, City Councilman Scott Paine declared, 'You will not have a great city unless you have a strong, vibrant downtown.'"[3] Other commentators have taken a different perspective, dismissing the downtown as "obsolete" — "a late-nineteenth-century creation that has no role in the late twentieth, a bad place to work, a worse place to live."[4] The latter view is evident in the lives of a perpetually increasing number of city dwellers who live their lives with little or no connection to their downtown, treating it as a place to be avoided.

The sorry state of the contemporary downtown has attracted much pious criticism. It is easy to lament streets of deserted, crumbling buildings that are home to poverty and crime. The lamenting seems all the more appropriate when one compares their desultory present to a prosperous past full of purpose and significance. But lamenting will do little to reverse the economic, political, and social trends that have produced deserted city centres. There is no easy solution for the complex problems that manifest themselves in the inner city. As many municipal governments and planners have discovered, it is especially difficult to resolve these problems in practice.

In a climate such as this, the story of Laurier in Brantford is a hopeful one. Against the odds, the city and the university are rebuilding a collapsed downtown. What they have accomplished is not a panacea for the problem with the North American downtown, but their progress has important implications for urban redevelopment and higher education. In Ontario, a series of cities have already noticed and are making "Post-Brant-Fordism" a key element of their development.

The story of Laurier Brantford has other implications for post-secondary education. The building and development of "satellite" campuses is an inherently difficult endeavour fraught with challenges and issues. Staff and students at satellite campuses often suffer from a feeling of isolation, a feeling that they are misunderstood or unappreciated, and not appropriately reflected in central budgets and priorities. In Brantford, these challenges were compounded by a decision to build a campus committed to the liberal arts at a time when they were increasingly out of favour. In the place of the general skills and knowledge they have traditionally emphasized, students, parents, and governments have increasingly preferred career-oriented programs. Within post-secondary education these trends have initiated a debate about the proper mission and goals of undergraduate education.

At Laurier Brantford the move toward career programming became a significant obstacle to the success of the campus, for it was designed to offer a different kind of education that did not fit this mould. In Brantford, the debate over the proper ends of university education were manifest in a struggle for survival, as the campus tried to find a way to attract the students needed to make the campus viable to programs that were not what they were looking for. In dealing with academic as well as urban issues, it was forced to struggle against the currents of the day.

My account of the birth of Laurier Brantford has, inevitably, been informed by my experiences in the role of dean, and then principal, of the campus. These roles put me in the middle of most of the decisions, conflicts, and events that affected the evolution of the campus. In both the city and the university I was a participant in key meetings that were sometimes characterized by tensions, arguments, and competing visions of the campus and the city. I have not tried to write a tell-all book, but have tried to present the history of Laurier in Brantford in a way that does not gloss deep divisions, obstacles, and debates sometimes evident behind the scenes. Developments were shaped and fostered by the clash of opposing views, conflicting political interests, and by forceful personalities, my own included. In hindsight, it seems obvious that the development of the campus and the redevelopment of the downtown was the right thing to do, but things were anything but clear or obvious when the key decisions were made, debated, and, in many quarters, resisted.

In presenting some of the key issues that characterized the development of the campus and the redevelopment of downtown, I have tried to present opposing points of view as sympathetically as I can. Inevitably, some may see particular events differently than I do. While I welcome any discussion this may

Courtesy of Wilfrid Laurier University.

The logo for Laurier's Brantford campus. The Latin motto under the Laurier coat of arms is Veritas omnia vinci — *"Truth Conquers All."*

engender, I believe it is more important to say that almost everyone involved in the evolution of Laurier in Brantford agrees that it has been transformative. Like the phoenix that rises from the ashes, the downtown is rising once again. The city has managed this rebirth by becoming a stirring example of how political will, perseverance, and post-secondary education can foster urban renewal and hope in a downtown that was, only a decade ago, a place of desolation and dismay.

| 1 |

BRANT'S FORD

The year 2000 marked the beginning of a new millennium. As the world waited for the Y2K problem to wreak havoc on the world's computers, others greeted the transition as the dawn of a new age. In Brantford, the end of the old millennium coincided with the arrival of a new university campus. I arrived the following year. The university's chief academic officer, Rowland Smith, had asked me to apply for the dean's position at the new campus. When I was interviewed and offered the post, my friends advised me not to go. A close colleague in Philosophy told me he was happy that the university had offered me "my own ship." Then he laughed and added, "Too bad that it's a sinking ship."

I quickly learned that pessimistic views of Brantford were a major obstacle to the success of our new campus. It was troubling to find such pessimism prevalent on the university's established campus in Waterloo, but much more troubling to find that it was an indelible part of Brantford's view of itself. Shortly after I moved to Brantford, Holly Cox, the campus's indefatigable recruitment officer, and I hosted a focus group that discussed Laurier Brantford with local high-school students. In a context in which we needed to attract applicants to sustain ourselves, we wanted to understand why local high-school students showed so little interest in a campus located close to home — so close that it could, at the very least, save their families thousands of dollars in annual expenses.

In the course of our discussion, the local students related a series of profoundly negative misconceptions. Laurier Brantford did not, we were told, award university degrees; it did not have "real" professors; it was not "really" Wilfrid Laurier University; it was not a "real university" at all. We arrived at the nub of the matter when one of the braver students took a deep breath, screwed up her face as though she had inhaled a bad smell, and blurted out, "Your campus is in Brantford, so we figured it can't be any good." Her fellow students nodded their heads in agreement.

The student's reasoning was an enthymeme — an inference based on an implicit proposition. The proposition was the general principle that whatever is in Brantford can't be any good. In the focus group it precipitated a discussion, not of Laurier's new campus and its challenges in attracting high-school students, but of Brantford itself — the students resolutely condemning the city in which they lived. It was strange to find myself, the interested newcomer, more enamoured of Brantford than its own inhabitants. Long-time residents I met in the course of my next few months were less surprised, telling me that Brantford had sunk so low that only outsiders seemed to appreciate what it could be.

The attitudes of the high-school students reflected a deep-seated pessimism that has been and is possibly *the* central theme in Brantford's recent history. As prevalent as it was, it was strangely out of step with Brantford's history, which has enjoyed more than its fair share of significant individuals and accomplishments. Even a cursory list is impressive. Among others, it must include Joseph "Thayendanegea" Brant, whose role in the American Revolution ultimately gave rise to Brantford; Charles Duncombe, one of the leaders of the Upper Canada Rebellion of 1837, who established Brantford's public library; Emily Howard Stowe, the first woman to practise medicine in Canada; Alexander Graham Bell, who invented the telephone in Brantford[1]; the celebrated poet Pauline "Tekahionwake" Johnson; Sara Jeannette Duncan, and Thomas B. Costain, two world-renowned authors;[2] James Hillier, the co-inventor of the electron microscope; Lawren Harris of the Group of Seven, one of Canada's most important painters; and Wayne Gretzky, widely known as the world's greatest hockey player.[3]

For most of its history, Brantford has enjoyed a proud prosperity. If it was anything, it was self-satisfied and sure of itself (sometimes too sure). Before there was Brantford, the first inhabitants of the region arrived some 11,000 years ago. They were ancestors of the maize-growing villagers who flourished along the flood plains of the Grand River as

Reprinted by permission of the *Brantford Expositor*.

James Hillier, the university's first honorary degree recipient in Brantford, speaking at the Brantford campus's first convocation, May 29, 2002.

early as 500 A.D. Their descendants occupied the valley in the first half of the seventeenth century, when the French named them The Neutrals — because they remained neutral in the bloody war between the Haudenosaunee (the Iroquois or the Five or Six Nations) and the Huron.

Despite, or arguably because of, their neutrality, the Neutrals were conquered and assimilated by the Haudenosaunee, who trace their history to "the Great Peacemaker," Deganawida, who founded the Confederacy of Five Nations sometime in the sixteenth century. This was an alliance among the Oneida, Cayuga, Onondaga, Seneca, and Mohawk nations that brought their warring to an end. The peace he established produced a powerful confederacy which, ironically, became a fearsome military alliance. In 1715, the Five Nations became Six when the Tuscarora were admitted to the union.

In the middle of the eighteenth century, shortly before the events that gave rise to Brantford, the Grand River Valley was the hunting ground of the Mississauga. In Brantford's very early years, the hill on which the settlement's first cabin was built (the downtown hill occupied by the Brantford Armouries) was still called Mississauga Hill, a name that recognized it as the Mississauga's favourite camping grounds.[4] But Brantford was not an offspring of the Mississauga but of the Confederacy of Six Nations. To the extent that the city can claim to have a founding father, it is Joseph Thayendanegea Brant.

In a globalizing era that has created "hybrid identities" straddling divergent cultures, Brant is a fascinating figure who was, at one and the same time, a feared Mohawk leader and warrior and a British captain and then colonel. In the latter role, he was completely at home in upper-crust British culture and society. His English leanings were nourished early by his sister, Molly Brant, who was the common-law wife of General Sir William Johnson, the British superintendent for Indian Affairs in North America. Johnson arranged Brant's admission to Eleazar Wheelock's School for Indians in Lebanon, Connecticut, an institution that became Dartmouth College. Brant attended and studied English, Greek, Latin, mathematics, and religion.

After leaving Wheelock's School, Brant served under Johnson during the French and Indian War of 1754–63, and received a silver medal in recognition of his service. He subsequently worked as a translator, interpreter, and aide for the British Indian Department. In 1775, he received a commission as captain and visited England, where he was presented at the court of King George III. All accounts suggest that he became something of a celebrity, maintaining his native dress, becoming a Freemason (receiving his apron from the King), and impressively matching wits with literati like James Boswell.[5] King George promised to support Brant and the Iroquois if they would fight on the British side in the growing American rebellion.

In its initial deliberations on the war, the Grand Council of Six Nations declared neutrality between England and America, but Brant became an impassioned spokesman for the British cause. In military actions, he led Brant's Volunteers, a band of Mohawk, Cayuga, Seneca, and Onondaga warriors, in sometimes fierce and bloody raids against American settlements. His war record included notable acts of bravery and compassion, but his name and his raids struck fear into the heart of white settlers, who referred to him as "the Monster Brant." When the Americans ultimately prevailed, they retaliated by invading Confederacy lands, burning villages, and confiscating Six Nations territory in the Mohawk Valley.[6]

Bitter about the end of the war, Brant faced a bleak future in New York. In return for the support he had provided to the British cause, he

In this 1807 portrait by William Berczy, Joseph Brant strikes a classical pose on the bank of the Grand River, pointing to the land he acquired for Six Nations. Berczy patterned the pose on statues of Roman emperors. Brant's portrait was also painted by Charles Willson Peale, who is widely known for his portraits of George Washington and Thomas Jefferson.

petitioned the English for territory in Canada. As the talks progressed, he wisely asked for land along the Grand River Valley, close to Seneca settlements in the Genesee Valley, situated between centres of commerce on the St. Lawrence River and the northwestern territories of British North America. On October 25, 1784, Sir Frederick Haldimand, the governor of Quebec, responded to the request by providing "the Mohawks and others of the Six Nations" with a land grant of 273,163 hectares — ten kilometres on each side of the Grand River, from its source to its mouth.[7] In securing this "fertile and happy retreat," the Crown paid the resident Mississauga £1,100 in return for their agreement to give up their claim to the land. At Buffalo Creek, New York, the Six Nations clan matrons decided to split the Confederacy. One contingent remained in New York State while Brant led the other to the new land he had acquired in Canada, laying the seeds for future Brantford.

Brantford is, quite literally, "Brant's Ford"— the place where Brant and his Six Nations followers forded the Grand River on the way to their new territory. The ford was connected to a thoroughfare used by Six Nations and by travellers, and sprouted a tiny settlement originally known as Grand River Ferry. In 1818, there were twelve people in the settlement, which grew quickly afterward.[8] One of Brantford's best-known early residents, James Wilkes, has recounted how Brantford was christened with its official name:

> It must have been in 1826 or 1827, when there were two or three hundred people, that the question of naming arose.... A meeting was called, when Mr. Biggar proposed that the name should be Biggar Town. Mr. Lewis, the mill owner, suggested Lewisville, and my father, who came from that city in the Old Land, stood out for Birmingham. It looked as if there might be a deadlock when someone suggested that as the place was at Brant's ford this title would prove the most suitable and the suggestion took unanimously. In the natural order of things the *s* speedily became dropped, and thus we have the "Brantford" of today.[9]

Economically, it was the possibility of trade with Six Nations and travellers crossing Brant's ford that gave rise to the settlement of Brantford. The key deed was sold to settlers after Brant's death (on April 19, 1830), but Brant himself had initiated and promoted the lease and sale of Six Nations land. The extent of the sales and the question whether he and others had a right to sell was a matter of difficult dispute then and ever since. Brant had hoped to attract farmers and establish an annuity for Six Nations, but the land that was sold "went for a mere song" and Six Nations of the Grand River Territory lost much of its original land grant. In Brantford, the extent to which it was legitimately acquired by others remains a source of great controversy and dispute.[10]

The first log cabin in Brantford was built by John Stalts in 1805. He erected it on a hill overlooking the Grand River, a few hundred yards from Brant's ford. Today, the site is occupied by a war memorial dedicated to the Brantford men who died in the Boer War. At the beginning of the nineteenth century, the location took advantage of the river, the hunting, and the trading opportunities, but the living conditions in the general area, known as Grand River Swamp, were not especially comfortable. In a reminiscence written in 1850, an observer recalled the frequently damp conditions on the low land around the river. The result was "decaying wood, stumps of trees and other vegetable matter," which "caused from the action of the sun, an exhalation of malarious vapour, which proved exceedingly injurious to the health, particularly of those unaccustomed to it."[11]

The noxious air did not prevent the growth of the fledgling settlement named Grand River Ferry. As it grew, it pushed its way down the thoroughfare on the north side of Brant's ford. The route became Colborne (pronounced Co-bornne) Street, the settlement's original main street. In the early 1820s, the village of Grand River Ferry consisted of a scattering of frame buildings, log houses, taverns, and trading posts on Colborne. In its early days, the settlement had a reputation as "a turbulent and at times lawless frontier village."[12] After an 1830 survey, settlers began to arrive in significant numbers. The result was a mix of English, Irish and Scottish immigrants, fugitive slaves from the United States, and Native Canadians and Americans that did not always mix well. The catalysts for conflict included rivalries across different ethnic groups, the easy availability of "whiskey and other spirits at trifling costs" and local gangs of ruffians. One of the latter, known as the "Swampers," "met on public and market days, and had it out with clubs and axe handles, often joining forces to club quiet citizens right and left."[13]

Despite its rough early years, Brantford began to prosper. Geographically, it grew north of the Grand River, down Colborne, spreading out on its east and west sides. Its proximity to the river was a key consideration in the nineteenth century, when the river served as a major thoroughfare for passengers and freight. In the middle of the nineteenth century, the Grand River Navigation Company built a canal to provide Brantford's downtown businesses with easy access to the river. The canal, which lay adjacent to present-day Wharf Street, was not successful because railways soon replaced the river as the major means of transport. A farmer's market, which was formally established in 1847, sold local produce and goods, and was a focus for mercantile trade and gossip. Hotels, industries, businesses, churches, law firms, local government, courts, and retail stores flourished, making downtown Brantford the true centre of the city.

One hundred years after its beginnings, Brantford was a town that was going places. Its success was rooted in the fertile agricultural land that surrounded it and in an entrepreneurial tradition that made Brantford an international centre for manufacturing. In 1877, Brantford officially became a city. In 1901, *The Industrial Recorder of Canada* ranked it "third of importance among the exporting cities of Canada."[14] By then, Brantford was a world leader in the production of farm machinery and well-known for the manufacture of many other products — sawmill equipment, paint and varnish, stoves, windmills, and bicycles. The companies that were the basis of the city's industrial success made up a veritable who's who of agricultural manufacturing in Canada: the Waterous Engine Works; the Cockshutt Plow Company; Goold,

Shapley and Muir; J.O. Wisner, Son & Co.; Verity Plow; A. Harris & Son; and ultimately Massey-Harris.

During the twentieth century, Brantford continued to flourish as a centre of agricultural manufacturing. Cockshutt Plow was bought by White Farm Equipment, which became a central component of Brantford's economy. Many of Brantford's other key companies were consolidated. Massey-Harris absorbed Wisener and Verity Plow and became Massey-Harris-Fergus, then Massey Ferguson. In the latter incarnation, it expanded to become the world's largest manufacturer of agricultural machinery, outperforming its closest competitor, the Ford Motor Company. In Brantford, Massey's positive economic

impact was augmented by the arrival of other businesses. In 1918, the Brantford mayor, Morrison Mann MacBride, met Herbert Fisk Johnson Sr., the head of S.C. Johnson and Son, Ltd., on a train

The cover of the 1897 catalogue for the Goold Bicycle Company presents an idealized image of rural living at the end of the nineteenth century. The caption under the stamp reads: BRANTFORD BICYCLES ARE THE HIGHEST STANDARD OF EXCELLENCE THE WORLD OVER. *The printing on the barn reads:* BRANTFORD. THE HOME OF GOOD MANUFACTURE. RIDE THE BRANTFORD. THEY ARE THE BEST.

Courtesy of Glen Norcliffe.

By the end of the nineteenth century, Massey-Harris was world-renowned for the quality of its products. This advertisement displays a Russian farmer harvesting his grain with Massey-Harris machinery.

going to Toronto and persuaded him to establish the Canadian headquarters of S.C. Johnson in Brantford. Brantford's economic punch was augmented by the success and growth of the Stedman Store empire, which began as a single store on Colborne and grew into one of Canada's largest retail chains by the 1960s, incorporating three hundred stores across the country.

Brantford never experienced the growth that characterized cities like Toronto and Hamilton, but it enjoyed a robust blue-collar prosperity until the 1970s. The citizens of Brantford were proud, even self-satisfied. They celebrated their participation in the World Wars; built monuments and parks and grand buildings; established a historical society dedicated to the history of Brant County; honoured Alexander Graham Bell, Pauline Johnson, and other Brantford notables; nurtured institutions like the nationally celebrated Ross McDonald School for the Blind and the Brantford Golf and Country Club; embraced social clubs, fraternal societies, and churches; promoted charities; formed unions; debated local, provincial, and broader issues with intensity; and had their significance (and the significance of Six Nations) repeatedly confirmed by royal visits.[15] In the historical core of the city — the core from which Brantford sprang — stately public buildings, an elegant Victoria Square, and a vibrant downtown reflected the city's history of success.

The unravelling of Brantford's self-assured demeanour began with the collapse of its industrial economy in the early 1980s. A history of good fortune began to reverse itself abruptly when a confluence of economic forces undermined the market for agricultural machinery. The casualties included the manufacturing operations that had traditionally defined Brantford. The starkly pessimistic attitudes that Holly Cox and I encountered when we met with Brantford high-school students in 2000 were a direct descendant of a series of developments that sent Brantford's economy — and with it, its downtown — spiralling downhill.

| 2 |

THE WORST DOWNTOWN IN CANADA

In Brantford, the fall of the downtown was rooted in the collapse of its manufacturing sector. In the early 1980s, low commodity prices and high debt charges produced an economy in which farmers could not afford to buy expensive farm equipment. The financial constraints this produced wreaked havoc on an economy built on the manufacture of agricultural machinery. One of the signs of trouble was local jokes about the rise of Brantford's own "red sea." It consisted of ever-expanding waves of Massey Ferguson's distinctive red combines, which rolled off factory production lines and, in the absence of buyers, accumulated in city parking lots.

Before Brantford's economy collapsed, the major employers in the city were White Farm and Massey Ferguson. Between them they maintained a workforce of more than seven thousand people in a city of eighty thousand. The unimaginable came to pass when their plants closed and they ceased their operations. In the wake of their demise, the companies that supplied them drastically reduced their workforce or shut their doors entirely. Mayor Mike Hancock, who was the manager of the local Human Resources and Development Canada office, remembers "desperate times" as unemployment soared to 24 per cent and he and others looked for ways to revive a defunct economy.[1] Speaking to the Canadian House of Commons in January 1994, the Brant member of Parliament, Jane Stewart, spoke of the problems that continued to persist. "Not very long ago," she said, "the city of Brant[ford] boasted having five thousand of the highest-paying manufacturing jobs in North America ... those jobs are all gone. Those companies are all closed and we ... are trying to rebuild our economy."[2]

It took years for Brantford to recover from the collapse of its economy. Downtown, the problems were compounded by the trends that have adversely affected downtowns everywhere. In the twentieth-century city, the rise of the automobile made transportation easy, making the suburbs the place to live and shopping malls the place to shop. In Brantford, the flight from the city core exacerbated the problems already evident downtown, producing derelict buildings and empty streets. In the 1980s and 1990s, the construction of Highway 403 began to revive Brantford's economy by placing it on a major thoroughfare that linked Brantford to Hamilton and Toronto to the east and Windsor and Detroit to the west. Like the Grand River during an earlier period, the highway became the major transportation corridor that spurred business, warehousing, and employment, but its benefits were localized in the city's north end, where they were manifest in outlying industrial areas, in sprawling suburban neighbourhoods, and in box-store retail outlets. Instead of helping to alleviate Brantford's downtown woes, the building of the 403 made them worse, drawing more people and businesses away from the city centre.

By the 1990s, the result of these developments was a downtown in a state of ruin. The city's once grand past was still reflected in Victoria Square, a historic square arranged in a Union Jack pattern in 1861 by John Turner, a famous Brantford architect. The celebrated statue of Joseph Thayendanegea Brant in the centre of the square was first proposed by the hereditary Six Nations chiefs in 1874, during a visit from His Royal Highness Prince Arthur. Sculpted by Percy Wood, it was cast from the bronze of thirteen cannon used at the Battle of Waterloo and the Crimean War. Brantford's population was twelve thousand when the statue was unveiled in 1886, but more than twenty thousand gathered to watch the unveiling by the Honourable J.B. Robinson, the lieutenant governor of Ontario. The ceremony included a poem written by Pauline Johnson. The poem was read by William Cockshutt, a member of one of Brantford's most distinguished families, who served as the president of Cockshutt Plow and as the local representative in the Canadian House of Parliament for fifteen years.

By the late 1990s, the Brant statue in Victoria Square was showing signs of wear. The square was still encircled by inspiring heritage architecture, but the historic pattern was abruptly interrupted by a centennial project — a 1967 city hall built on the northeast corner of the park. It is ironic that the City of Brantford chose to celebrate Canada's one hundredth birthday by demolishing two buildings from the Confederation period — a classic 1877 church that had been turned into the Brantford YWCA and a heritage house locally known as "Old One Hundred." The city hall that replaced them has been hailed as an example of an architectural style that is tellingly called brutalism.[3] It looks like a concrete spaceship that has, by some strange twist of fate, landed on a heritage Victorian square.

The brutalist aesthetics of the new city hall were disappointing, but they were the least of the downtown's worries at the end of the twentieth century. On the east perimeter of Victoria Square its problems were more sharply evident in two empty historic buildings that bordered the park — the city's former public library, a 1904 gift from the Andrew Carnegie Library Foundation, and Park Church, a Gothic revival building that dated from the 1880s. Their architectural details included a large silver dome on the library and a unique stained-glass window built above the church vestibule in 1910. The architectural merit of both buildings was still obvious, but both were vacated in the course of the downtown's decline. As businesses and people migrated outward, it proved impossible to attract new occupants. Because "location, location, location" is what matters in real estate, the asking price for the church was seventy-five thousand dollars — half the cost of a modest suburban home.

On the south side of the square, across the road from Park Church, one could see the downtown crumbling. The Wyatt, Purcell & Stillman

Courtesy of Brant Museum and Archives, cat. no.1998102_01.

Courtesy of Brant Museum and Archives, cat. no. 97922331g.

The old YWCA on the northeast perimeter of Victoria Square, circa 1900–05, was replaced with a "brutalist" city hall in 1967. Built as a centennial project, the city hall was a stark sign of Brantford's declining interest in its own heritage and history. Some embellishments and greenery were subsequently added, but they could do little to soften the radical move away from heritage architecture.

Law Office on the corner was still doing business, but it was located in a once-grand but now decaying Second Empire pre-Victorian home built by Edward L. Goold, an important Brantford industrialist involved in the manufacture of bee keepers' supplies, windmills, gasoline engines, tanks, lookout towers, concrete mixers, pumps, and bicycles. The look of the building had been undermined by age and wear, and by the addition of an out-of-place concrete block extension that lacked the character of the original home. One-half block to the west of the law office was a forlorn and dilapidated mansion that had been built by the Wilkes family, one of Brantford's founding families. In its later incarnations the building had served as an Odd Fellows Temple and the Brantford Boys' and Girls' Club. A once stately dwelling soaked in Brantford history had acquired the look of a haunted house, complete with broken and boarded windows and doors, peeling paint, sagging wrought-iron railings, unkempt lawns, stray animals, and overgrown weeds.

Brantford's 1880 post office and customs house was situated on the same block. A superb example of Second Empire architecture, the building was designed by T.S. Scott, the federal government's chief architect in the Public Works Department. While the building operated as a post office, it was a source of civic pride. When an even grander post office was built in 1913, the Post House was bought by Holstein-Friesian Association of Canada and used as their national headquarters until 1989. In this instantiation the building underscored the agricultural significance of Brant County. At some point during its occupancy, the Holstein Association extended the original post office by adding an art deco extension.

They left the building in good condition but it deteriorated quickly when they left in the late 1980s. Ten years later, it was bereft of major tenants and in a state of poor repair. By the year 2000, it and the law office beside it looked like an ailing old couple standing, or rather sagging, together on the southeast corner of the park.

South of the 1880 post office lay Dalhousie Street. (Locally, the Brantford pronunciation — Da-loo-sey — is taken as proof that someone was a Brantfordian.) A thriving farmer's market established in 1860 used to be located on the south side of Dalhousie, across from the post office. In 1985 the outdoor market was replaced with a downtown Eaton's mall which quickly failed. John Winter, a Toronto retail consultant who has studied malls, included the mall in his list of Ontario "ruins of failed downtown shopping centers."[4] Rod McQueen, author of the definitive history of Eaton's, grouped it with others that were opened in the 1980s, as part of "a wrong-headed Ontario government experiment that drew Eaton's in to help revitalize downtown urban cores that had been disemboweled by suburban malls."[5] McQueen concluded that "the idea was a miserable failure." So did Pierre Filion and Karen Hammond in their study of downtown malls.[6] In Brantford, a local twist attributed the failure of the downtown mall to a Mohawk curse cast when it extinguished the Six Nations' traditional right of access to the earlier market it replaced.

Across the street from the empty mall were a dilapidated old hotel, a row of rag-tag buildings, and a smoky bar called Rumbles. On an early trip to Brantford, one of the campus's first professors, Gary Warrick, and I looked for a place to drink a beer and ended up in Rumbles. We smiled when one of the characters in the bar came over and asked us if we were bikers, in town for a motorcycle rally. With few options available downtown, we sometimes returned to Rumbles, but quickly developed two key rules of engagement. The first was to stay away at night, when the owners hired four or five young women to dance simultaneously on the downstairs bar. The second kept us away from the second floor, where so much smoke accumulated that it was difficult to see, much less breathe.

Like Rumbles, some businesses found a way to survive downtown. Most of them were marginal, but one of them was the city's most successful redevelopment project, the Sanderson Centre. Located east of Rumbles and the empty Eaton's mall, it opened as a vaudeville house in 1919. The architect was the celebrated Thomas Lamb, whose buildings included New York's Ziegfeld Theatre and the original Madison Square Garden. He designed a theatre with acoustics and lavish looks that could compete with theatres around the world. When it ceased to operate as a vaudeville hall, it was turned into a movie house — known first as The Temple Theatre and then as The Capitol. In an attempt to save a deteriorating heritage building, the city acquired ownership in 1985. Despite some public criticism, a six-million-dollar restoration project lovingly restored the building, recreating a dazzling theatre complete with ceiling murals, wood panelling, and a magnificent chandelier. In honour of a local family known for philanthropy, the city renamed the restored building The Sanderson Centre for the Performing Arts.

As impressive as the restored Sanderson Centre was, it struggled to attract patrons when it opened in 1990. It sustained itself with an annual subsidy from the city. One of its problems was the stark contrast between its spectacular interior and the bleak city blocks that surrounded it — blocks dominated by crumbling asphalt parking lots and a seedy strip club (Moody's) located across the street. Circumstances were even bleaker one block further south, where the downtown's fall from grace culminated on Colborne, Brantford's original main street. Older Brantford residents could remember a time when Colborne was a series of bustling shops and businesses that were "the place to be" on Saturdays. But retail trade was fading already in the 1970s. In a move that was a sign of the times, the Stedman bookstore that had operated on Colborne for almost ninety years closed its doors and went out of business in 1974.

As retail shopping moved away from the downtown, Brantford's weak economy provided nothing to replace it. On Colborne, the problems were compounded by two renewal projects — the mall and a new office building — both of which failed, reinforcing the conviction that Brantford's downtown was a lost cause with no future. In 1997, the Royal Bank built an eye-catching branch at the end of Colborne, across from the Lorne Bridge spanning the Grand River, but a single building could not revive a street caught in a precipitous decline. With the exception of the bank, the half-kilometre from the bridge to Market Street — an intersection locals called "Crack Alley" — was made up of block after block of crumbling, boarded-up buildings. It was this line of more than fifty decrepit buildings that was uppermost in Mayor Chris Friel's mind when he described downtown Brantford as "the worst downtown in Canada." It was a label the city could not shake.

Courtesy of Wilfrid Laurier University.

One of Laurier's student ambassadors, Sarah Innes, in the Sanderson Centre for the Performing Arts today, after its restoration. The centre opened on October 2, 1986, with a performance of Evita. *The restoration of the theatre won a Theatre Preservation Award from The League of Historic American Theatres.*

When I went to Brantford, the urban blight on Colborne Street was a shock to see. I had walked through slums in Toronto and Montreal, but they were not as hopeless as the blocks of boarded-up buildings on Colborne. They reminded one of the worst streets one sees, not in Canada, but in cities like New York, Detroit, and San Francisco. This kind of streetscape seemed eerily out of place in a small Canadian city with a proud heritage. When the directors of the 2006 horror film *Silent Hill* searched for a bleak setting for their movie, they decided to feature a block of dilapidated Colborne buildings. In the trivia included in a listing for the film, The Internet Movie Database (IMDb) writes that "Filming in Brantford,

Some sections of Colborne Street were still in decline in 2004. Vacant and dilapidated buildings lined downtown streets when Laurier arrived in 1998.

Ontario, Canada, lasted four days. The decaying downtown strip that was used for most of the film is a section of Colbourne [sic] St. It was picked as such because not many modifications were needed as that area of the downtown was already in a state of decay … and consisted mostly of abandoned buildings that could be 'dressed' easily for filming."[7]

The desperation and disillusionment on Colborne was especially intense in a few scattered restaurants and businesses that continued to try and eke out a living in the midst of the decay that surrounded them. Most had moved to Colborne in the good times and

could not afford to leave now that the state of their street and the downtown frightened away customers and undermined their property values. The owners I spoke to were bitter. They felt trapped, with nowhere else to go. When I asked other Brantford residents what the city should do to address the problems downtown, a number of them told me that the best idea was a fire or a bulldozer "let loose on Colborne Street." As fate would have it, Colborne got both within the next few years, when arsonists set some of its empty buildings on fire, and the city bought and demolished a sequence of vacant properties.

Colborne Street demarcates the southern end of downtown Brantford. Beyond it, the land slopes down to a flat that was the location of the canal the Grand River Navigation Company[8] constructed to ferry goods to the Grand River. Many years later, the waterway is gone. The flat that has replaced it is the site of a multi-storey concrete parking lot that exits onto a major thoroughfare called Icomm Drive. It was named after the Icomm Centre, a twenty-four-million-dollar project built with funds raised from the provincial government, Bell Canada, the City of Brantford, and local fundraising. Originally planned as a telecommunications museum that would house the Bell archives, the building is located on a field beside the river. At one point both it and a provincial government centre for electronic processing on Colborne Street were parts of a two-step plan to bring a new kind of development to downtown Brantford.

Like other plans to resuscitate the downtown, this one failed. The provincial plan for an electronic processing centre in Brantford was abandoned by Bob Rae's newly elected NDP government after the 1990 provincial election. The construction of the Icomm Centre proceeded until Bell Canada decided to pull out of the project in a period of financial difficulty. The result was a centre that never opened. With the Province of Ontario giving up on the processing project and Bell giving up on the Icomm building, Brantford pessimism had another leg to stand on.

The silver lining in the dark cloud was the interest that the empty Icomm Centre generated outside Brantford. It was the building that caught President Rosehart's eye when Wilfrid Laurier University was first approached about expanding into Brantford. Rosehart had come to Laurier from Lakehead University determined to expand his new university. During his ten years in office he initiated a series of construction projects that earned him the moniker "Bob the Builder," an epithet that pleased him. When approached about the possibility of a Laurier campus in Brantford, he was interested but skeptical of the university's ability to persevere downtown. The Icomm Centre was not exactly what he wanted, but he was intrigued by the suggestion that the university could create a campus in a just-constructed, never-used building beside the river. One of its principal advantages was a location that removed it from the intimidating streets, dilapidated buildings, deserted sidewalks, bars and strip clubs that infested downtown Brantford.

| 3 |

IN ANDREW CARNEGIE'S FOOTSTEPS

In many ways, the plight of downtown Brantford in the 1990s was epitomized by the condition of the 1904 Carnegie Library on the border of Victoria Square. Like much of historic Brantford, the building tied the city to a famous historical figure. Today, Andrew Carnegie is still revered as one of America's "rags to riches" heroes. In 1848, his family emigrated from Scotland and he found a job working as a bobbin boy in a cotton factory for $1.20 a week. When he retired fifty-three years later, he was famous (and, in the world of unionized labour, infamous) as "the world's richest man."

Inspired by a "Gospel of Wealth" that dictated that the rich should help others, the retired Carnegie decided to spend his remaining years giving his wealth away, sometimes worrying that he would fail to do so.[1] His most famous gifts were the libraries he established. According to Joseph Frazier Wall, who wrote a biography of Carnegie, his Library Foundation established 2,811 libraries.[2] The great majority (1,946 of them) were given to cities across the United States, but 106 were given to Canada. In the spring of 1902, James Bertram, the secretary who oversaw requests for Carnegie library funds, received a letter postmarked Brantford.

Carnegie's interest in libraries reflected his own experience as a boy, an experience he recounted on a monument he erected in front of the Carnegie Library in Allegheny, New York. The inscription reads:

> To Colonel James Anderson, Founder of Free Libraries in Western Pennsylvania. He opened his Library to working boys and upon Saturday afternoons acted as librarian, thus dedicating not only his books but himself to the noble work. This monument is erected in grateful remembrance by Andrew Carnegie, one of the "working boys" to whom were thus opened the precious treasures of knowledge and imagination through which youth may ascend.[3]

In his autobiography, Carnegie wrote that "This is but a slight tribute and gives only a faint idea of the depth of gratitude which I feel for what he [Anderson] did for me and my companions. It was from my own early experience that I decided there was no use to which money could be applied so productive of good to boys and girls who have within them the ability and ambition to develop it, as the founding of a public library in a community which is willing to support it as a municipal institution."[4]

In Brantford, the first library was organized by Dr. Charles Duncombe in 1835, when he set up the Brantford Mechanics' Institute. Duncombe, born in Connecticut in 1792, moved to Upper Canada in 1819. Although he lived in Burford Township in Brant County, he also owned property in Brantford. An ardent Reformer, Duncombe became a member of the provincial legislature in 1830, and worked actively in support of progressive ideas in education, prisons, health, and other areas. In 1824, he established Ontario's first medical school in St. Thomas. In Brantford, the Mechanics' Institute he founded was located in a small basement downtown and circulated one hundred donated books put on loan to the public. Duncombe sowed the seeds of its and his own undoing in 1837 when he supported the Mackenzie rebellion, gathering a force of five to six hundred men, who quickly abandoned him when they met real troops, failing to achieve anything of significance. In the aftermath, he fled back to the United States.

When Duncombe left, the Mechanics' Institute closed but it was revived in 1840, and merged with the Zion Church Literary Society in 1866. The church's minister, William Cochrane, one of the founders of Brantford's Young Ladies' College, served as president for twelve years. After a fire destroyed the Institute and most of its books in 1870, it was relocated above an early YMCA building on Colborne. The Institute operated in this location until 1884, when it was dissolved by a city council motion that replaced it with the Brantford Free Library. The motion passed by a decisive majority, though some worried that the library would turn Brantford's wives into "novel readers."[5]

It was Judge Alexander Hardy who brought a Carnegie library to Brantford. A brother of Ontario Premier Arthur Sturgis Hardy, Alexander was a prominent local figure who was dedicated to public education, and to the library in particular. In March of 1902, at a meeting of city council, Alderman J. Inglis forwarded a motion to petition Andrew Carnegie for a library, a city hall, or both. The motion was defeated, but Judge Hardy had already written Carnegie on behalf of the Library Board. In April, Hardy heard back from Carnegie's secretary, James Bertram, who offered funding of thirty thousand dollars. As soon as the offer was received, any doubts about the building of a library appear to have evaporated, and the project proceeded. On two later occasions, Hardy secured further funding — a visit to New York secured an extra five thousand dollars for the original construction, and a third request, in 1913, secured another thirteen thousand to enlarge the basement.

As planning for the library proceeded, a debate arose over the appropriate location. Newspapers, politicians, and the public participated in a heated discussion over two different sites: their relative costs, which was most suitable for women and children, and so on and so forth. After a great deal of debate and some manoeuvring by vocal members of the public, the newspapers, the city council, and the Library Board, the "park site" on George Street, on the eastern side of Victoria Square, was chosen.

Reverend G.C. Mackenzie, the rector of Grace Anglican and chair of the Library Board, laid the cornerstone for the new library on December 16, 1902. The Brantford *Expositor* reported that Mayor D.B. Wood spoke at the ceremony, describing "the splendid building that is now being erected and of what it meant to the beauty and progress of the city. The building would be large, spacious, beautiful, ornamental and useful. It would be a building that would rank among the best in Canada for architectural beauty.… Every detail of the building had been gone into … and when the building was completed it would be one of which every Brantfordite would be proud."[6]

Ironically, and somewhat unfairly, the official cornerstone recorded the names of the city councillors who voted down Inglis's motion to approach Carnegie, but not the name of Judge Hardy, who secured the funding. The oversight was not remedied until after his death, when a memorial stone recognizing his role was included in the north side of new library steps.

The finished library, built by Stewart, Stewart & Taylor Architects and Shultz Bros. Construction,[7] did not disappoint. The day after it opened, *The Expositor* reported that "vast sums" had been expended, and that their "careful investigation" had revealed that the "outlay is much greater than was first anticipated."[8] The story hints at public scandal, but not in a way that diminished the paper's enthusiasm for the finished building: "The new Carnegie library in this city was informally opened, and last evening a very large number of prominent people took advantage of the opportunity to inspect the building.… It presented a unique appearance, and those who saw it from a distance or gave it a critical inspection while going through

were more than delighted. The building is complete in every particular."[9]

The Expositor's "Library Notes" of the same day reported that "The free library opened yesterday and was crowded as a result, all day long. Hundreds visited the building and expressed themselves as delighted with the interior furnishings. The library is certainly fitted up in magnificent shape and everything has been done with a view to the comfort of the patrons." The only negative note sounded complained of some "considerable trouble" with "dogs which were brought in." To ensure no similar problems in the future, a new library regulation prohibiting dogs in the building was immediately established.

Right from the start, the Brantford library was recognized as one of Canada's finest examples of the Beaux Arts style that it embodies. Situated on the edge of one of the country's finest Victorian squares, its architectural details included a mansard roof, a dome, and a grand entrance. The entrance was set in a large portico at the top of a long, imposing stairway. At the top of the stairs, four Ionic columns supported a triangular pediment in front of the building's dome. The interior featured archways, pillars, a mosaic, and a rotunda with a stained glass skylight with Islamic tracery situated underneath the dome. Above the main entrance, the builders inscribed a boast from Virgil, who wrote, "I have erected a monument more lasting than bronze." The names Shakespeare, Dickens, Milton, Tennyson, Burns, and other English-speaking writers were embossed in pediments above the first floor windows.

Lavish details like those in the Brantford library were common in Carnegie's early buildings. It is not

Details of the Brantford Carnegie Library. The quote from Horace above the front entrance translates as "I have built a monument more lasting than bronze" — Odes, 3.30.1. The 1902 cornerstone commemorates the dedication of the library. In 1956, when the stairs were redone, a stone inscription was added to recognize Judge A.H. Hardy's role arranging Carnegie funding.

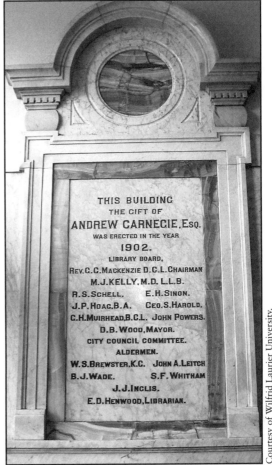

clear what his secretary, James Bertram, thought of the details of the Brantford library, but he grew impatient with cities which, in his opinion, spent Carnegie's money on unnecessary architectural embellishments. In 1911, he issued a pamphlet entitled *Notes on the Erection of Library Buildings*, which included written advice and standard designs, and warned against "aiming at such exterior effects as may make impossible an effective and economical layout of the interior." The pamphlet was sent to municipal authorities when they were notified that they had received a Carnegie grant. Looking at the library in Brantford, one wonders if Bertram was too concerned about architectural extravagances, for the fine details of the Brantford building very successfully confirmed its significance.

In downtown Brantford, the Carnegie Building housed the public library for almost ninety years. It served, not only as a centre for reading and the borrowing of books, but as a place of culture and public education, sometimes serving as a home for the city's museum, archives, and art gallery. During its tenure as the public library, the building was one of Brantford's most successful public buildings, but it was showing signs of wear by the 1980s. In 1979, the public library's chief librarian, Lavinka Clark, complained that "the premises have been put to the fullest possible use and the building is grossly inadequate for our ever-expanding needs and programs beneficial to the public."[10] After repeated entreaties, complaints, and submissions to city council, it agreed to move the public library.

The Carnegie Building was closed in December 1991. Its impressive exterior remained, but the interior of the building was worn out from almost ninety years of constant wear and tear. The Brantford Public Library was moved to less elegant but more spacious premises in an empty Woolco store on Colborne Street. The library won an award for its clever renovation of its new building. In other cities, vacated Carnegie libraries were converted into banks, office buildings, law offices, government buildings, and even private homes, but the architectural masterpiece that Carnegie gave Brantford sat empty and forlorn, unable to attract a tenant. Local rumours suggested that the building would become a provincial courthouse. The president of the Historical Society, David Judd, proposed that it become the home of the Brant County Museum and Archives.[11] He was successful in attracting some support but not the necessary funding. At one point the city put the building up for sale and

a local firm, MMMC Architects, looked at a possible renovation on behalf of a private insurance group. In 1996–97, the city considered turning the building into offices for the Planning and Building Department.

As the 1990s progressed, the building seemed to have no future. The future of its setting seemed even bleaker. On one side of the building, the harsh aesthetics of the 1967 city hall undermined the historical integrity of Victoria Square. On the other side, the integrity of the square was being challenged by a new owner who had bought Park Church and decided to demolish it in favour of a parking lot. As Peter Muir wrote in *Brant News*:

> The Carnegie building is part of an impressive grouping of buildings that surround Victoria Square in the centre of Brantford. The "neo-classical" building with its temple like front steps, massive pillars, domed hall and mosaic floor, now sits vacant and lifeless beside Park Church.
>
> The Church has brought attention to the fate of "one of the most impressive public squares in the Province of Ontario." It has been granted a temporary reprieve from the wreckers' ball but is slated for destruction in the spring. The Carnegie building may be next on death row. It has been empty for three years and needs work if a suitable tenant is to be found.[12]

These were difficult times for Brantford's most historic square. The old YWCA and Old One Hundred

Park Baptist Church, beside the Carnegie Library, circa 1900–05. *The church was saved from demolition only when the province assigned it a heritage designation in recognition of its unique stained glass window above the vestibule. The building now houses Brant Community Church.*

were already gone. The city hall had not retained any vestiges of heritage. The Carnegie Building had been vacant for almost a decade. Park Church was slated for demolition. The impressive home that E.L. Goold had built across the street from Park Church was in a state of serious disrepair. And the decline on the perimeter of the square was compounded by the deterioration in the buildings that lined the blocks surrounding it.

In the midst of these discouraging circumstances, the Brantford Heritage Committee initiated a push in a better direction. In a context in which most of Brantford favoured the demolition of the old buildings downtown, it opposed such action and did its best to save the architectural heritage that could still be found in downtown Brantford. The committee found a way to save Park Church from the wreckers' ball by securing a provincial heritage designation that prevented its new owner from demolishing the building. The designation was awarded in order to preserve the unique circular stained glass window on the front of the church. With the church saved, at least for the foreseeable future, one could not help but wonder whether the former Carnegie Library, so long a sign of Brantford's prominence but now quickly deteriorating, might be saved as well.

| 4 |

A NEW DIRECTION

According to a local story, Winston Churchill bought his cigars in Brantford. Like many urban legends, this one contains some strands of truth. Churchill did go to Brantford. He visited on January 3, 1901, while on a lecture tour he had arranged before taking his seat in the British House of Commons. In the United States he met with President McKinley, Vice-President Theodore Roosevelt, and Mark Twain. In Canada, he came to Brantford. You can still see his signature on the registry at The Brantford Club, an exclusive downtown club (for most of its history, too exclusive to allow women members).

Churchill became a serious cigar smoker during a trip to Cuba in 1895. Afterward, he smoked eight to ten cigars a day, so he must have smoked in Brantford. His iconic image as a cigar-smoker was established by a famous portrait by Yousuf Karsh in which he scowls after Karsh has taken his cigar away. In Brantford, Churchill must have smoked cigars. It is possible that he smoked a Brantford-made cigar, but he did not come to Brantford to buy cigars; he imported them from Cuba. The Brantford legend ties together a local visit, a popular image of Churchill that made him the world's most famous cigar smoker,

and one forgotten facet of the city's manufacturing past: Brantford was once the home of a number of successful cigar manufacturers — the Alexander Fair Cigar Company, S.W. Cornell and Company, Halloran and Haskett, and Bunnell and Busch.

Other local folklore is relevant to the rise and fall, and the subsequent rebirth, of Brantford's downtown. In the end, the turnaround downtown, which began with the saving of the Carnegie Building, was rooted in the idea that Brantford should have a university. This was an idea that represented a major break from the city's past. When I went to Brantford and asked why the city did not already have a university, I was told two stories. One attributed the lack of a university to Brantford's industrial, blue collar past, and, more particularly, to the wealthy owners of Brantford's manufacturing interests who were said to vehemently oppose the development of a university because they did not want to deal with an educated workforce that might not do what it was told. The second pointed the finger at the provincial government, which was alleged to have rejected Brantford's requests for post-secondary education in favour of other cities in Ontario — London, Guelph, St. Catharines, Peterborough, et cetera.

When I looked for evidence that might support these accounts, it was difficult to avoid the conclusion that they are, like the story of Churchill buying his cigars in Brantford, the stuff of urban legend. Historically, Brantford's focus on industry and especially manufacturing made it a city that showed little interest in universities. So as far as I can determine, it was city, not provincial attitudes that made Brantford a place without a university. The historical record suggests that the key attitude was indifference — Brantford had no university because it had, in the course of its history, shown little interest in having one. It was only when the city's industrial base began to collapse that those who cared about the city showed some interest, but this was too late, long after the government had founded the province's most recent universities in the 1960s.

Through most of its history, Brantford saw higher education as unnecessary or, at most, a vehicle for technical training. In a study of post-secondary trends in Brant County from 1784 to 1933, Walter Szmigielski argues that this emphasis on practical utility reflects a uniquely American influence on education in Brant County.[1] One might debate the view of British and American education he assumes, but it would be difficult to deny Szmigielski's claim that Brant County adopted a view of education that emphasized vocational opportunities. This is evident, not only in the kinds of educational institutions that operated in Brant County, but in histories of Brantford and Brant County, which show little interest in higher education. The most advanced education that merits comment in F. Douglas Reville's classic history of Brantford, written in 1920, is industrial classes and technical training.

Historically, the institution in Brantford that most resembled a university was the "Young Ladies' College" (officially, the Ladies' College and Music Conservatory). Founded by the Presbyterian Church in 1874, it was established at a sumptuous three-and-a-half-acre property that was owned by the Honourable E.B. Wood before he left Brantford to become the chief justice of the Supreme Court of Manitoba. The college was well-known, attracting well-heeled students from across the country. It incorporated a Preparatory Department for women under fourteen, and a Collegiate Department that granted teacher and university-level certificates. It was notable also for the quality of instruction and a highly regarded music conservatory. Alexander Graham Bell attended the musical performances. The conservatory continued to operate after the college closed in 1900, and was affiliated with the University of Western Ontario in 1911, but its operations dwindled gradually and ceased in the early 1930s.

The curriculum at the Ladies' College emphasized the classics, the fine arts, and "elevated" sensibilities: "Through the prominence given to English, the Classics and History, it aimed to cultivate a taste for the reading of a pure and elevating literature which in after years, shall continue to be a source of pleasure and profit."[2] It is not difficult to imagine a sequence of steps that could have turned the college into a university (or a college of a university), but this never came to pass. Instead, the Ladies' College flourished as a centre of women's learning and art and music for a quarter century, and then closed its doors. Afterward, the most advanced education available to women (and men) in Brantford was found at the local high school, the Brantford Collegiate Institute.

Brantford's next endeavour in post-secondary education was a satellite campus of Mohawk College, which opened in 1970. It took applied career training to a higher level but still reflected the city's focus on vocational education. The quest for a university, which represented a step in a new direction, came later. In a Brantford context, it is tempting to search for the person who came up with the bold idea that the city should have a university. But the truth is more complicated. Over the course of more than twenty years there was a whole cast of Brantfordophiles — citizens, mayors, would-be mayors, councillors, government officials, business leaders, professors, and educators — who pushed Brantford in this direction. Many others opposed their proposals, which went against the grain of history, and they themselves proposed conflicting plans that sometimes came to naught. Their differences notwithstanding, their joint efforts ultimately culminated in the moves that brought Laurier to Brantford.

Lobbying for university education began in 1975. At a time when the local economy was beginning its slide downhill and the downtown was already in a state of shambles, a group of concerned citizens established a Council on Continuing Education. The membership included prominent local figures, among them Mary Stedman, the head of the eminent Stedman family, and Mike Hancock who was destined to become the Brantford mayor.[3] Stedman remembers that many outside the group were skeptical of "high falutin'" ideas about higher education. Not so their members, who worried about Brantford's low level of educational attainment, a

Photo reprinted with permission of the *Brantford Expositor.*

Mary Stedman has been a major supporter of the development of post-secondary education in Brantford. She, her family, and the Stedman Foundation have been generous supporters of Laurier Brantford.

feature of the city that distinguished it from its more successful counterparts in Canada. Endorsing education as the ultimate solution to Brantford's many problems; the Council organized a literacy project

Courtesy of Kevin Klein.

Mike Hancock, in the mayor's office, sits with three student politicians who played a prominent role in the Students' Union in Brantford: Zachary Mealia, Amanda Flanagan, and Melissa Burke. Mayor Hancock and Mayor Friel were strong supporters of post-secondary initiatives downtown.

and initiated discussions with McMaster University and the University of Western Ontario, which taught courses in the city. More courses were offered, but continuing students had to transfer to their home campuses in Hamilton and London. Neither university sustained their operations. The Council's most enduring success was not local university courses, but an annual lecture series that featured prominent intellectual figures, among them Margaret Atwood, Linus Pauling, W.O. Mitchell, and David Suzuki.[4]

The concerns about the future that had motivated the work of the Council on Continuing Education were magnified as Brantford suffered through the collapse of White Farm and Massey Ferguson. As the economy and the downtown spiralled downward, a number of prominent figures promoted higher education as a solution to Brantford's problems.[5] The most significant initiative was orchestrated by Robert "Bob" Nixon when he served as provincial treasurer. He and his father, Harry Nixon, were a Brant County political dynasty, having represented the region in the provincial government for seventy-two consecutive years. His daughter, Jane Stewart, was part of the dynasty, representing Brant in the federal government. At the apex of her career, she served as a minister in the federal cabinet and was touted as a candidate for prime minister before she was mired in a scandal about the operation of Human Resources Development Canada, an agency in her portfolio. Popular sentiment in Brantford saw her as the victim of a backfired attempt to clean up issues that others had ignored.

The Nixon family had deep roots in Brant County. Their farm, located outside St. George, raised Holstein cattle, a milking breed that played a key role in the development of agriculture in the region. It was St. George and then Brantford that served as the home of the Holstein Association of Canada, which oversaw the propagation of the breed. When Bob Nixon retired, he moved into a small heritage home on the family farm, where he took up painting, producing canvases that won him some acclaim. After his daughter gave up her political career in federal

politics, she lived in a different house on the farm, and began commuting to New York City, where she works for an international labour organization associated with the United Nations.

During a long career as an elected politician, Nixon established himself as an influential member of the Liberal Party of Ontario, but found it difficult to interest the provincial government in Brant County. He sighed and rolled his eyes when he told me so. In 1985, after he was re-elected and became the treasurer in a Liberal government, he was determined to do something for Brantford, which was in a state of financial turmoil. In 1987–88 he sent one of his treasury managers, David Trick, to a series of meetings with a local committee interested in bringing a university to Brantford.[6] Mohawk College and McMaster University were included in the discussions. Trick was struck by all the empty buildings downtown and suggested that they house the new post-secondary endeavour.

The stage seemed set for a university initiative in downtown Brantford. An influential cabinet minister backed the idea, the local committee was eager to support it, and the downtown was discussed as a possible location. But the possibility was never realized and the trajectory of the discussions moved in a different direction under the influence of Mohawk and McMaster. McMaster was not interested in an independent university in Brantford or a satellite campus. Mohawk viewed the situation as an opportunity to expand but argued that a downtown campus would, like George Brown in Toronto, be landlocked and unable to expand. Others accepted the argument that it would be too expensive to renovate vacant older buildings. Like most of Brantford, the committee had given up on the downtown.

The end result was a proposal that did not recommend a university campus, but a new campus of Mohawk College. As a concession to the idea of a university, Mohawk agreed that it would make arrangements with already existing universities, allowing them to offer programming in Brantford. When the idea of a Brantford university resurfaced a decade later, Caroline Freibauer recounted the discussions:

> Back in the 1980s ... Mohawk had its satellite campus downtown in the Beckett Building on Colborne Street where adult upgrading and retraining classes were held in six classrooms and a conference room. Other job readiness and retraining courses for women were offered at the YM-YWCA. The Brant-Elgin campus, then called Braneida, was gaining a reputation for industrial training. Nursing programs were run out of the Brantford General Hospital. The next logical step was to unite all these campuses.
>
> Thus a campaign began — the first of several — to bring a full-fledged post-secondary school into Brant, a community with half as many university graduates as the provincial average. In 1987, a $24-million facility was proposed.... By 1988 the price tag for the dream campus had grown to $35 million. At that time,

Mohawk's president Keith McIntyre began negotiating with universities to offer degree completion programs in Brantford.... In 1989, the effort switched to an expansion of the existing campus and the price tag went up again, to $38.9 million.[7]

In the end, the effect of the Nixon initiative was limited. The provincial government rejected the plan for a new Mohawk campus, which it deemed too ambitious and expensive. As a kind of consolation prize, it provided a grant (of $6.2 million) to expand the college's operations on its Brantford campus, which was located in a warehouse district away from the downtown.

A number of prominent Brantford figures continued to push for a university. John Starkey was a colourful city councillor in love with Brantford history. He had gained a reputation for speaking his mind, not hesitating to criticize his fellow councillors, the mayor, or the city government. One avid reader of the commentaries Starkey had written for *The Expositor* told me that he had used Starkey as his "crap detector," counting on him to illuminate civic issues by playing devil's advocate.

Starkey was deeply committed to all things Brantfordian and believed in radical reform. In 1994, he ran for mayor on a platform that included a commitment to a university. In his speeches he argued that the money spent on attempts to reinvigorate Brantford's economy had been wasted, and that tax dollars should be put to a different end: "Brantford needs a university."[8] This position was emphasized in his campaign:

As a community, we should make a commitment to begin raising funds and accumulating assets to enable Brantford to eventually attract or establish a local university. This will make our city more competitive as an attractive place to live, locate, and invest, and provide the option of a higher education to those who cannot afford to go away to school. The importance of leadership is essential to the success of such a crucial project, and so from the Mayor's 1995 income, I pledge the first $40,000 to establish the "University for Brantford Foundation."[9]

Others began thinking of post-secondary education as a solution to the downtown's problems. One of the problems was the empty downtown mall, a nondescript brick fortress that sprawled over more than two downtown blocks, protecting its interior space from the deteriorating downtown beyond its walls. One city manager I talked to complained that the mall was not "porous" enough to create an integrated downtown. "It functions," he said, "like a constipated brick in the middle of downtown." The mall's fortress-like walls might not matter if it had successfully created a vibrant retail market, but it quickly failed. By the 1990s, it was eminently usable downtown space bereft of stores and customers. In an effort to promote downtown revitalization, a group associated with Mohawk College proposed that the college move into the empty space. Skip Stanbridge,

the vice-president in charge of Mohawk's Brantford campus, said that administrators were willing to discuss all possibilities. "There are people in the city of Brantford and at all three levels of Brantford," he said, "who feel there's a natural link between the revitalization of the downtown and the development of post-secondary education in Brantford.[10]

The success of any of the plans for Brantford post-secondary initiatives required popular support. A long and involved attempt to establish a broad community consensus on Brantford's future began with a mayor's task force on the future of the city. It proposed a county-wide strategic plan that was undertaken by a not-for-profit group (a local Community Futures Development Corporation), which hired a planning company and a local coordinator who played a key role in subsequent developments. John McGregor came to Brantford after working on development issues in the Kalahari Desert and the Northwest Territories and on projects with Six Nations. He was staggered by Brant County's profound pessimism when he arrived, which struck him as more negative than the attitudes he had experienced in his work in the Kalahari and the North. He saw an underlying defeatism as the principal barrier to change, and welcomed a strategic plan that might get the city talking and thinking in a more positive way. In an effort to push in this direction, the discussion material he and the planning committee produced presented the city and the county as a community driven by "a fierce independence and unshakeable pride" and a "continuing tradition of genius" rooted in a proud history.[11]

The strategic planning exercise was an ambitious endeavour that began with a detailed survey of seven

hundred residents and fifty community leaders, and
twenty workshops attended by three hundred people. The final strategic plan, released in April 1997,
noted that the county's levels of post-secondary education were lower than the provincial average and
listed "brain drain" as one of its major problems.
In its positive recommendations it encouraged the
establishment of a university in Brantford as a way
to "provide an opportunity for young people to get
an education locally," and to "raise overall education levels in the County."[12] Other recommendations
supported the proposal that Mohawk College move
into the empty Eaton's mall, promoted lifelong learning and formal education (in particular, the use of
new technology and distance education), and advocated programs focused on business training.

The details of the Brant Community Strategic
Plan were not realized. The proposed Coordinating
Committee which was supposed to oversee the
achievement of its various components never materialized. It is difficult to see how such a committee
could have managed the sweeping scope and the
myriad details of the plan's proposals. But at the
same time, the creation of the plan did what good
strategic planning does — it made Brantford and
Brant County rethink what they could be. In the
aftermath, BOBB — the Big on Brantford/Brant
Committee — organized a series of local forums
on key strategic issues. In May 1997, one discussed
the idea that Mohawk College should move to the
downtown core. In September, another discussed
the need for a Brantford university. The notion that
Brantford needed post-secondary downtown had by
this time taken root.

| 5 |

CHASING "UBC"

Even in the tough times, Brantford has enjoyed a strong identity. In the campaign to establish a university, this expressed itself in a desire to have a university of its own. Everyone in Brantford nods knowingly when I tell them that there are those in Brantford who did not want a satellite campus of Laurier or some other existing university but a new "UBC"— a University of Brant County.

In the quest for a university, the local desire to have a Brantford institution was manifest in a proposal to establish a private university. This was a radical idea in a country which defines university education in terms of public institutions. In this respect, Canadian education has developed in a different way than its American counterpart, where some of the nation's best known universities — Harvard, Yale, Stanford — are privately funded institutions. The idea that Brantford should have a private university proposed a new educational paradigm for Canada, but this was not what motivated the city. From its point of view, the plan to found a private university was not an attempt at educational reform, so much as an attempt to circumvent a system of publicly funded institutions which excluded Brantford. One way or another, those who wanted a local university were bound and determined to secure one. If this meant breaking the mould that defined university education in Canada, this was fine with them. To some of those involved, this made the proposal more attractive.

But the proposal for a private university did not begin as a Brantford initiative. It was an idea forwarded by three renegade arts professors who were inspired by a desire for educational reform. Gordon Morrell, Edmund Pries, and Ronald Sawatsky were part-time professors at the University of Waterloo. Morrell and Pries were members of an ever-expanding army of part-time faculty who worked at Canadian universities. Squeezed between limited provincial funding and the demands of full-time faculty, universities increasingly relied on part-timers, who were paid a fraction of the salary of full-time professors, taught larger classes, and did not enjoy the security and the benefits that accrue to tenured faculty (benefits that included sabbaticals and research opportunities). This was a difficult lot for part-timers who had successfully survived the rigours of a Ph.D. in the hopes of full-time employment. In a situation where some of them engaged in the research associated with a job as a professor more than their full-time

PART-TIME   ASSOCIATE   TENURED

Andrew Toos on the evolution of the academic, a parody on the traditional illustration of "the evolution of man." Like the original, it assumes a male stereotype.

counterparts, it was difficult, even unjust, to have to endure working conditions so inferior to those of their full-time colleagues. The more radical decried "tenure as injustice" and described themselves as the "lumpenproletariat" of the academic workforce, a term that Marx used to described the rabble that makes up the bottom layer of the working class.

Most part-time professors toiled in the hope that they would eventually land a full-time position. Many did. Others organized unions to fight for better working conditions for part-time faculty. In Kitchener-Waterloo, Morrell, Pries, and Sawatsky came up with a radically different strategy. Instead of working as perpetual part-timers in an existing university, they decided to launch an initiative to establish an institution of their own. They wanted a model that could compete with existing universities

and decided that it would be a small liberal arts institution that would offer a different model of education than the one that characterizes Canadian universities. Like private liberal arts colleges in the United States, the City College they first proposed for Kitchener was designed to emphasize teaching over research, general education, undergraduate rather than graduate programs, student/professor interaction, and, in the spirit of humanism, the development of the whole person. When the Kitchener option did not work out, they partnered with Brantford. The partnership was a marriage of two outsiders: a city and a group of part-time faculty determined to do an end run around existing universities in their attempt to find a way into the Canadian university system.

Even before it came to Brantford, the City College Project had attracted national media attention. At a time when a Conservative government in Ontario was seriously considering the possibility of private universities, the City College proposal was swept into a heated debate which pitted the City College group and others who wanted private universities against the existing public universities and their faculty associations. The locus of the debate moved to Brantford after two members of the Education Committee of a local development board,[1] Doug Brown and Vyrt Sisson, heard Gordon Morrell interviewed on a national radio broadcast. In a situation in which the Brant strategic plan had already flagged a local need for more post-secondary education, Brown and Sisson were intrigued by the idea of a private university and arranged for Morrell and his two colleagues to speak to their committee. Unable to establish the college they wanted in Kitchener, the City College group was determined to make the most of the Brantford opportunity. When they met with the education committee on September 20, 1996, they requested $291,000 to establish a private college. In return for the funding, which would be used to pay for salaries, a marketing plan, and the development of a curriculum, they promised to open the college in September 1997.

At a special meeting on October 10, 1996, the local board enthusiastically noted that the proposed college was in keeping with other Brantford initiatives (among them, the plan to move Mohawk College downtown) and encouraged the education committee to pursue the idea further. The board was less enthusiastic about the proposed price tag, which they thought extravagant and not well worked out. One of the key board members, a retired bank manager, told me that the City College professors did not know how to write a business plan. He raised his hands, looked to heaven, smiled, and quipped: "What can you expect from arts professors who haven't studied business?" (In the wake of the collapse of the North American stock market after questionable business practices in 2008, I poked him in the ribs and asked him: "What can you expect from business leaders who haven't studied ethics?")

The Board offered the City College professors fifteen thousand dollars to prepare a preliminary plan for a private university. They accepted the offer and submitted a *University College of the Grand Valley: Business Plan* two months later. The "Executive Summary" outlined an ambitious plan to establish a university "in the heart" of downtown Brantford.

> The City College Project Group-Brant, in cooperation with Brant Community Futures Development Corporation, plans to develop an accredited university college, University College of the Grand Valley (UCGV), in the heart of the City of Brantford by September 1, 1997. UCGV will become one of the first private, tuition-driven, liberal arts colleges in Ontario. This model, based on other similar institutions in British Columbia and Alberta, as well as the United States and Great Britain, is a new model for Ontario post-secondary education. UCGV is not intended to supplant the existing public post-secondary education system, but rather to supplement it and to increase the options available to students.[2]

In explaining why a private university should be established, the plan emphasized Brant County's low level of educational attainment, the need to avail local students with access to a university, and the economic and cultural benefits of a university. The mission statement for University College of the Grand Valley was committed to "a high quality undergraduate university degree with a strong emphasis on creative teaching, smaller classes, a high degree of professor-student interaction, and experiential learning." It promised that UCGV would "be an active participant in the Brantford community, culturally, intellectually and economically."

The City College's forty-three-page business plan attempted to work out, in a more detailed way, how a private university would operate. The plans included a proposed liberal arts curriculum,[3] library services provided in partnership with the Brantford Public Library (a plan discussed with Wendy Newman, the Library's CEO), an agreement with Mohawk College that would allow college students to transfer to degree programs, and suggested linkages with the downtown YMCA (to provide recreational facilities) and the Woodland Cultural Centre, a Brantford institution that houses one of Canada's largest repositories of aboriginal artifacts. In its discussion of possible locations, the City Group had no doubts about their preference. The empty Carnegie Library had caught their eye, convincing them that an association with the history and heritage of the downtown could be a key component of the new college. "It is the goal of UCGV to locate in the heart of the old City of Brantford. UCGV hopes to contribute to the ongoing process of the revitalizing of the downtown core

of Brantford.... To date, the Carnegie Library is the best and most appropriate building which may be available for use."[4]

In a rudimentary way, the College of the Grand Valley business plan successfully addressed the issues that a new university would have to face in Brantford. But it faced a major obstacle. To function as a university it would have to be accredited by the government in a province that had no tradition of secular private colleges. In attempting to navigate a way around this problem, one of the City College professors, Edmund Pries, met with administrators from the University of Waterloo, proposing an affiliation. When the university's president, James Downey, told them that Waterloo would not be interested until City College had an established reputation, Pries told him that the college wouldn't need an affiliation when it reached that point. As a clever but improbable alternative to Waterloo, the business plan proposed an affiliation with Northland Open University, a somewhat shadowy correspondence university which was incorporated in Whitehorse, Yukon, in 1976, but ceased its operations. In lieu of an agreement with an existing university, the College business plan proposed a direct application to the Ontario government.

In view of financial and accreditation concerns, the Brantford development board that had commissioned the College of the Grand Valley business plan decided that it would not release it to the public, but use it as a basis for a revised plan that would include additional details. To keep the initiative going, they hired John McGregor, who had coordinated the Brant Community Strategic Plan, and formed a University Committee to work with him.[5] In an attempt to establish some momentum, McGregor personally contacted sixty prominent Brantford citizens. In December 1996, shortly after the College of the Grand Valley business plan was presented to the board, the Ontario Premier's Advisory Panel on Future Directions for Postsecondary Education raised the hopes of McGregor and the committee when it recommended that the Degree Granting Act of 1983 be amended to allow the province to accredit private universities. McGregor and others travelled to Toronto to discuss Brantford's plan to establish a private university and were told (by the deputy minister of training and education) that the City College proposal looked "excellent," but that it could not be supported immediately, and would have to wait until provincial legislation was changed to allow for private universities.

McGregor and the University Committee made some significant attempts to mobilize support for the Grand Valley initiative. With the help of the local member of Parliament, Jane Stewart, McGregor and his committee established the Grand Valley Education Society (GVES) as a charitable organization to raise money for their new initiative. Ontario's former minister of education, Bette Stevenson, was contacted. She was sympathetic to the project but was already engaged in a similar venture in Newmarket, where she was helping David Strangway, the former University of Toronto and University of British Columbia president, who was attempting to establish a private institution called Wolfe University. Strangway's experience at two of Canada's major universities made him a passionate advocate for the kind of education provided by private liberal arts institutions: an interdisciplinary education focused

The Grand Valley Education Society played a central role in bringing the university to Brantford. Key members pose outside the GVES office: (left to right) Susan Vincent, Colleen Miller, Stuart Parkinson, Vyrt Sisson, Bruce Hodgson, and Douglas Brown.

on high quality undergraduate teaching. When the Newmarket project did not succeed, Strangway took his mission to British Columbia, where Quest University became Canada's first accredited secular private university in 2005.

After months of work on their project, the Brant University Committee decided it needed to mobilize public support for the founding of a private university. It announced a public meeting that took place in September 1997, the month originally proposed for the opening of the new university-college. The meeting inaugurated a series of public meetings that discussed all aspects of the project — the need to raise eight hundred thousand dollars in start-up funds; the character of the proposed college

Courtesy of the Brantford Heritage Inventory.

The Bell Building on Victoria Square was one of the buildings suggested as a home for University College of the Grand Valley. After Laurier arrived, the university had positive discussions with Bell Canada over its use. The discussions came to an end when security restrictions the company introduced in the wake of the 9/11 attack on the World Trade Center in New York would not permit public access to the building.

(specializing in small classes, emphasizing teaching and student-professor interaction); and possible locations (a number of sites were proposed). The publisher of *The Expositor*, Michael Pierce, promised to support the committee by sending a reporter to all public meetings.

A few weeks before the first meeting, the city's most outspoken councillor, John Starkey, published an *Expositor* article entitled "Brantford Needs a University." Comparing the economic woes of

Brantford to those of Newfoundland, he singled out Brantford's lack of a university: "Unlike all of our principal neighbors, we have no university. And so the city looks to a future without the best, the brightest, the most ambitious, the most determined, the most fortunate. Brantford's youth is taught that the road to success is a one-way route out of town to someplace with a university."[6]

Starkey went on to support the University College of the Grand Valley, favouring the vacant Carnegie

Library as the right place for its campus: "The open-ing of Brantford's 'University College of the Grand Valley' is an event of exciting promise. Follow the announcements as they are made. And when the call goes out for volunteers and donations, work hard and dig deep."[7]

The Expositor contributed to the momentum with an editorial entitled "School of Hard Knocks." Observing that "to date the community seems less than inspired by the idea" of a private university, it granted that "It is certainly understandable that there would be a certain amount of healthy skepti-cism about the plan. For one thing, this is Brantford, where the unofficial motto is "I'll believe it when they open the doors."[8]

The Expositor itself begged to differ: "For decades Brantford has felt inadequate because it lost out during the explosive period of university growth in the 1960s. Subsequent attempts to develop a uni-versity presence in Brantford in conjunction with existing universities have largely been unsuccessful. So, if half-measures have failed to work, why not go all the way and dream big — the University College of Grand Valley? There's little to lose, and the poten-tial rewards are great."

| 6 |

THREE WAYS

By the end of 1997, Brantford was abuzz with activity aimed at bringing post-secondary education to the old downtown. While the University Committee worked on the proposal to establish a private university, the Downtown Renewal Group lobbied to move Mohawk College to the vacant Eaton's mall. The latter had toiled on the details of a proposal for two years. The plan that they proposed was influenced by discussions with Mohawk College, the old YM-YWCA, the mayor, the city, members of the federal and provincial governments, the mall owners, and the public library, which said that it was ready to serve the new location by transforming its undeveloped third floor into a multi-media study space.

Caroline Freibauer, a reporter with an interest in downtown developments, recounted the developments in *The Expositor*:

> …with the downtown economy virtually deflated, yet another group of concerned citizens is crusading for Mohawk's Elgin Street campus to move into the vacant Eaton Market Square mall.

And despite the many failed attempts at creating a post-secondary presence in the city, this group is just as earnest, committed and unflagging as the crusaders who have gone before.

"If we have a problem, our problem is explaining to the people of Brantford exactly how good a deal this is," said Frank Matthews, a retired businessman, entrepreneur and member of an informal concerned citizens committee called the Downtown Renewal Group. The group's long-term objectives are to encourage and bring new initiatives to Brantford's core. The short-term objective is to make a proposal for a joint Mohawk College and YM-YWCA development work….

Terry Jones, executive director of the YM-YWCA, which is in dire need of a new facility, likes the partnerships a Mohawk plan creates. "It's a community initiative which addresses our problem with the downtown and our problem with post-secondary education."[1]

In the end, Downtown Renewal Group took the Mohawk/Y proposal to city council, asking it to provide a $3.4 million share of the project cost. Once they had secured this commitment, they planned to turn next to the provincial and then the federal government, asking them for the same amount. City council decided to postpone a decision so it could consider an alternative plan which would create a new YM/YWCA, a high-rise condominium overlooking the river, and a soccer court and recreational complex at the end of Colborne Street.

As the Downtown Renewal Group and the University Committee pushed downtown Brantford toward post-secondary education, the mayor began pursuing initiatives of his own. Chris Friel was only twenty-seven when he was first elected — the youngest mayor ever elected in Ontario. He was fresh, good-looking, and had a penchant for striking suits. In his speeches, he could captivate an audience. Sometimes with affection, and sometimes with derision, he was known as The Boy Mayor (one admirer I talked to described him as The Boy Wonder). After he left politics, and made the rounds as a speaker, he entitled one of his speeches "The Confessions of The Boy Mayor." Friel's detractors said he was a vain autocrat who did not build consensus, but found ways to out-manoeuvre the councillors he did not agree with. Some described him as obstinate and pig-headed. Others said that this was why he was able to change Brantford.

Before he became mayor, Friel had earned a BA in Political Science from the University of Waterloo.

After graduation, he began working on an MA in political economy. When he had to decide the subject of his thesis, he picked the ultimate Brantford topic — the collapse of Massey Ferguson/White Farm. He left before he finished, going to work for the development group that organized the Brant Strategic Plan. Not long afterward, he entered the mayoralty race as an unknown and unexpected candidate. In a city desperate for change, he surprised the pundits and won. When he became mayor he was determined to turn Brantford — and especially its downtown — around. He believed that post-secondary education could play a role in reshaping the city, but he was skeptical of the attempt to establish a private university, worrying that it might negatively affect the city's relationship with the provincial government.

Fifty kilometres away, there were others who shared Friel's skepticism about Brantford's attempt to establish a private university. At Wilfrid Laurier University, a new president, Bob Rosehart, thought that the Brantford attempt to create a private university was intruding on territory that belonged to his new institution. The president was someone who liked to keep busy. At any one time, he juggled as many balls in the air as he could manage. Driving with him was an adventure as he conducted a conversation, drove, talked on his cell phone, and kept track of his text messages. I will not forget an occasion when I breathed an inward sigh of relief when we entered a section of an obscure highway with no connectivity, as this prevented him from trying to do all this at once. On an ordinary morning, one of the things he did to keep busy was read newspapers and news clippings. One of the threads that he was following was the discussion of a private university in Brantford.

Two buildings away, one of the university's best-known History professors, Terry Copp, was following the same events through his personal connections. Copp gained renown as one of Canada's best military historians, arguing, in a series of bestselling books, that our accepted views of the Second World War, of D-Day, and of the Normandy invasion, were radically mistaken. But Copp's interests were broader than military history. When he first came to Laurier, he worked on labour history. Under his tutelage, some of the students he supervised studied Brantford. In the 1970s, he himself visited, and was appalled at the deterioration he saw downtown. It made a riveting impression he did not forget.

In 1997, Copp visited again. On this occasion, he accompanied his wife, Linda Risacher Copp, an artist who was working on a series of paintings entitled *A Year on the Grand*. While in Brantford, Copp was struck by the talk of a private university downtown and wondered why it couldn't be a campus of Laurier. Back in Waterloo, he asked Arthur Stephen, the vice-president of Advancement, how he might sell the idea to Laurier's new president, Bob Rosehart. Stephen told him that the president was already watching the developments in Brantford closely. When the two of them met with Rosehart, the president was open minded. He had not yet earned his nickname, "Bob the Builder," but he was already intrigued with the possibility that he might expand Laurier's presence in southern Ontario.

Rosehart invited Copp to investigate the situation further. He contacted one of his former students, Robert Campbell, who taught high school in

Brantford. Campbell took Copp to meet Brantford's new mayor.[2] Friel was delighted with the suggestion that Laurier establish a campus in Brantford and immediately committed himself to doing what it would take to make it happen. When Copp reported back to the president, Rosehart called the mayor and took a delegation to meet with Friel and the two councillors on the city's Post-Secondary Education Committee (Mike Hancock and Vince Bucci).[3] When they came to Brantford, the Laurier contingent was given a tour of the empty Icomm Centre, which was proposed as a site for a new Laurier campus. Rosehart went back to Waterloo impressed with the building, thinking that the Brantford idea was an idea worth pursuing.

Rosehart has always said that he saw his work at Brantford as a continuation of his work at Lakehead University. In Thunder Bay, a small city in Northern Ontario, he enjoyed the close-knit community, the chance to be a central "mover and shaker," and the opportunity to represent the city and the whole northern hinterland to the world beyond. In southern Ontario, he found a "new Northern Ontario" in Brantford. He was soon immersed in Brantford goings-on and was brainstorming with the mayor and the city about the possibility of a Laurier campus. As an engineer by trade, he wanted new buildings to be the cornerstone of any new developments. In Brantford, he wanted a new campus on a greenfield site, but warmed to the idea that Laurier might establish itself in the Icomm building. He did not like the layout but was impressed with the new construction and the electrical engineering in a building that had been built to serve as a state-of-the-art telecommunications centre.

The Icomm Building after it was turned into the Brantford Charity Casino. The community debated whether the building should be used for the casino or the university. Though city council decided in favour of the casino, the decision spurred the development of the university, which the city helped fund with its portion of the casino profits.

To move the project along, Rosehart drafted a tentative agreement with the city. It proposed a ten-year lease of the Icomm building at a price of one dollar a year, with Laurier gradually taking over the building's operating costs. To cover capital renovations, the university and the city would apply to the federal government's Community Futures Program. Rosehart himself would approach the provincial ministry for funding to cover Brantford students. A Laurier Advisory Board would steer the development of academic programs and the university would hire a senior administrator from the university as "principal dean" of the new campus.

By the first months of 1998, a flurry of activity, much discussion and debate, and some intrigue consumed Brantford as three distinct post-secondary proposals vied for the right to its downtown. For those in the know, a little epic with a pantheon of colourful characters was well underway. Piloted by someone who had worked in the Kalahari and reinforced by Waterloo's renegade arts professors, the University Committee was attempting to establish a private university in the Carnegie Building. A different coalition of citizens and leaders who made up the Downtown Renewal Group were committed to a plan that would put Mohawk College and the YM/YWCA into the empty shopping mall. A short distance away, Brantford's "Boy Mayor" and "Bob the Builder" were, on the fringes of downtown, aiming to claim the Icomm Centre in the name of Laurier.

This was a heady moment for a downtown to which everyone had turned a blind eye for so long. Three different post-secondary groups were actively pursuing a location in the old downtown. And yet, for all of this, in the midst of so much activity and discussion, each of the proposals began losing its momentum. The labour of the Downtown Renewal Group notwithstanding, Mohawk College pulled the rug out from under the Mohawk/Y proposal when it decided that it would need an additional six months to study the plan, and would begin its study only after the municipal, provincial, and federal governments had committed their share of the proposed funding. Mohawk's vice-president, Cal Haddad, commented, "We still haven't had the time to do a definitive study on whether it will help Mohawk College and its students.... We're willing to listen to any concrete proposals. But we have no money, not even for a moving truck."[4]

As the Mohawk/Y initiative died, the proposed date for the opening of the University College of the Grand Valley came and went. The provincial government was clearly interested in making room for private universities, but put off any policy decisions in the wake of political pressure from existing universities. The three City College professors were pulled in other directions, by other demands and interests. Morrell secured an appointment at an existing university.

At Laurier, the idea of a satellite campus in downtown Brantford was not enthusiastically endorsed by the university community. Outside of Professor Copp, a determined President Rosehart, and a small circle of administrators the president brought on board, the prevailing mood was one of indifference and skepticism. Waterloo was preoccupied with Waterloo. Those who talked about the Brantford developments, and few did, asked why anyone would want to go to Brantford. Even among the senior administrators, some were skeptical, questioning the suitability of a campus in the Icomm Building. Further obstacles arose in February when Brantford City Council decided that it would consider a proposal to turn the Icomm Building into a charity casino.

With all three post-secondary proposals confronting obstacles, the plan to bring a college or a university downtown seemed poised to become the latest in a string of failed attempts to stop the slide of Brantford's city centre.

LEANING TOWARD LAURIER

A key component of the Brantford attempt to establish a downtown university was the community support for the idea provided by the University Committee. When Laurier's interest in the downtown was made public, the committee was faced with a decision — should it back the new initiative or maintain its commitment to a private university? Not everyone welcomed the Laurier possibility. In a patriotic spirit that was in keeping with Brantford's historic sense of self, some argued that a university based in Brantford was preferable to a satellite campus of a university based in Waterloo. In the subsequent discussion and debate, key members of the committee argued that its proposal for a private university should be maintained but broadened in scope to incorporate a range of possibilities that included a satellite campus of Laurier, or some other university.

One of the key voices to emerge in the discussion was that of Colleen Miller. She lived in Paris, Ontario, and operated a human resources firm that aimed to help its clients transform their careers and working lives. Miller was equally dedicated to the attempt to transform Brantford. Among other things, she broke through the gender barriers at the city's established gentlemen's club, The Brantford Club, to become the first woman member. Speaking for the University Committee, she took the lead welcoming Laurier's interest in Brantford: "The exciting thing is that there are big universities out there hearing about this community, and now we have the option of looking at two possible paths."[1]

Despite the growing local support, the plan to bring Laurier to Brantford faltered as the proposal to turn the Icomm building into a casino gathered steam. At a meeting in February, city council voted to give a professional casino company, RPC Anchor Gaming, an option to purchase the Icomm. When President Rosehart heard of the initiative, he hesitated but was not ready to give up on the idea of a satellite campus. The university was "still interested" he told *The Expositor* in early March. "We've emotionally put the Icomm building behind us. I admit it was Icomm and the work of the university committee that got our interest. But even with the building gone, it's not like we're going to give up. We've just switched to Plan B."[2]

On March 4, the University Committee and the Grand Valley Education Society came out in support of "the golden opportunity" at Laurier, which

Courtesy of Wilfrid Laurier University.

LEFT: *Colleen Miller, who has served as president and director of the Grand Valley Educational Society, has been one of the key community supporters of a Laurier campus in Brantford.* RIGHT: *Kate Carter was one of the campus's first professors and later served as associate dean and dean. She received her Ph.D. from the University of Alberta and then taught at Duke. As a girl growing up in Paris, Ontario, she never imagined that it would be possible to teach at a university in Brant County.*

it decided to pursue as part of a two-pronged push to attract a private or a public university downtown. At a meeting that discussed the Laurier option, "The 44-member Community University group quickly pledged to help Rosehart in any way possible.

Members have been scouting out possible locations for the campus, among them the former library, the Bell Building and the third floor of the federal building. 'We'd love to see [Laurier] come here,' Doug Brown said. 'The trick is not to lose the momentum [for a private university] if it chooses not to come here. We are committed to a university in Brantford no matter what.'"[3]

A week later, seven months after the University College of the Grand Valley had been scheduled to welcome its first class, the University Committee released a one-hundred-page *Revised Business Plan* for a private university now called "Brant University." The proposal was an expanded version of the City College plan. The mission statement and curriculum remained the same; similar partnerships were proposed (the library partnership was now backed with a detailed prospectus compiled by Anne Church, a professional consultant hired by the library); and similar buildings were suggested as a home for the university (among them, the Icomm — which was already optioned to the casino company and no longer available — the Carnegie Library, and the old Boys' and Girls' Club). The plan was well-intentioned, but some of its details show that it was thrown together in haste, in an attempt to respond to all the developments in the drive for a university. Some aspects of the plan were simply impossible — further revisions were to be made by January/February 1998, one month *before* the plan was released, and two million dollars in fundraising would have had to be organized and initiated as soon as the plan was released. The details of the plan included an ambitious timetable for the development of Ontario's first private university: a detailed curriculum and governance structures by June, an application for a provincial charter in one year, the appointment of a president by June 1999, the hiring of full-time professors by March 2000, and an opening in September 2000 or, if necessary, September 2001.

Like the plan for a University College of the Grand Valley, the Brant University Plan did not provide a convincing business plan for the building and operation of a university. But this did not prevent it from underscoring, yet again, the reasons to bring a university to Brantford. By now, anyone who followed local news and events knew and understood some of the sixteen reasons given for establishing a university downtown. These included Brant County's low participation rate in post-secondary education, the access to university education it would provide for local families, and the role that a university and its graduates could play in the economic and cultural development of the region. The economic benefits were calculated at twenty-four million dollars a year. In a city that had not recovered from the collapse of its industrial economy, with a downtown still mired in urban decay, these were compelling reasons to support a Brant University.

Like the proposal to establish University College of the Grand Valley, the Brant University Plan was innovative. There was much that could be said for it but there was no way to change the fact that a private university in Brantford would have been an anomaly that would face many challenges. It was not easy to see how any university could attract students to Brantford's crumbling downtown, but much more difficult to imagine a successful private university managing it. In a university system in which the existing institutions were locked in a perpetual competition for interested students, how would a (secular) private institution lure them with no reputation, higher tuition costs, and a foreign view of education? The answer to this question remains a central issue in the Canadian university system, but it was quickly moot in Brantford, where the city's civic officials and the public advocates for a university turned their attention to the Laurier initiative. The two plans for a private university are now forgotten, though one aspect of their trajectory intersected with the Laurier initiative when one of the original City College professors, Edmund Pries, took up a position at Laurier Brantford.

Within the Laurier community, the Brantford cause was pushed by a determined Professor Copp, who returned to visit Brantford after city council voted to sell the Icomm Building to RPC Gaming. In the course of his private campaign to push the university in a Brantford direction, he met with city officials, took eye-catching photos of the Carnegie Building and the square, and did his best to create some enthusiasm for an elegant "campus around the Square." In Waterloo, the university's chief academic, Rowland Smith, warmed to the idea that Brantford could be an innovative campus with the potential to allow Laurier to develop a university education that would distinguish it from other Canadian universities. Laurier's longest-serving dean, Art Read, was looking for a new challenge and began to discuss the Brantford possibility with Copp, Smith, and President Rosehart.

As the Laurier community discussed what the university might do at Brantford, the fate of the Icomm Building hovered as an unsettled detail in the background. City council had granted RPC Gaming an option to buy the building, but this did not end the debate. Financially, the construction of the building had been supported by many Brantfordians who believed that downtown revival should include a new home for the Bell archives. They had a personal stake in what happened to the Icomm, which seemed to be headed in a very different direction than the one that they envisaged. A member of the Grand Valley Education Society who had contributed to the project told me he felt "betrayed" by the city's actions. With emotions running high, the disposal of the building became a matter of controversy and debate. The proposal that it become the site of a Laurier campus only added fuel to the fire. Council had voted to give RPC Gaming an option to purchase the building but it had not been ratified and now they were being inundated with objections. The mayor, some council members, and a host of critics began to argue that the city should withdraw its commitment to the option.

Some of those objecting to the sale of the Icomm opposed the proposed price — four million dollars for a building that had cost twenty-four million to construct. A city-wide referendum had voted in favour of a casino, but many more commentators objected to the sale on moral grounds. Letters to the editor of the Brantford *Expositor* argued back and forth. Dale Fisher, president of District 5 of the Ontario Secondary School Teacher's Federation, wrote that teachers were concerned that a casino would wield a negative influence on their students. He did not convince another letter-writer who argued that casino jobs were the most important part of the equation. Someone else wrote that a university would, in the long run, be more valuable than a casino.

Max Sherman, a former city councillor, proposed a compromise between the two sides, suggesting that the Icomm be sold to the casino, but that some of the proceeds be used to support a university. When it was argued that the university had expressed its interest in the Icomm too late — after the RPC option was finalized — Councillor Starkey obtained and circulated an internal Laurier memo that proved otherwise. At a heated council session held to discuss the Icomm sale, the vast majority of the delegations loudly opposed the sale. President Rosehart followed the debate from Waterloo, refusing to be drawn into it. He was still interested in the Icomm, but his experience as a university president had taught him to keep his head low in the midst of public controversy.

Despite all objections, which included Mayor Friel's arguments in favour of the university option, the pro-casino forces prevailed on April 15, 1998, when city council ratified RPC's option to purchase the Icomm. The decision required the company to purchase the building before January 1, 1999. For some, including President Rosehart, this kept alive a glimmer of hope that the sale would not be consummated. In the meantime, a resolute mayor and University Committee continued to court Laurier. After a meeting with Professor Copp on April 20, Friel and the city's chief administrative officer, Geoff Wilson, began to work earnestly on a plan that would give the university the Carnegie Building.

The agreement had to be worded in a way that managed some sensitive concerns on both sides. In a city full of doubts about itself, some worried that Laurier had ulterior motives in pursuing Brantford land and funding. Some argued that the university could sell any building it acquired, and use the proceeds to fund operations back in Waterloo. There was some illogicality in this line of reasoning — it is difficult to see how the university could have made a profit selling a building that no one had been willing to purchase for almost a decade — but it was an emotionally charged suspicion deeply rooted in the Brantford psyche. As fate would have it, this was not a barrier to an agreement because of the university's own insecurities — it did not want to own property in Brantford. Instead, the university preferred the ownership to remain in Brantford, as this would make it easier to leave if the new campus did not take off.

On May 14, city council tried to reconcile the Icomm sale with the Laurier initiative, agreeing to dedicate two million dollars, half of the proceeds, to the development of a local Laurier campus. At the same meeting, council approved a draft agreement among the three participants: the city, the Grand Valley Education Society, and Laurier. The agreement offered the university the Carnegie Library on the understanding that the city would renovate the building to make a suitable building for a campus. The provincial courthouse attached to the city hall, two buildings down the street, was identified as a location that could accommodate future expansion.

The city's proposed agreement included appendices designed to show support for a Laurier campus. Appendix A was the business plan for "Brant University." Appendix B was a description of the Sanderson Centre and other community facilities. Appendix C included letters of support from the local member of Parliament, Jane Stewart; the County of Brant; Six Nations of the Grand River Territory; and some supporters who had little connection to post-secondary education (as a joke, someone told me that the Brant Synchro Club and Gatquatic Divers, who were in reality trying to be supportive members of the community, signed up in the hopes that some classes would be held in the Grand River). In return for its support, the city's proposed contract required Laurier to: commence operations by September 1, 1999; offer "a distinctive full university degree program within the community"; report annually on the progress of the campus; and ensure community involvement and participation in its operations. The desire to create a truly Brantford institution was evident in a proposal that the university "set up the operations of the Brantford campus as a Federated independent college with autonomy and independent decision-making capabilities within 10 years."[4]

At Laurier, President Rosehart struggled with some details of the plans. He was impressed by the strength of Brantford's desire for a university, most evident in its willingness to provide financial support for a campus. But he did not like old buildings and was not captivated by the neoclassical grandeur of the Carnegie Library. He preferred the Icomm Centre or, even better, a campus made up of new buildings. In order to maintain the momentum he had generated in Brantford and accommodate these preferences, he insisted that the proposed agreement outline two phases of development. He was willing to accept buildings around "beautiful Victoria Park" as "Phase One" of a Laurier campus, but he did not envision them as the campus's final site. That was expressly outlined in a proposed "Phase Two," which would "identify and procure green space of approximately 50 acres and undertake fundraising to construct brand new facilities of approximately 30,000 square feet. The greenfield site that would house Laurier's final campus would incorporate,

as much as was possible, space for future growth, ready access to transportation routes, sufficient on-site parking, close proximity to existing parks and recreation facilities, easy site servicing, and a view of the Grand River."[5]

The Glebe lands, parkland in central Brantford owned by Six Nations, were cited as a potential property that met all of these requirements. A possible partnership with Six Nations was envisioned, but, as it was not clear whether Six Nations of the Grand River Territory were interested, it was not made the subject of the detailed negotiations that would have been required in a community where land claims remain a controversial issue both in the city and at Six Nations. As things played out, the discussion of this possibility was obviated by subsequent developments which abandoned the idea of a greenfield campus in favour of a downtown site.

In the wake of all the controversy over the disposal of the Icomm, city council's discussion of the draft agreement with Laurier was characterized by voracious wrangling over procedure. This was a sign of things to come. Councillors took exception to Mayor Friel's handling of the situation, arguing that he had negotiated with Laurier behind the scenes, that they had been improperly excluded from the discussions, and that he had not adequately informed council of the agreement. A local journalist, Ross Marowits, wrote an opinion piece on the meeting in which the agreement with Laurier was approved, entitling it "Council's Infighting Spoils Moment." In lambasting council, he wrote that "process is only part of the problem. The circus-like atmosphere of recent council meetings, political grandstanding, posturing for the television cameras, rambling

questions, childish pouting and lack of discipline
have devalued the institution itself."[6]

The vehemence of the debate notwithstanding, the political infighting vanished on May 15,
the day after city council approved an agreement
with Laurier, a day when the city and the University
Committee presented the agreement to President
Rosehart, Professor Copp, and Dean Read at a joint
presentation at Brantford City Hall. To mark the
occasion, the city's council chamber was dressed in
flowers and festooned with balloons and decorations
featuring Laurier's official colours of purple and gold.
A Chamber of Commerce wine and cheese reception followed. On behalf of the university, President
Rosehart received the city proposal and promised
to take it to Laurier for study and approval. But he
emphasized that the studying must at some point
stop: "Then you get like the Nike commercial and
you 'Just Do It.'"[7]

| 8 |

A TIMELY MOVE

On June 29, 1998, six weeks after Brantford's city hall presentation to Laurier, the university, the city, and the Grand Valley Education Society signed a formal Declaration of Intent which committed them to work out a formal agreement that "will lead to the creation of a campus of Wilfrid Laurier University in the City of Brantford." President Rosehart, Mayor Friel, and Colleen Miller signed the agreement. The three parties agreed that they would aim for an agreement to be signed by September 1998, to allow a campus to open by September 1999.

A key component of the agreement was the participation of the Grand Valley Education Society, which represented the community's support of the initiative. The members worked well with President Rosehart, who liked to roll up his sleeves and work with the local community. Inside Laurier, however, some did not like his unassuming style. On an occasion when I asked him what had happened to his glasses, which he had taped together after a minor accident, he laughed and said that he had worn them that way for three weeks. There were those at Laurier who wanted a presidential style that was more lofty and remote, but Rosehart's demeanour worked well in Brantford, where the community was impressed by his unpretentious manner and his interest in local goings-on. The interest was genuine; he wanted to ensure that a new Laurier campus would be enmeshed in the Brantford community, and could rely on it for political, social, and much-needed financial support. From his perspective, the broad coalition of citizens who made up the Education Society was a key component of his new initiative.

The June Declaration of Intent, designed to create positive momentum for the idea of a Laurier campus in Brantford, more than succeeded, receiving a great deal of media attention. It was commented on locally, provincially, nationally, and even internationally, when it was mentioned in an article about Canadian universities in the *Economist*.[1] On the day of the signing, the *Globe and Mail* published a photo of GVES members on the steps of the Carnegie Building, reporting that "University Plan Excites Brantford — WLU to Open Branch Campus."

> Brantford, Ont. — The industrial legs of this lunch-bucket city were chopped off a decade ago. Its downtown core, pitted with empty store

fronts, is a withered reminder of better days.

But despite economic setbacks and false starts in recent years, no one could kill the dream of a university for this community of 81,000 people.

At a ceremony here today, the dream will begin to feel real when the city and the Grand Valley Education Society, which spearheaded the campaign, sign a letter of intent with Wilfrid Laurier University to establish a campus next year in the 96-year-old Carnegie Library, which dominates the city's picturesque, tree-filled main square.[2]

A successful Brantford campus would have to be supported by provincial funding for the students who attended (whose tuition could not cover the cost of running a contemporary campus), and, ideally, for building projects. Two months after the declaration of intent, on August 28, 1998, President Rosehart wrote to the minister of education and training, Dave Johnson, requesting funding for a new campus. "This is an innovative approach to community-based university access," he wrote, "and I think it is fair to say the initiative has captured the minds of the citizens in the Brantford area." In his letter, the president compared the university's decision to open a Brantford campus to the government's decision to launch a new university in Oshawa. Begun as the Durham University Centre, the project was given sixty million dollars of provincial start-up funding when it became the newest university in

the province, the University of Ontario Institute of Technology. Administrators at other universities saw the project as a political handout, and griped that too much money had been spent on the project — money that would have been better spent on their own institutions. They pronounced the new university's acronym UOIT as "you-owe-it."

UOIT set a precedent for the development of new university campuses, but Minister Johnson ignored Rosehart's request for funding in Brantford. The government's cold shoulder, however, did not change attitudes at Laurier or Brantford, where the planning of a campus continued unabated. As questions turned to the details, two prominent university figures were drawn into the planning process. One was the vice-president academic, Rowland Smith. The other was Art Read, the dean of arts and science. Smith was a Rhodes Scholar who loved opera (sometimes singing librettos at his meetings) and liked to sign his memos as "Orlando Furioso" ("Mad Orlando"), after the hero of an obscure sixteenth-century Italian epic. Dean Read was one of the dedicated people who had made Laurier what it was. He began his career teaching in the Physics Department, became chair, developed a special interest in the physics of music and moved on and up, becoming the longest-serving dean of the university's largest faculty.

In the planning of the Brantford campus, Smith and Read were unlikely bedfellows. An old adage about university politics has it that "If one and one made only one, there would be something to be done." At universities, one and one rarely make one because they are free-thinking institutions full of clever individuals who rarely agree about the right way forward. This is the root of the disagreement

Taking the next step

Our new program on the Brantford campus offers students in the Brantford area a first-class liberal arts program, close to home. Its innovative elements are really exciting: All will share the educational experience of the core courses and will, as a result, quickly develop an identity as Brantford students. I am exhilarated at the prospect of fashioning this unique program, and am confident that the students who join it will be seen—years later— to have been specially distinguished by their experience in the development of such a progressive venture.

Rowland Smith

Dr. Rowland Smith
Vice-President: Academic

BEYOND FIRST YEAR

More advanced courses will be added over the next two years, giving second- and third-year students access to the classes they want and need to finish their degrees. Some of those courses will likely be core courses, and senior students will also be required to take advanced-level, subject-specific courses.

We expect to develop concentrations in four key areas at the Brantford campus. These are: Computing, Communications, Cultural Studies, and Management.

HOW TO GET IN TOUCH WITH US

ADMISSIONS: Gail Forsyth, Manager
(519) 884-0710, Ext. 6099 E-mail: admissions@mach1.wlu.ca

STUDENT AWARDS: Pauline Delion, Director
(519) 884-0710, Ext. 4256 E-mail: pdelion@mach2.wlu.ca

ASSISTANT VICE-PRESIDENT AND DEAN OF STUDENTS:
David McMurray (519) 884-0710, Ext. 3319

CAREER SERVICES: Jan Basso, Director
(519) 884-0710, Ext. 4137

GENERAL QUESTIONS: Dr. Arthur Read
Dean of Arts and Sciences (519) 884-0710, Ext. 3602

OUR WEB SITE IS: www.wlu.ca

Wilfrid Laurier University has received a very warm welcome from Brantford and its residents, and now I'd like to extend an equally warm message to the people of Brantford and area: Welcome to Laurier! We're glad to be here and together we're going to make great things happen! This publication answers many of the questions you may have about Laurier and about being a Laurier student. We hope you like what you see, and if the information you want isn't here, please feel free to contact any of the Laurier staff members listed here. Hope to see you in September!

Robert Rosehart

Dr. Robert Rosehart
President and Vice-Chancellor
Wilfrid Laurier University

"Starting a new campus with an innovative curriculum has been a challenging and exciting experience. We're pleased to be part of the Brantford community, and we look forward to a great future for a great program."
Dr. Arthur Read
Dean of Arts and Science
Director, The Brantford Project

LEFT: *President Rosehart and Vice-President Smith in Laurier Brantford's first recruitment brochure.* RIGHT: *Dean Read in a photograph for university advancement.*

and political manoeuvring that makes universities infamous. At Laurier, the internal politics revolved around two sides of a political divide represented by Read and Smith respectively. Read became an administrator at a time when the university was run by "home-grown" talent — professors who taught and then ascended to administrative ranks. The result was a crop of leaders who were intimately attached to the university — to its history, its values, and its very strong sense of community. Smith belonged to a new cohort of leaders who arrived when Laurier began to hire outsiders to senior administrative positions. The new set of leaders, Smith among them, did not see themselves as leaders imbued with a responsibility to preserve and sustain what was good about the old Laurier. More often than not, they were prone to change it, in ways that were frequently inspired by their experience at their previous institutions.

In a period of transition, Laurier's "old" and "new" guard often clashed. In the case of Smith and Read, their conflicting allegiances were manifest in differing attitudes toward the university's largest faculty, the Faculty of Arts and Science. At his previous institution, Dalhousie University, Smith had divided its Faculty of Arts and Science into two separate entities: a Faculty of Arts and a Faculty of Science. He saw this as one of his key accomplishments and believed that this was the right way for universities to operate. Read believed the opposite, seeing no reason why the university should split its most important and successful faculty. Among the rank-and-file faculty, one could find professors on both sides of the debate. As it proceeded, the result was two clever leaders, one from the old guard, one from the new, trying to strategically out-manoeuvre each other in favour of the arrangement they preferred.

In the midst of the battle over the fate of the Faculty of Arts and Science, some were surprised to find Smith announcing that he was appointing Read the director of the Brantford project. Their deep differences were a portent of what was to come in Brantford, but Read's appointment in September 1998 was a positive move for both of them. Smith needed an experienced administrator for the Brantford project but this was a case where there was more going on. For him, a veteran administrator who knew how to get what he wanted, the appointment was politically expedient; it moved Read out of the Faculty of Arts and Science, where he continued to be the major obstacle to Smith's passionate desire to split the faculty. This did not mean that the appointment made no sense for Read, for this was a battle he could not sustain as he was coming to the end of his third and final term as the dean of the faculty. The Brantford appointment intrigued him and provided him with a bold way to extend his fifteen-year career in administration.

Once appointed, Dean Read became the focal point for all aspects of the Brantford plans: curriculum development, liaison with the City of Brantford, relations with Grand Valley Education Society (GVES) and other local groups, student recruitment, and building renovations (which he oversaw with Ron Dupuis, the director of the university's Physical Plant and Planning). Under the guidance of Read and Smith, a curriculum committee began work on a three-year interdisciplinary BA and a program in musical theatre that aimed to take advantage of the Sanderson Centre as a Brantford venue. By now, the university was committed to Brantford, but not in a way that settled the location of the campus. With his penchant for tradition, history, and classical refinement, Smith saw the Carnegie Library as one of the few assets that downtown Brantford could provide. Read and President Rosehart were skeptical, and continued to covet the Icomm, which they saw as a more utilitarian and a better long-term alternative.

In an interview in *The Expositor*, Read acknowledged that the vice-president academic "loved" the Carnegie, but:

> "The president and I still like Icomm for lots of reasons, not the least of which is the long-term usefulness of the building," said Read. "I'm being optimistic, but I think we're going to grow out of the Carnegie building quickly and I hate to see the city put a lot of money into it and then have us leave." Read said the city feels it will have to invest in renovating the Carnegie building anyway, so the money won't be wasted. "But in terms of WLU's identity and how it will fit into the community, a long-term site would be more desirable," said Read.[3]

Despite Read's and Rosehart's lingering desire for the Icomm, its impending sale meant that it was not available, and Laurier and the city signed a formal agreement to turn the Carnegie Building into a Laurier campus at the end of October. Rosehart continued to envision it as a temporary arrangement.

Sensitive to his views, the city promised to provide the building for the purpose of establishing "a degree granting program," on the understanding that the university had "the intent of establishing at some time in the future a permanent campus in Brantford." When the number of students attending the University in Brantford increased "to four hundred or more students per annum," the city promised to designate two million dollars in proceeds from the sale of the Icomm building "towards the establishment of a permanent campus or towards the capital costs of the expansion of the University's activities."[4]

The new agreement was conditional on a fund-raising agreement with the Grand Valley Education Society, which was quickly negotiated and signed. In return for a commitment to establish a general Bachelor of Arts program, the society agreed to "assist Laurier in soliciting funds from the public in Brant County for the maintenance and support of the Program, and for scholarships for students attending the Program."[5] The university promised to "give serious consideration to taking such actions as may be necessary to have the Brantford Campus evolve into a federated college of Laurier ... at such time as there are in excess of five hundred (500) full-time students (or their equivalency in part-time registrations) enrolled."[6]

As the city, the university, and the GVES worked on the different components of the new campus, the agreements they signed generated a great deal of comment and publicity. Locally, there were some grumblings of dissent, most of them objecting to the money the city was using to fund Laurier's move to Brantford. In a letter to *The Expositor*, one critic complained that "This city must have money to burn, judging by what was signed between this city and Wilfrid Laurier University. Who at city hall was the genius behind this financial sink hole...? Services are being cut, surcharges are added and taxes being raised, but the decision makers at city hall have seen fit, putting the taxpayers of this city on the hook for close to three million dollars, so far."[7] But the nay-sayers remained a small minority. As it became clear that something was really going to happen, most of the city embraced Mayor Friel's remark that "This is a timely move: there is no better way to start the next 150 years of Brantford's existence than with the establishment of a new university campus for our students. This sets a clear agenda for the future of our community."[8]

Outside of Brantford, the optimism was endorsed by the Royal Bank when it awarded the GVES and the development board that created it a first-place prize in their 1998 Community Economic Development Awards. In the flush of all the energy and enthusiasm, it was easy to forget that it was not yet clear whether a university campus was viable in downtown Brantford. No one knew whether Laurier would be able to attract the students needed to make the campus work. At the provincial legislature, it was a worrisome sign that the provincial government continued to ignore what was going on in Brantford.

| 9 |

THE LIBERAL ARTS

Brantford saw Laurier's downtown campus as an experiment in urban renewal. President Rosehart saw it as an opportunity to expand Laurier. For Rowland Smith, the advent of Laurier Brantford was something different. He was charmed by the Carnegie Library and Victoria Square but blasé about the City of Brantford. What interested him was not the city, but the chance to create a new campus with a distinctive mission. He believed that more of what was available on the Waterloo campus would not give Brantford a strong *raison d'être* and make it difficult to attract students to the new venture. Why, he asked, would students go to a fledgling campus in gritty downtown Brantford if they could get the same programs in a well-established campus with a great reputation, and more students, courses, professors, and resources only fifty kilometres away?

Smith wanted to answer this challenge by creating a campus that would have an academic mission that distinguished it, not only from Laurier Waterloo, but from other universities. As Laurier's chief academic, he wanted to turn the Brantford project into an opportunity to change Canada's post-secondary system. He and Read agreed that they would do so by reviving an ideal that had, like the downtown in cities like Brantford, fallen on hard times. It was incorporated in the loosely defined set of disciplines known as the "liberal arts" or, as Read the physicist liked to emphasize, "the liberal arts *and sciences*." When they decided to move in this direction, they were, unknowingly, following in the footsteps of the renegade professors who had put together the Brantford plan for a University College of the Grand Valley. This was not coincidence so much as a conviction they shared with many critics of contemporary education: that we need to reclaim the liberal arts and sciences and reassert their role in university education.

Viewed from the street, the story of Laurier Brantford is one of urban redevelopment. As important as that story is, it is intertwined with a parallel narrative about university education and the attempt to push it in a particular direction. Much of the latter took place behind the scenes, in meeting rooms and offices at Laurier. It began with Smith's decision to build the Brantford campus around the liberal arts, a decision that favoured the first of two competing views of higher education — the belief that it should aim at the education "of the whole person" versus the belief that it should aim at more pragmatic objectives like employment. The ideal that Smith, then Read, then Laurier advocated was rooted in the very birth of universities in the Middle Ages, when the *artes liberales* defined the educated person. They consisted of seven basic subjects (usually Grammar, Rhetoric, Logic, Arithmetic, Geometry, Music, Astronomy, and Cosmology), which aimed, at least in theory, to make the educated person someone who was urbane, culturally and historically aware, and able to speak, write, and argue well.

In North American universities, the liberal arts ideal has been associated with the study of the "great books canon," made up of texts like the Bible, Sophocles, Plato, Tolstoy, Shakespeare, Maimonides, et cetera. In an era that has raised deep questions about gender and cultural biases, it has been roundly criticized for its emphasis on "Dead White Guys," but variants of liberal arts curricula and canon persist, especially in the United States. More generally, the term *liberal arts and sciences* has come to designate higher education characterized by a few key themes — an emphasis on general education; writing and reasoning and communication skills; the study of historically significant texts; and an attempt to instill in students an understanding and appreciation of the world of ideas, history, culture, science, and contemporary issues. In most Canadian universities, what remains of the liberal arts tradition is found in the disparate disciplines with which it had been traditionally associated — English, literature, philosophy, classics, religious studies, history, music, and so on. This has made faculties of arts and humanities the prime inheritors of the liberal arts tradition.[1]

In contemporary education, debates about liberal arts education raise fundamental questions about

Drawing by the author.

This is a copy of a detail from the Herrad of Landsberg illustration "The Seven Liberal Arts" in Hortus deliciarum, *folio 32, circa 1180. Herrad was the Abbess of Hohenburg Abbey. The detail presents Dialectics as one of seven liberal arts (Dialectics, Music, Arithmetic, Geometry, Astronomy, Grammar, and Rhetoric). The barking dog Dialectic holds represents the dialectician's ability to respond (with arguments) as quickly and forcefully as a barking dog.*

the purpose of a university education. Should it aim at general knowledge, which creates informed, well-rounded citizens of tomorrow? Or should it provide students with preparation for a particular job? As the citizens of Brantford worked to establish a physical campus for Laurier's new experiment, these were the questions discussed by Smith and Read and an interdisciplinary committee made up of Laurier professors from History, Biology, Religion and Culture, Geography, and Philosophy (my own introduction to Brantford was as a member of this committee).[2] Against liberal arts education, many commentators complained that it does not provide students with entry into meaningful jobs and careers. In favour of it, others maintained that specialized job training was not the most important part of university education, even from the point of view of career development. In a rapidly changing world in which specialized knowledge was quickly outdated, and often constrained one, they maintained that the aim of undergraduate education should be general knowledge, a love of ideas, and the ability to read and think and create in a rigorous and sophisticated way.

In the world of careers and employment, the liberal arts were often derided. Jokes declared that the difference between a pizza and a liberal arts degree was that a pizza can feed a family of four. As employment councillors tirelessly pointed out, the reality was different. In the course of their careers, most liberal arts and science graduates ascend to management or professional occupations. Many of them enjoy remarkable success. In Canada, the career of the chief justice of the Supreme Court of Canada, Madam Chief Justice Beverley McLachlin, illustrates the point:

> After entering the University of Alberta in 1960, McLachlin became smitten by philosophy.... "At that

Courtesy of Drew and Toothpaste for Dinner.

One cartoonist on how to make the most of a liberal arts degree in one's employment.

point in my life — I was eighteen, I suppose — I felt my brain was very muddled. I had a lot of ideas, and I was having trouble putting structure and order on things," she says. "It helped me learn to order my ideas better, because philosophy is insistent on approaching things in an analytical, logical way. You have to be able to defend or analytically attack a position, and you have to be able to set out either process in clear terms that other people can understand."[3]

80

At Laurier, the curriculum committee charged with the development of Brantford programming came down firmly in support of Smith's vision of a campus that emphasized the liberal arts and sciences. As the Brantford community worked on the details of the financing and design of a campus in the old Carnegie Library, the curriculum group was busy designing a version of the liberal arts ideal that would provide it with its academic content. In the process, Read and his committee took on a challenge that was, in the world of higher education, as unlikely as the one that Brantford had embarked on. In Brantford, the city was trying to revive its historically important but devastated core. In Laurier, the curriculum committee was trying to revive the historical centre of university education at a time when it was precipitously on the wane.

The decline in the liberal arts was especially evident in faculties of arts and humanities which were struggling. As Professor David Bentley of the University of Western Ontario noted in a much-lauded 1999 address to the Canadian Congress of Social Sciences and Humanities, the departments they contained were "seldom prosperous and often just getting by as a consequence of reduced funds, declining enrolments, decimated faculty and staff complements, and mounting government and public skepticism."[4]

One might, and many did, debate the root causes of the problems within the liberal arts at the end of the twentieth century. Whatever one's analysis, it was clear that one of them was economic. As globalization, a rapidly changing economy, and economic ups and downs of the sort that undermined the city of Brantford raised worries about employment, university students and their parents increasingly favoured programs they viewed as a route to a job or professional career. In the climate this produced, their focus shifted from the liberal arts to disciplines and programs that claimed to have more practical utility — business, social work, law, medicine, health studies, engineering, nursing, teacher training, computing, information technology, and other career-specific programs.

In the course of this evolution, the values that shaped universities shifted. In medieval times, the liberal arts were liberal because they were studied by the free man, the man who had the liberty (the freedom) to engage in study for its own sake. They were contrasted with the "illiberal" arts — arts which consisted of applied disciplines designed to teach a practical skill that would help a student earn a living. In the midst of economic uncertainties at the end of the twentieth century, post-secondary students and their parents turned the hierarchy of programs in the original university on its head, making the illiberal arts their primary purpose, making the liberal arts the university's less favoured offspring.

As the popularity of applied programs increased among students and parents, their leanings were reinforced by governments, which no longer embraced the idea that the central aim of higher education should be the well-rounded, cultivated person. Instead, funding decisions favoured career preparation and applied research. In Ontario, successive Mike Harris governments championed such a view, pushing higher education in the direction of job training. In the fall of 1999, the year that Laurier's Brantford campus opened, the Ontario throne speech announced that "Your government believes that students deserve to graduate with the skills and knowledge they need to get jobs. It will expand the number of college and university courses with direct job links. And it will start measuring and publishing job placement results for graduates of all college and university programs."[3] In the climate this produced, universities repackaged their operations, presenting themselves as economic engines that should be supported as a means of economic development.

As governments and students pushed universities away from the liberal arts, they were pulled in other directions by their search for supplementary funding, which was manifest in "development" (at universities, a euphemistic term for fundraising) activities. In comparison with their American counterparts, which enjoyed strong philanthropic traditions, Canadian universities had relied on more generous public funding. As the latter declined, they turned to private donations as a way to bolster budgets. This move enjoyed some success, but in a manner that had a marginal impact on the liberal arts, primarily because the most significant philanthropists were successful business people, corporations, or professional organizations, who used their donations to support the programming that mirrored their own interests. Most significantly, they supported initiatives in business schools and medicine. Once again, the remnants of the liberal arts were left with a steadily decreasing portion of an ever smaller pie.

In the financial climate these different trends produced, the liberal arts felt increasingly neglected and ignored. In university planning, the "action" was elsewhere, in applied subjects and disciplines that attracted more money and more attention. The

liberal arts and sciences continued to persist, but with prospects that were, in Professor Bentley's words, "gloomy," as they were forced to get by without the funding, the resources, and the attention needed to maintain them as vibrant and dynamic enterprises. Like the sagging old buildings that lined the streets of downtowns like Brantford, they looked forward to a future of continuing decline.

At Laurier, the issues raised by the decline of the liberal arts played themselves out in academic planning for the Brantford campus. The City of Brantford aimed to revitalize its downtown by reinventing it as a home for higher education. In the process it hoped to dispel prejudices about the futility of downtown. At Laurier, the Brantford curriculum committee aimed to revitalize the liberal arts by reinventing them in the form of an interdisciplinary program that would be designed to show, in opposition to the current prejudices, that the liberal arts and sciences were relevant in contemporary education. Smith wanted the new program to be a "core" curriculum — a program and set of courses that all students in Brantford would enroll in — devoted to the liberal arts. It would emphasize writing and reasoning skills, and expose students to culture, history, and the discussion of science and contemporary issues. In Canada, where university students have a relatively free hand deciding on the courses that they take, the notion of a core curriculum was a radical idea. The idea that it should be a program devoted to the liberal arts and sciences was even more so.

Read and his curriculum committee designed the Brantford core curriculum. Like Smith, he rejected the prevailing notion that the liberal arts and sciences should be replaced by specialized training for particular careers. When he advised incoming under-graduates, he told them that thirty-plus years as a professor and administrator had taught him that it didn't really matter what majors they took. Whatever discipline they chose, their future would be enhanced by better thinking skills and general knowledge. It was not the knowledge of a specific career that mattered, but the ability to learn, to assess data, dissect an issue, to address an argument, et cetera that would be the basis of their future successes.

In designing the Brantford curriculum, the Laurier professors charged with this task were determined to create a curriculum that appealed to students. Their own teaching had taught them that today's students were "allergic" to many of the texts that made up the traditional liberal arts curriculum. Most found Virgil, Hobbes, Newton, and Aristotle impenetrable and irrelevant to their lives. To ensure that this did not undermine the Brantford curriculum, which could survive only by attracting students, the curriculum committee organized its version of the liberal arts and sciences in the form of a program it named Contemporary Studies. As the name suggests, it was designed to provide a general education that focused on contemporary issues and concerns, aiming to illuminate them by applying the kinds of skills and knowledge — and to some extent the texts and problems — that were the basis of the study of the traditional arts and sciences. A student in the program might still study Aristotle or Newton, but Contemporary Studies was designed to allow them to do so in the context of contemporary issues and concerns, a context which would underscore their relevance.

The Contemporary Studies curriculum was designed to make Laurier's Brantford campus a campus that was, in the words of its mission statement, dedicated to "the liberal arts and sciences and their ability to provide students with the skills and knowledge relevant to contemporary issues and concerns."[6] The decision to create a campus centred on a core program of this kind was more daring than the original committee realized. It meant that every Brantford student would have to choose the liberal arts and sciences at a time when their value was in question and interest in them was on the wane. In order to be successful, this meant that the new campus would have to attract students and interest, not only to an urban centre in decline, but to a historically important component of university education that was also spiralling downward. In an educational and an urban context, the Brantford campus was an attempt to revive a faltering, diminished core that had lost its pride of place.

| 10 |

A GRAND OPENING

As Laurier worked out the details of a curriculum in Waterloo, a flurry of activity unfolded in Brantford. In less than a year, Laurier, the City of Brantford, and the Grand Valley Education Society needed to complete a multi-million-dollar fundraising drive, as well as create a fully functioning campus with a finished building, a curriculum, staff, professors, and students. Despite the complexity of the endeavour, everyone committed to an opening in September 1999. Colleen Miller and the other members of the Grand Valley Education Society were full of energy and enthusiasm. Miller saw her dream of a Brantford university becoming a reality, and she and her colleagues made the most of the myriad of connections that tied them to every facet of the Brantford community, jumping in to help whenever something needed to be done.[1]

The GVES decided that Laurier needed a physical presence in Brantford, and set about trying to arrange it. The Carnegie Library was their preferred location but it was being readied for renovation and thus not available. The group talked to their local MP, Jane Stewart, and then applied to Human Resources and Development Canada (HRDC) for funding. In the end, the Royal Bank offered an empty downtown office they had vacated when they moved to their new building on the end of Colborne Street. The well-located site, half a block from Victoria Square on Market Street, became the nerve centre for Laurier activities in Brantford.

The director of the Brantford project, Art Read, had been working on his new initiative for months, both in Waterloo and in Brantford. In Waterloo, he became an ambassador for Brantford, exploiting the network of relationships he had established over many years at Laurier (some joked that he had become "an advertisement for Brantford"). In Brantford, he embraced the local leaders who were driving the university initiative. At the beginning of February, he was appointed the dean of the Brantford campus, an appointment designed to make him an integral member of Laurier's senior administration. With the opening scheduled for seven months away, one of the key tasks he supervised was the hiring of campus staff and faculty. To foster the local interest in what was happening, he wanted to hire locally, but it was even more important to find qualified staff who understood universities, which are peculiar institutions that retain a medieval structure.

Read assembled the kind of mix that he was looking for. A number of his new employees lived in Brantford (one had been born at Brantford General; one had graduated from Pauline Johnson Collegiate, and another from North Park). The librarian had previous experience at Queen's, the campus manager at McMaster, and the recruitment officer at Laurier's own liaison office. The campus's first professors brought doctorates from Oxford and McGill. To complete his staff, Read asked another faculty member to move from Laurier's theatre program to the Brantford campus, hoping to take advantage of its proximity to the city's restoration of the Sanderson Centre, now one of Canada's finest performance spaces.[2]

An ambitious GVES fundraising campaign set two million dollars as its target — one million to furnish the Carnegie Building and another for scholarships and bursaries. It was a daring goal for a campus with no track record, no reputation, and especially no alumni, for a university's standard source of donations is its own graduates. The Society proceeded by connecting the campaign to key members of the Brantford community. One of the city's greats, James Hillier, was appointed honorary chair. He provided credibility built on his invention of the electron microscope, his years as the head of RCA Laboratories, and his work as a professor at Princeton.

The real work of the campaign, though, was led and supervised by two co-chairs. Brendan Ryan had been a local director of education and was admired for his work on charitable projects, the "gift of the gab" he brought from his native Ireland, and the self-deprecating way in which he bragged about his latest mishaps on the golf course. Bruce Hodgson was a former vice-president and secretary of Gates Canada Inc., a subsidiary of an international manufacturer of automotive and industrial supplies which was headquartered in Brantford. The company was an avid supporter of education in the community. Hodgson himself had served as chair of the Board for Mohawk College and chaired the Council of Governors of the Colleges of Ontario. In a quiet, industrious way he was a key figure in the attempt to push Brantford in new directions.

With the help of the Laurier Development Office, the campaign committee used the well-connected members of the Grand Valley Education Society to identify potential donors. They meticulously established a list of possible contributors in Brant County and approached them. Ryan and Hodgson made key requests and brought Dean Read and President Rosehart in to help with major "asks." One quick ask involving Ryan and the president, a strategically planned meeting in a company parking lot, produced a quarter of a million dollars. A carefully orchestrated campaign to bring a university to Brant County attracted widespread media attention. To the delight of the fundraisers, all segments of the community contributed — the city and the county, major corporations, individuals, and volunteer organizations. Vyrt Sisson, who was instrumental in setting up the Brantford Community Foundation, described the campaign as an idea that "caught fire." One year after it commenced, on November 26, 1999, the GVES announced that it had reached its two-million-dollar target. Pledges and donations continued to come in for another month, making the final tally $2,337,629.[3] Five years later, Arthur Stephen, who was ultimately responsible for the Laurier side of the campaign, told me that his only regret was that they had not set a much higher target.

While the campaign progressed, the president lobbied the provincial government for funding. The GVES looked, as it always did, for ways to support him. On November 18, 1998, the Society met with Ron Johnson, the Brant MPP, to solicit his help in pushing the government for start-up funding. He contacted the minister of education but no promises were forthcoming. Three months later, Rosehart provided the Ministry with detailed information on the Brantford initiative. In his communications he emphasized the similarities between the proposed Brantford campus and Durham University Centre, which had received sixty million dollars in government funding. Two months later, on April 12, the coordinator of the University Committee, John McGregor, met with the deputy minister of education. The province ignored all of the entreaties.

Everyone was disappointed with the attitude of the provincial government. In Brantford it felt as if the city was, once again, going to be ignored. This was a source of great frustration but did not dampen the local enthusiasm for the birth of a new campus. The failed government requests built camaraderie between the university and the community members working on the project, who were buoyed by the success of the fundraising campaign. Without provincial funding, President Rosehart could not pursue the full-scale campus he wanted, but work continued on the Carnegie restoration. The solid relationship with the city and the fundraising campaign meant that there were no financial issues in the short term.

The resounding success of the fundraising campaign and the frenetic pace of campus planning[4] kept everyone's mind off more ominous issues that emerged as Laurier began recruiting students for the campus. Like every other campus in the country, Laurier Brantford would have to pay its way. To sustain its operations it would have to attract students whose tuition, coupled with government grants, would make this possible. Administrators described this reality as the need to put "bums in seats" to offset the costs of running a university. The Brantford campus could be no different. If it was to be successful, this meant that Laurier must find some way to bring students to downtown Brantford, which still consisted of run-down streets and dilapidated buildings. Its approach to this problem was creative — design a ground-breaking program, in this case the Contemporary Studies Program, and use it to attract students to its new campus.

In the run-up to the campus opening, there was a great deal of speculation on the number of students who would enroll in its first year. Various figures were proposed — fifty, seventy-five, one hundred. With no past precedent, it was difficult to judge. In a GVES/Laurier planning meeting on March 8, 1999 — six months before the campus was due to open — President Rosehart would only say that there had been many enquiries about Brantford. "The challenge," he added, "was to turn the enquiries into applications." In an article in *The Expositor* the same month, the newspaper noted that "No one is saying exactly how many students have so far applied for full-time Brantford positions."[5]

No one was saying for good reason — because no one wanted to spoil all the positive progress by saying that the situation did not look promising. Behind the scenes, the university was concerned. At the end of the month, on March 29, it tried to improve the situation by holding a student reception and a focus session to brainstorm on the question of how the university could make the Carnegie campus work for students.

Dean Read began to aim for fifty first-year students. In an effort to combat what was turning out to be an alarming lack of interest in a Brantford university campus, Holly Cox took him to every local high school. Read was engaging but it was a tough sledding. The students bound for university had never heard of the Brantford campus. When they thought of university, the cities they thought of were Hamilton, Toronto, Guelph, and Waterloo. In an effort to encourage applications, the university announced a five-hundred-dollar "pioneer" scholarship for students who enrolled on the campus. Even with this inducement, the Contemporary Studies Program, the program that was supposed to make the campus a success, proved to be a tough sell. At a time when students wanted applied programs with a career focus, the university decided to let students take the first year of Laurier's popular Bachelor of Business Administration in Brantford. Read announced plans for a one-year business diploma.

From an enrollment point of view, the future looked bleak. Read took some consolation in a greater-than-anticipated interest in part-time courses. Unexpectedly, the arrival of a university was a hit with seniors in Brantford, who saw it as an opportunity to enliven their retirements with courses they could take for general interest. The topics covered in the liberal arts courses the campus had chosen to emphasize — the Second World War, modernism, the ecology of the Grand River, contemporary social issues — appealed to them. More than fifty joined the campus as part-time students. This was a welcome development that would fill seats and bring interesting perspectives to the classroom, but it could not resolve the impending financial issues with the campus because all seniors were permitted to enroll in courses at no charge.

In early June, the normal date for university admissions, the Brantford campus was still struggling to attract students. A newspaper article reported that the "first trickle of applicants to Laurier Brantford has swelled to 35 full-time students ..." This was described as "exceptional news,"[6] but the report was incorrect. Laurier Brantford had attracted thirty-five *applications* for admission, not thirty-five full-time students. In any university, the number of students who attend is a small percentage of the number of students who apply. Assuming a 20 per cent take-up rate — an exceptionally high rate of return — the Brantford application numbers would yield a first-year class of seven students. This was a sobering possibility with only two and a half months left before the campus was due to open.

As Laurier hunted for students that would go to Brantford, the Waterloo campus was inundated with more applications than it could handle. In dire circumstances in which the future of Laurier Brantford was in jeopardy, Dean Read and President Rosehart began to look for ways to take advantage of the overflow. Why not, they asked, redirect some applicants to Brantford? In a move that raised some eyebrows in Waterloo, they decided to award "alternative offers" to Brantford to Waterloo applicants whose grades were slightly below the Waterloo requirements.

Looking at the longer term, the president pointed to the "double cohort" that would arrive in 2003, the year in which Ontario planned to eliminate grade 13. This promised to be a watershed year for all universities in Ontario, for it would create a situation in which two years of students — grade 13 students in the old system and grade 12 students in the new — graduated at the same time, producing tens of thousands of extra university applications. "When we started work on the Brantford campus," Rosehart said, "we didn't think of the double cohort, but now we're looking at the proposal and realizing we have some probable growth for the long term and not just two or three years. That's good news for Brantford."[7] Laurier Brantford would, the president said, be Laurier's "ace in the hole" when the post-secondary system had to cope with the upcoming enrollment bulge.

Though student recruitment loomed as an issue that would make or break the Brantford experiment, it was worried about quietly in a few Laurier offices and was not allowed to emerge as a focus for media attention.[8] As the university was determined to ensure it did not dampen the enthusiasm for the impending marriage of Laurier and Brantford. This was not something that mattered at the university's Waterloo campus, where Brantford was barely a blip on the radar screen, but it mattered in Brant County, where the university's arrival was the talk of the town. Every week, and sometimes every day, the newspaper and the local radio stations had something to say about the coming of the university: the work on the Carnegie Building was progressing; the fundraising campaign had reached a new milestone; Art Read was speaking

to this or that group; professors were hired; and so on and so forth. Laurier Brantford was a tiny operation by any standards, but it was well-recognized that its arrival heralded a major change in Brantford.

The significance of all the work of local volunteers seemed to be confirmed in January, when Colleen Miller was one of the final nominations for Brantford's Citizen of the Year Award, in recognition of her work as chair of the GVES. An article about her noted her work in training and development, which was marked by her ability to instill confidence and enthusiasm in her clients. "I see the same confidence problem in the community," she said, "and yet we've got so much going for us here! I believe a university can help with that confidence …"[9]

In his own unique way, Rowland Smith, Laurier's vice-president academic, gave Brantford something to talk about. An inveterate traveller, he had spent a good portion of his life attending performances in theatres and opera houses around the world. When he came to Brantford, he was impressed by the seating, the murals, and the acoustics in the Sanderson Centre and decided to boost the Brantford project by funding a performance there by the Opera Program in Laurier's Faculty of Music. He wanted something special so he arranged, in March, the first full production of Jean-Baptiste Lully's opera *Thésée* since 1779. The production contributed to the revival of the works of the father of French opera and was reviewed in *The Expositor* and the Toronto *Globe and Mail*. A very different, but equally enthusiastic sign of Laurier's arrival was the work of Vey Cartage and Signtech, which took one of Vey Cartage's semi-trailers and turned it into a monumental billboard welcoming the university to Brantford.

President Rosehart and the Vey Cartage trailer welcoming Laurier to Brantford, in front of the Carnegie Building.

As Brantford celebrated and the university worried about the impending opening of the campus, the Carnegie renovations proceeded. In January 1998, the city leased the building to the university for one dollar a year. This allowed the provision of the building without allowing its ownership to leave Brantford. Once the lease was signed, MMMC Inc. Architects, an established Brantford firm known for its work on other heritage renovation projects, was hired to oversee the renovations. Craig Newsome, who had studied the Carnegie Building, became the supervising architect. Though President Rosehart and the university (with the notable exception of Rowland Smith) saw the Carnegie site as a temporary, even makeshift, home, Newsome set out to recapture the architectural glory of the original library. The final MMMC design did not stray from this ideal, proposing a one-building campus that included tiered seating in two upper-floor classrooms, a "wired" one-hundred-seat lecture theatre, seminar rooms, offices for administrators and faculty, a computer lab, common areas, and a tuck shop that became a small café.

The renovations required a significant reworking of the interior of the building, which was done with great care in a manner designed to highlight its neo-classical features. Arched entrances, elaborate mouldings, and high ceilings were preserved. The stained-glass skylight in the dome, the Islamic filigree at its centre, and the Romanesque mosaic underneath it were cleaned and repaired. On the first floor, missing pillars were rebuilt. In key locations, glass partitions were used to keep the building's original details visible. The rooms were painted in Edwardian colours — slate green and plum — chosen from tiles in the mosaic in the rotunda. The work progressed well until February, when the city announced that the money that had been set aside for the Carnegie renovations would not cover the MMMC renovations. Fortunately, the city was able to increase the amount from $910,000 to $1.3 million by securing the additional four-hundred thousand dollars from the two million that had been set aside from the proceeds of the sale of the Icomm Building, thus allowing the project to continue. It was a challenge to complete the work in time for classes in September. Barely, they succeeded.

The computer lab was in the final stages of construction when classes commenced on September 13, 1999, but the building was ready. Like the original Carnegie Library that had opened ninety-five years earlier, the renovated Carnegie was an immediate success. The extra costs of the renovations were forgotten as MMMC and the university were congratulated on an inspiring restoration, which drew a Commendation Award from the Brantford

Courtesy of Wilfrid Laurier University.

The main entrance to the Carnegie Library opens into an inspiring rotunda capped with an Islamic-styled skylight. After the building was renovated, the rotunda became a focus for special events. Here, Rachel Anderson, the first student to graduate from Laurier Brantford, poses in the rotunda in 2002.

Heritage Committee. Like the city's renovation of the Sanderson Centre, the new Carnegie recaptured the grandness of Brantford one hundred years earlier. In the process, the Laurier project retained stylistic and symbolic links with the Carnegie Library's (and Brantford's) heritage, but managed to do so in

TOP: *The ribbon-cutting at the Grand Opening of Laurier Brantford: (left to right) Art Read, Chris Friel, Colleen Miller, and Bob Rosehart.* RIGHT: *The poster for the Grand Opening of the Brantford campus.*

a manner that successfully transformed it into superior teaching and administrative space. Eight years after the public library fled the Carnegie Building, it reemerged as a university campus, all very much in keeping with the spirit of Carnegie's original gift, which had promoted the library as a vehicle for popular education.

The Expositor described the 1999 renovation of the Carnegie Library as "a grand makeover." At the Grand Opening of Laurier Brantford on October 1, the city's celebrated town crier declared the campus open, and speaker after speaker praised the building. In a conversation with *The Expositor*, President Rosehart said that he and Dean Read were still considering other sites for future expansion, but "had

Friday, October 1, 1999 starting at 2 p.m.
Campus Grand Opening
LAURIER
BRANTFORD

Courtesy of Wilfrid Laurier University.

been captivated by the thought of expanding around Victoria Park, into vacant space, and perhaps closing off the streets surrounding the park for a true campus atmosphere." Standing on the steps of the Carnegie, one could imagine an elegant campus-around-the-park. "But we won't get ahead of ourselves. Remember, I was one who was initially keen on the Icomm (building), things change. Now this building seems just right for what we have developed."[10]

THE WOW AND THE OW FACTOR

At the Grand Opening of the Brantford campus, the federal minister of Human Resources Development, Jane Stewart, captured the sentiments of everyone, declaring that it was "the most significant thing that is going to happen in our community in the next century."[1] With the exception of a minor typographical error in the Laurier student newspaper, which remarked on the "doomed" rotunda in the Carnegie,[2] the only wrinkle in the proceedings were some remarks by the newly elected Brant representative in the provincial government, Dave Levac.

Levac was not on the official program and neither Mayor Friel nor President Rosehart wanted him there. Their concern was political. In Brantford, the president's prime goal was provincial funding for his new campus. To secure it he needed the support of the Conservative government, which continued to elude him. Rosehart was a Liberal (he seriously considered running for the party after he retired), but he was sensitive to the politics of the day and worried that the provincial government would be offended if Levac, a Liberal MPP, was included in the formal program at the opening of a new university campus. Friel agreed with him and they decided

to ask Elizabeth Witmer, the MPP from Kitchener-Waterloo, to represent the provincial government.

As a long-standing Conservative cabinet member with an impressive record, Witmer had the pedigree and influence the president and mayor were seeking. But things looked different on the ground in Brantford, where Levac was a popular politician with deep roots in the community. He was widely known for work with community organizations and was elected Citizen of the Year in 1997, a year in which he organized a visit to Brantford by the Queen, founded Brantford's Walk of Fame, and served as the vice-chair of the United Way. As the duly elected provincial representative for Brant, some of those involved in the Brantford campus Grand Opening wanted him recognized, all the more so given that he had a special interest in education, having worked as a teacher and then principal for twenty years prior to becoming MPP.

Through the intercession of members of the GVES, Levac got his chance to speak at the opening ceremonies. As someone who had completed his first degree at Laurier, this was a doubly special moment for him, but his remarks emphasized his Brant, not his Laurier, roots. Like Colleen Miller and so many others who had worked on the campaign to bring a university to Brantford, he saw the day as a special moment in the history of Brant County. When asked to speak, he told the audience that the new campus was a major step for the city and that he looked forward to a day when it became an independent university. Like Charles De Gaulle's infamous "*Vive le Québec libre!*" Levac's separatist sentiments struck a chord with many in his audience, much to the chagrin of others, the Laurier president included.

Levac's remarks notwithstanding, the media coverage of the opening was positive and upbeat. In an editorial entitled "The Best Is Yet to Come," *The Expositor* described the opening as an event that would change the history of Brantford. The arrival of Laurier would provide a university education for students who couldn't leave the city. More deeply, it would change attitudes toward Brantford: "Brantford has a long and illustrious history; over the years it was an economic powerhouse, its name known across the continent for its manufactured wares; it has sent premiers to Queen's Park and top-ranking cabinet ministers off to Ottawa."[3] Despite this impressive history, Brantford never achieved the cache of college towns, where "the province's best were educated and went out to conquer the world." What was Brantford? "[W]ell, it was a place where you packed your lunch bucket before going out onto the factory floor." With a university in town, Brantford had finally arrived.

Like the coverage of the Grand Opening, positive media reports were a key component of the Brantford initiative from the start. *The Expositor* and CKPC, the local radio station, followed developments avidly, presenting the arrival of a university as an important, positive event that could be a turning point in Brantford history. Their attitudes fostered excitement in the city. Any way you measured it — in terms of enrollment, number of programs, budget, size of the campus — Laurier Brantford was a tiny operation, but it was one that enjoyed a more elevated status than established universities located in other cities where the existence of a university was old news.

The Brantford campus staff called the city's buoyant enthusiasm "the wow-factor." It was evident when neighbours, friends, and acquaintances discovered that they were working for "the university," an association that accorded them instant status. The wow-factor reinforced the positive attention in the media (and vice-versa). Arthur Stephen, who ran the university's Public Relations, very consciously nurtured the positive relations with the media, providing regular updates and press releases, ensuring that the media had access to Laurier representatives when they wished, and that the university always put "its best foot" forward.

A number of initiatives maintained the honeymoon with the community and the media. A study of the downtown conducted by a part-time professor, Laurence Hewick, instigated some positive discussions of the downtown, attracting the attention of the media and the mayor. The university announced its interest in residence accommodations. An innovative agreement signed with Brantford Collegiate Institute allowed its students to take a course at Laurier Brantford in their last year of high school. This unique arrangement laid the foundation for a "Laurier" program that attracted high-performing students to a downtown school with a declining enrollment. The campus's first professor, Peter Farrugia, began planning an international conference on "The Lessons of History," to be held at the Brantford campus. Holly Cox visited local schools and organized education and career days. The GVES established new scholarships and bursaries, hosted a Brantford speaker's series (headlined by Rex Murphy, Gwyn Dyer, and Ann Dowsett Johnston) that drew more than two hundred people, and organized a high-school essay contest — 14 Windows On Laurier — that invited students to write about the literary greats whose names were emblazoned on the pediments above the Carnegie Building's exterior windows.

Impressed by the success of the GVES fundraising drive, Laurier's Development Office suggested an additional one-million-dollar campaign to raise more funds for the university. The Society, not wanting to be primarily a fundraising organization, took on a strategic planning exercise five months after the Grand Opening. Its members committed themselves to a new vision: "In ten years, Laurier Brantford will be a thriving campus of 1,000 students located in renovated state-of-the-art facilities surrounding Victoria Park, teaching a broad range of needed courses, operating as an independent federated college, and offering a full range of student services."[4] The same month, the *Hamilton Spectator* published a major spread on revitalization in downtown Brantford entitled "Brantford Fights Back." It featured a large photograph of Mayor Friel on a dilapidated Colborne Street and another of Dean Read on the steps of the Carnegie Building.[5]

In its academic operations, the tiny size of the Brantford campus (in September there were thirty-nine full-time students, in January the number rose to forty-six) fostered close relations between professors, staff, and students. Everyone on the campus knew everyone else by their first name. This promoted a family-like atmosphere characterized by great camaraderie, though it precipitated some issues of its own. One student complained to the campus manager, Tracy Arabski, that "you just can't get away from anything here," visiting high-school students being courted as future students wondered about a one-building campus, and relations between a faculty member and a student that were *too* close precipitated a complaint of sexual harassment. In other areas the campus faculty and administration faced many practical challenges. As soon as the building opened, Arabski had to invent ways to orchestrate mail delivery, student registration, textbook sales, student awards, campus maintenance, and more.

Partway through the year, work on a Laurier/Sanderson Centre collaboration on the musical *Gypsy* fell through because of disagreements over the financial arrangements. The production had been organized by Professor Leslie O'Dell, who had been "on loan" from the Waterloo campus for the year. There were tears and disbelief at one of the rehearsals when she told a shocked cast — she had already chosen 155 players and hired a professional set designer, light designer, wardrobe coordinator, choreographer, and musical director — that the production was cancelled. One consequence was strained relations between the downtown's two major revitalization projects. Dean Read diagnosed the root of the problem when he remarked that "This project has floundered for lack of a very carefully thought out agreement between Laurier and the Sanderson Centre. We have nothing in place to say who provides what, who pays for what, and what happens to any profits or losses."[6] The cancellation raised questions about the idea that the Brantford campus would launch a program in musical theatre. The proposal was quashed when the Faculty of Music came out against the idea, questioning the expertise in Brantford and arguing that there was no market for the program. In the aftermath, O'Dell decided to move back to friendlier territory on the Waterloo campus.

Among the Brantford challenges, the most serious — the "Ow factor" — was recruitment. No university campus can survive without attracting students. Caught up in the excitement and the hustle-bustle of opening, everyone dismissed the campus's troubles attracting students in its first year. It was more difficult to dismiss the problems a year later, when Brantford could boast a tiny but eye-catching campus and was fully integrated into Laurier's annual recruitment campaign. By then, the university had designed professional, even lavish, marketing materials, but they garnered little interest. The campus had only thirty applications when the January deadline for applications arrived. Prospects were bleak. Judging by the application pool, Brantford's second year of recruitment would be even less successful than its first. The situation was discussed at the GVES and meetings with them and the city, where projected student numbers became a touchstone for success. The university made a conscious effort to be positive, fearing that bad news might make it even harder to attract new students, but it told the society and the city there were problems.

Many proposed remedies were explored, some well-intentioned but unhelpful. The campus recruitment officer was pushed to visit Rotary Club meetings throughout the province — an unlikely place to find students. The university ultimately decided

A *student view of an early open house.*

Cartoon by Grayson Sherritt. Courtesy of *The Sputnik*.

it would try to entice students to come to Brantford with cash, upping the Pioneer Award available to all students to a thousand dollars. The GVES supported this push, announcing sixteen additional scholarships and an entrance scholarship that was made the prize in the local high-school essay contest they sponsored. In a move that smacked of desperation, the campus decided that it would try to lure second-year students from the university's Waterloo campus through advertisements published in its student newspaper, *The Cord Weekly*.[7]

None of the moves had much impact, primarily because they did not address the real issues that were the root of Brantford's ow-factor. To understand the dearth of applications for Brantford one had to understand the issues the Brantford curriculum committee had wrestled with when designing the campus's liberal arts curriculum. In Brantford, these were evident in a survey the GVES conducted when attempting to raise support for a private university. It asked high-school students and the general public what they considered important when choosing a post-secondary institution. Both groups had cited future job prospects/potential as their top consideration. In the case of high-school students — the primary pool for university enrollment — job concerns ranked higher than any other consideration. Sixty-seven per cent of all survey respondents said that job potential was what mattered most. In a distant second place, only 42 per cent ranked quality of curriculum as a key consideration.

In a blue-collar town like Brantford, it was not surprising to find that education was seen through the lens of job potential,[8] but such attitudes were not unique to Brantford. In 1998, when Laurier was at work on the opening of the Brantford campus, a survey of students at York, one of Canada's largest universities, found that 83 per cent of entering students came to enhance their chances of getting a better job.[9] In Brantford and at York, students were openly not interested in the kind of liberal arts curriculum designed for Brantford. It was this that lay at the root of the problem of attracting students. The attempt to persuade them to enroll in a program they did not want in the middle of an intimidating downtown proved to be too great a task even for Laurier's Advancement Office, which had won many accolades and awards for its ability to attract students.

As Brantford struggled, the educational issues that were the root of the problem were a hot topic in provincial debates about higher education. In a throne speech that caused great consternation in universities across the province, the Ontario government declared that it would push the whole post-secondary system away from the liberal arts. In opposition to such views, the chancellors of Ontario's universities met at the Glendon campus of York University in March 2000, emerging with a statement reaffirming the value of the liberal arts and sciences. "The liberal arts and sciences," the statement read, "must continue to be a seminal part of Ontario's higher education. This is a practical idea as much as a philosophical one. A number of recent studies have clearly underlined that a well-rounded, general education — learning to think, to write and to express one's ideas clearly — is as valuable to future employability as technical or technological training."[10]

A few weeks later, a group of hi-tech CEOs meeting in Toronto released a statement echoing the same sentiments. At York University, the Senate approved a three-part resolution expressing its gratitude for their support. The resolution was forwarded to the senates of other Ontario universities, which in many cases expressed supporting views. When Paul Davenport, the president and chancellor of the University of Western Ontario addressed convocation at the University of Toronto in June, he decided to speak on the importance of the liberal arts in the knowledge society.

Led by Rowland Smith, Laurier had responded to the challenges to the liberal arts by developing a whole campus devoted to a core program in the liberal arts and sciences. As Art Read put it, the core curriculum in Contemporary Studies "provides a background against which students can build competencies in reasoning, communication, research, and other critical skills."[11] The Brantford curriculum committee had tried to package the liberal arts in a new way that emphasized its relevance to contemporary issues and concerns, but this was not a hit with students, who showed little interest in Contemporary Studies. Combined with all the social problems that still surrounded the Carnegie Building, the result was a recruitment and enrollment crisis that threatened the future of Laurier's new campus.

In Brantford, the issues at the heart of a provincial debate over the value of liberal arts programming were played out in a life and death struggle for enrollment at the only campus in the province exclusively devoted to the liberal arts. In a climate in which such programming was, whatever its merits, falling out of favour with students, the Brantford campus was in trouble. As the university tried to minimize the problems in its relationship with the community — an attempt to maintain the wow-factor — different constituents in the university debated what to do. Rowland Smith remained steadfast in his commitment to the liberal arts. He never wavered in his opinion that it was the core program in Contemporary Studies, not the revitalization of downtown Brantford, which made the campus educationally unique, significant, and worthwhile.

In virtue of his position as vice-president academic, Smith ruled the day. Those who shared his vision saw him as a champion and saw Brantford as an important attempt to reassert the value of the liberal arts in post-secondary education in Ontario and beyond. Others grumbled, dismissing the new campus as Smith's attempt to create an "Oxford on the Grand." In the midst of it all, the university struggled unsuccessfully to find a solution to Brantford's recruitment problems. When it looked as if Brantford might attract fewer students in its second year than its first, the tensions began to mount. Within the corridors of the university, away from the public eye, the battle lines began to form.

| 12 |

THE TROUBLE WITH BRANTFORD

Although the university's initial idea for Brantford envisaged a greenfield campus away from the downtown, its future lay in the Carnegie Building. Thoughts about a move away from Brantford's most historically significant, most destitute, and most impoverished neighbourhood were forgotten as the campus focused on more immediate concerns. Unless it found a way to stir more student interest in Brantford programming, its very existence was in question.

The problem was exacerbated by two circumstances. The final details of the Contemporary Studies Program were winding their way through the university's different levels of approval at a snail's pace. Without final approval, the campus could not provide prospective students with a full description of the program. In September, at the major recruitment event in Ontario, the Toronto University Fair, Brantford could only tell students that more was coming. Here was a university trying to sell them something in the liberal arts, but what it was, was not entirely clear.

A second problem was the consequence of the Brantford recruitment strategy that saved the campus in its first year of operation. The university had managed to get students to Brantford by diverting

them from Waterloo. The students who were given offers had come to Brantford because they did not meet the Waterloo admission requirements and this was the only way they could attend Laurier. As the second year progressed, this became a problem, for students in the university were allowed to transfer from one program to another and there was nothing to stop them from migrating back to Waterloo, their original destination, when they moved from first to second year. Some students tried to transfer before the year was over. In this way, the admission strategy that had kept Brantford afloat now threatened to turn Brantford into a "back-door" route to Waterloo. It did not help that it threatened to tag Brantford with the label "Last-chance U."

Art Read wanted to tackle Brantford's issues head on by diversifying the campus's curriculum. The alarming lack of interest in Contemporary Studies convinced him that the campus needed programs that students wanted. He decided that he would achieve this goal by broadening the curriculum to include some standard arts and science majors, and, ideally, some of kind of career-oriented programming.

In its first year of operation, Brantford had flirted with the possibility of career programming when a handful of students were allowed to go to Brantford for the first year of Laurier's most sought-after program, the Honours Bachelor of Business Administration (BBA). Smith allowed the students on the proviso they combine the program with first-year Contemporary Studies courses, a measure that was originally intended as a stop-gap measure to get "bums in seats." But enrollment problems continued in Brantford's second year. As applications failed to materialize, the university considered a Brantford wing of the BBA program. This could have solved the recruitment problems in one fell swoop, but the dean of business rejected the idea. He had been on assignment elsewhere when arm-twisting by Vice-President Smith had pushed the BBA to Brantford. Upon his return, he insisted that the business students in Brantford complete their programs in Waterloo and cancelled first-year Brantford offerings. He was blasé about the success or failure of the university's Brantford operations, and aligned his faculty's future with an attempt to establish an upscale business program in Toronto.

In Brantford itself, a different kind of career programming was suggested by Joe Rapai, the director of education for the Brant Haldimand Norfolk Catholic District School Board. On October 27, 1999, he wrote President Rosehart. He was, he said, "delighted" to have been able to "share in the enthusiasm and excitement that has been generated by Laurier coming to Brantford ..." and proposed that the university and the school board "work together to develop a Faculty of Education on the Brantford Campus."[1] His letter outlined a number of reasons why: a shortage of teachers in the local area; the large number of Ontario teachers forced to earn their credentials in expensive foreign programs; Brantford's location, which would allow it to serve areas of Ontario under-serviced by existing teachers' colleges; and the potential for collaborations with the W. Ross Macdonald School for the Blind and the schools located on the Six Nations and New Credit reserves.

Someone leaked Rapai's letter to *The Expositor*, which wrote an editorial (on November 12, 1999) challenging Laurier to take up his offer. In a situation where the problems with enrollment were increasingly evident, the Board of the Grand Valley Education Society added to that pressure by deciding, on the same day, to make "assisting [the university] in the development of a Faculty of Education" one of its strategic goals. A letter published in the newspaper four days later urged the public to get behind the proposal, providing President Rosehart's email address so that *Expositor* readers could contact him directly. The head of the Downtown Business Improvement Association, Cheryl Parker, called on the local school boards and Laurier officials to make it happen.[2]

President Rosehart was interested in the possibility of a Faculty of Education, but he passed the matter over to Vice-President Smith, who was in charge of academic programming. Smith was not moved by the local pressure. He saw this as a move that would tarnish the liberal arts ideal that had been planned for Brantford. In personal conversation, he did not hide his disdain for education programs, which he saw as academically "light" and unsophisticated. In a formal letter to Rapai dated March 24, he was more careful. He and the president were, he said, willing to concede that a Faculty of Education might be a possibility for Brantford in the future, but not in current circumstances. Laurier was not, he pointed out, accredited for teacher training and it would be difficult to secure provincial funding. In an effort to dismiss the possibility once and for all, he warned that putting Brantford's eggs in this basket could be "suicidal."[3]

The GVES did not receive Smith's refusal well. Its members were by now most anxious about Brantford's enrollment problems and believed that they could not be resolved without significant curriculum developments. In a March memo from the group's central advisory committee to the rest of the organization, Brendan Ryan, who had played such an important role in the local fundraising effort, reported that the committee had "expressed disappointment ... at the report in the newspaper that there would be no immediate progress in the notion of a Faculty of Education at Laurier Brantford." This did not satisfy the Committee, which proposed that "planning work should continue and contacts be established so that the idea would not have to start from square one, at a future date."[4] In the rest of his memo, Ryan raised pointed, but prescient, questions about the growth of a Brantford campus devoted to the liberal arts:

> The Provincial Government recently made some scathing remarks with respect to the values of a Liberal Education as opposed to a more utilitarian type of education in computers, business or engineering. There was a strong reaction from a large segment of the education community who stressed the importance of a Liberal Arts Education. This position was backed by a number of C.E.O.'s of major companies who were having a convention at that time. It should come as no surprise that the Harris Government is not run by a group of Renaissance-type thinkers. They are bottom line type of people who put a value on everything....
>
> What are the implications for Laurier Brantford? Well, it seems to me that if we are to have a limited course offering, we are limiting our growth potential.... If the Program is to be only Contemporary Studies ... it will be a difficult one. Certainly, promotion and advertising for Laurier Brantford would probably have to be extended outside of Ontario if one is to achieve ... [desired] numbers while offering such a small market niche.[5]

Within Laurier, one administrator sympathetic to the local desire for an education program was Dean Read. He could not overrule Smith and Rosehart's decision not to pursue a Faculty of Education, but he was anxious about Brantford and tried to expand its programming base by introducing a program to prepare students for entry into faculties of education at other universities. The Primary/Junior Education Preparatory Option (or PJEP Option) was designed to complement the Contemporary Studies Program. By combining it with other courses relevant to teaching at the primary/junior level, he hoped to attract students who saw themselves as future teachers. At the university Senate, the proposal had to weather hostile challenges from professors who argued that Brantford and Laurier did not have the proper expertise to develop it. Read weathered the storm and the program was approved. In the aftermath, the idea behind the program proved to be a good one: it did generate some student interest in Brantford, but it did not pack sufficient punch to turn things around.

Distressed by the campus's failure to attract students, Dean Read began to reconsider the campus's liberal arts and science mission. He had no doubts about the value of education of this ilk, but the future of the campus rested on his shoulders and it could not be successful without attracting more student interest. Without the approval needed to introduce diverse new programs to the campus, he took matters into his own hands, allowing Brantford students — both new students and those already enrolled at the campus — to register in programs other than the campus's core program in Contemporary Studies.

Like Brantford, Laurier was a small community. News spread quickly, often with embellishments. Read's decision to allow students into majors other than Contemporary Studies was a major move that quickly made the rounds, producing a clash Read was trying to avoid. The campus recruitment officer mentioned what was going on to her supervisor, who told the vice-president of advancement, who immediately went to Smith and told him what was going on. Smith was upset by what he saw, correctly, as an attempt to push Brantford away from its liberal arts mission. This exacerbated already strained relations between the dean and the vice-president. All came to a head when Smith talked to the university registrar, who looked at the numbers and reported that less than half the students at Brantford were registered in the core program in Contemporary Studies. An angry Smith decided he was going to remove Read from his position.

As with many conflicts, there were two sides to the story. Smith saw a campus designed to champion the liberal arts abandoning this vision. This was a travesty given that it was this mission which, in Smith's mind, made Brantford significant. Read saw things from a different perspective. As the administrator on the ground, it was his job to ensure that the Brantford campus did not become yet another failed project in the ruins of downtown Brantford. The decision to admit students into programs outside the core program was a way to save, not dismantle, the campus and its future.

What was looming as an ugly institutional battle over the control and direction of the Brantford campus was averted by Art Read. Instead of fighting Smith, he decided to leave his post and return to the Physics Department on the Waterloo campus. At a fragile time when the campus was struggling — unsuccessfully, a public spat between its two senior administrators could have had serious consequences. In the wake of the local community's frustration over the decision not to pursue a Faculty of Education, overt wrangling would have made it even more difficult to attract students and maintain local support, adding ammunition to the cynics who continued to dismiss the idea of a university in Brantford. Read's decision ended the strife before it accelerated into a public debacle. In dealing with the media, he very

deliberately took the high road, telling the press that
he had, after fifteen years as a dean, decided that it
was time to take a leave and return to teaching.

| 13 |

TWO CHALLENGES

I went to Brantford early in 2000, as Dean Read's successor. My first assignment in the city was a talk on the importance of liberal arts education. I presented it to the local University Women's Club. Their enthusiasm was infectious, but it could not erase the worries I was privy to in a series of meetings with the president and his two vice-presidents (Rosehart, Smith, and Stephen) — a group of senior administrators the faculty called The Gang of Three. President Rosehart had looked at me in a fatherly way and told me to "take a direction," any direction: the direction didn't matter as much as the taking. Smith emphasized the campus's liberal arts curriculum. Stephen told me he could sell Laurier Brantford if I gave him "more to work with." The president told me that the university would have to leave Brantford if we did not find a way to resolve the current enrollment issues.

At Brantford, one could not escape the enrollment problem, which followed one like a shadow, intruding into every aspect of one's life. At a party I attended at the University of Western Ontario, someone discovered I was a dean, asked for the details, and laughed uproariously when he discovered that I was the dean of forty students. Others were more sensitive and more helpful. At an open house we held for interested students, the turnout was devastating — less than a dozen showed up. At a session in the Carnegie Lecture Hall, a handful of students listened to the president, myself, and others pontificate on the advantages of attending Laurier Brantford (we could very honestly say that the classes were small). It was not easy to look out and see the rows and rows of empty seats. The situation turned embarrassing and potentially calamitous when a photographer from *The Expositor* showed up to take a photo. We did not need negative publicity about our difficulties recruiting students. He saved the day for us when he surveyed the room, sized up the situation, and solicitously asked the students to sit in a cluster of seats that allowed a photo that looked like a detail of a full house.

In the midst of the search for an answer to our recruitment issues, one of Brantford's compelling challenges was the running of a tiny, inexperienced young campus. Today, it would be difficult to find students and professors who could imagine life at the Brantford campus in its very early years. When I arrived, there were five other employees — two professors and three staff. A third professor joined the campus shortly afterward.[1] On such a small campus, the roles were broadly defined. As dean, I supervised fewer professors and staff than I had supervised when I was the chair of a very small department, but was responsible for a vastly larger range of responsibilities covering every aspect of the campus's operations. The campus manager, Tracy Arabski, handled everything from finances to academic support to computing services to the bookstore. In such a small setting, professors, staff, and students were extremely close. Campus meetings with *all* full-time faculty and staff were held in my office. All of us knew the students on a first-name basis, enjoying a friendly camaraderie which is rarely, if ever, found on a larger campus.

The atmosphere on the campus was lively and informal. When a cat showed up on a winter's day, we adopted it and named it Orlando in honour of Vice-President Smith. It lived in the dean's office for a month and disappeared the day before we planned to give it to a student who was going to take it home as a pet. Students, professors, staff, administration, and community supporters knew one another personally and understood one another's issues.

Students enjoyed an exceptional atmosphere for learning. Faculty crossed disciplinary lines very easily. One result was discussion, a conference, and then publications on ethical issues in archaeology. In a single building, students had easy access to professors, staff, and administration. They talked to professors in offices downstairs, went to lectures and tutorials in classrooms upstairs, and visited the administration office for any other matter. They received personal, virtually immediate, attention. The local media maintained an active interest, and campus ties to the community remained remarkably strong. The GVES, usually in the form of Vyrt Sisson, a retired local banker, seemed to be waiting around every corner when the campus needed another photocopier, art for the walls, or help with student activities.

Laurier Brantford faculty, staff, and students were active participants in local events. Here Jim Dimmick, Robert Feagan, Garry Warrick, John Murnaghan, Stephen Haller, and Jamie Dimmick (front) participate in a charity event in Victoria Square.

Photo courtesy of the author.

Like any small community, Laurier Brantford had its idiosyncrasies. On one occasion Vyrt Sisson brought me a pile of application forms for student bursaries available from the Stedman Foundation. The Stedman sisters, the heirs to the Stedman fortune, were major contributors to the donor campaign that launched the campus. They sent Sisson to tell me that their foundation would welcome applications from our students. Determined to see that Laurier Brantford students responded to the offer, the campus manager, Tracy Arabski, identified sixteen suitable students whom I asked to apply. To ensure that Laurier Brantford would put its best foot forward, I reviewed each application, helping the students to improve them.

At the end of the process I was dismayed by the unprofessional look of the handwritten applications. To improve the applications even further, I had my assistant create an electronic template of the application form and type each application. We called the students back to sign the printed applications, minus the scrawls and blotches and messy handwriting that had marred their handwritten counterparts. The result was a stack of clean and professional quality copies submitted to the Foundation. Feeling satisfied with a job well done, I was surprised a day or two later, when the applications were returned by an apologetic Sisson, who told me that that the Stedman Committee believed that one "could tell a great deal" by someone's handwriting, and wanted handwritten applications. Fortunately, my recycle bin had not been emptied and I was able to reclaim the discarded applications, which we forwarded to the committee. The handwriting on a number of successful applications apparently impressed the adjudication committee.

In the midst of the friendly, almost cozy, atmosphere, the fly in the ointment was an ominous understanding that the campus could not survive if we did not find a way to generate enrollment. This grim reality intensified camaraderie, pulling the faculty and staff together even more. Together, we saw Brantford as an underdog fighting against stiff odds: the campus was a drain on the university budget, the professors had contractually limited appointments, and our future was uncertain. The only secure job at Brantford was my own. And it was not secure because of Brantford, but because I had a position in Philosophy in Waterloo — a position I could return to if things went awry.

To solve the enrollment problem, we needed to expand Brantford's academic programming. The few students already enrolled were frustrated over our limited curriculum. Some transferred to Waterloo to gain access to a broader range of programs, courses, and professors. The problem was compounded by limited student services and activities. With such a limited enrollment, we could not provide the extensive health services, learning services, athletic and recreational opportunities, et cetera available at other campuses, thus making it more difficult for us to compete with established campuses. It did not help that we struggled with these issues in the middle of a still-devastated downtown. When I enthused about future possibilities in an interview with *The Expositor*, a letter to the editor noted that my "upbeat" list of what struck me when I came to Brantford failed to include many negatives, "not the least of which is falling debris from our deteriorating structures." Many were skeptical of our ability to attract students to a neighbourhood made up of "bombed out" buildings.

The challenges were real, but the campus could also claim some assets. In the midst of a difficult situation, everyone who worked on the Brantford campus shared a sense of purpose. The recognition that we needed to change the way we did things to avert disaster made the campus open and receptive to new ideas and direction. In the local community, the problems downtown made us an important revitalization project that many people, including the mayor and most of city council, were determined to support. Though most of the downtown was disconcerting, even frightful, the renovated Carnegie Building and Victoria Square retained a sense of dignity and elegance in the middle of all the turmoil. In comparison with the university's Waterloo campus, which was a hodgepodge of uninspiring buildings, we enjoyed first-class architecture and an ivy-league-like setting (in Brantford, the Waterloo campus was described as "architecturally challenged"). In recruiting students, we soon learned that a visit to the Carnegie Building could work wonders. Visitors were very quickly captivated by the idea of an elegant campus around a historic downtown park.

The strategy for turning Brantford around was multi-faceted. Job one was making sure the campus had students for its second year of operation. When the deadline for applications to the university's other programs came and went in January 2000, we extended the Brantford deadline — up until the following September. We were still admitting students one week before classes started, having made a special effort to target those who applied to the Waterloo campus but missed the admission cut-offs by 1 or 2 per cent. Every professor and staff member on the campus participated in recruitment.

In a Senate meeting that presented enrollment figures in September, the chair of the Psychology Department nudged me in the ribs, smiled, and said that the applicant/entrant ratios for Brantford showed we had accepted 140 per cent of our applicants. How, he wondered, was that possible? What the figures really showed was that we accepted 40 per cent more students than had applied by the official deadline in January. We managed this by accepting applications for another nine months. At Brantford, we worked harder on recruitment. We had to. The campus's survival was at stake.

While courting individual students for September, we worked on long-term strategies. We reviewed, rewrote, and remodelled the campus's promotional material, and worked with the GVES and the community to expand our limited student services and activities. I made program development our first priority. After a prolonged approval process, the university Senate finally approved all the details of the Contemporary Studies Program in November 2000. While this was not a solution to our problems, it was a starting point. In expanding our options I decided to develop "companion" programs that would complement the Contemporary Studies core.[2] This was an approach to programming purposely designed to avoid the conflict that brought the relationship between the vice-president and Dean Read to an end. It allowed the campus to diversify its programs in a way that elaborated, instead of stepping away from, the idea that Brantford would be a campus committed to a core program in the liberal arts.

The campus already had one companion program in primary education that allowed students to combine preparatory courses in primary/junior education with the Contemporary Studies Program. To provide others, we arranged courses with majors in a range of disciplines: Anthropology, Communications Studies, Development and International Studies, English, Geography, History, Philosophy, Psychology, and Religion and Culture. In keeping with the campus's commitment to Contemporary Studies, these were not offered as "stand alone" programs, but as options students could *combine* with the core program. To deal with sensitivities on the Waterloo campus, where questions were asked about Brantford offering Waterloo programs, we advertised the new courses with titles like Anthropology and Contemporary Studies and Communications Studies and Contemporary Studies.

Companion programming created a campus in which all students shared a core program in the liberal arts and sciences, but did so in a way that allowed us to develop further programs to attract enrollment. We envisioned an integrated package that would incorporate a series of programs that combined well with the Contemporary Studies core. In designing new programs, we also looked for those that were a natural fit with downtown Brantford. We made much of the fact that the North American downtown is, even in decline, the centre of many of those things that merit study at a university: government, courts, the news media, social support services, poverty, and the history of a place, and consciously set out to integrate such topics in our course offerings. In keeping with our proximity to the New Credit and Six Nations reserves, we developed a program in Indigenous Studies. To take advantage of our proximity to Mohawk College, we began investigating the possibility that we could create programming that would allow our students to combine our core program with college programs and diplomas

It is difficult to imagine a campus working harder than Brantford did during its difficult early years. Teaching, the running of a new campus, and the drive for more students consumed us. Morale was sustained by an atmosphere that was friendly, informal, and relaxed. Social cohesion was maintained with laughter and bonhomie. The atmosphere was nourished by parties, visiting speakers, joint research projects, debates on public issues like 9/11, and the storming of the Bastille, which was reenacted by Professor Farrugia's students. On a night of "Guerilla Music" organized by one of the students, fifty people, six of us in guerilla suits, drummed on the lower floor of the Carnegie Building.

Occasionally it may have gone too far. On one Halloween, when the campus was full of costumed staff and students, the students asked me to don a frilly wedding gown. I balked but they eventually prevailed — it would be the highlight of the day if they could see me in a costume. Somewhat sheepishly, I put the gown on and emerged from my office. Judging by the laughter, I had indeed made the students' day. My own feelings were more mixed, however, when the president walked through the door to the administrative area on an unexpected trip to Brantford. He looked at me and seemed, just for an instant, to be weighing his support for me as dean. But the president was a master of decorum. He looked at me only for a second, then turned and talked to the campus manager, carrying on as though nothing had happened.

I slunk back into my office and removed my wedding gown.

| 14 |

TAKING UP RESIDENCE

On my first official day in Brantford, I walked down the street and discussed the campus with the mayor. When he asked me what we needed to make the campus grow, I told him that we needed a residence. Without a residence, the campus was not a realistic possibility for students who lived outside Brant County. The mayor said that he would make it happen.

In acquiring a residence, I wanted to broaden the horizons of the campus. It had, again and again, been justified as a way to create a university for local students. Especially for students with limited resources, this was a worthy goal. But Laurier Brantford could not, in any realistic way, satisfy the needs of local students bound for university. With three full-time professors and a limited selection of courses, there was no way that the campus could provide the programs most of these students sought. More profoundly, I worried that an emphasis on local students was at odds with one of the essential goals of university education —to broaden the horizons of its students. This should happen, not only in the classroom, but in campus life, where students learn by meeting and talking with other students; ideally, by exchanging opinions and working and living and befriending

students different from themselves. In Brantford, the desire for a residence was a desire to promote this cosmopolitan ideal by fostering a campus with students from a variety of places and backgrounds.

As the mayor promised, he launched a search for a potential residence. In the meantime, we rented two floors of an apartment building — an experiment that went badly because the students and other tenants did not mix well. The students felt that they became scapegoats for any issues in the building; the tenants thought the students stayed out too late. In the search for a stand-alone Laurier residence, the mayor favoured a 9,000-square-metre office complex at the corner of Colborne and Market streets. The site had been occupied for more than 150 years, but fires had destroyed first the initial 1837 tavern and then the hotel that replaced it.[1] In the 1980s, the intersection was the site of a major attempt at downtown renewal orchestrated by Mayor Dave Neumann and Phil Gillies, the local MPP. By 1986, two major projects were completed — a thirty-five-million-dollar Eaton's mall, which aimed to revive the downtown as a shopping district, and the office complex, which was built to renew Brantford's ties to the manufacturing empire that had been Massey Ferguson.

Massey House was the result of a deal the city made with Campeau Corporation and Varity Corporation. Varity had become the owner of what remained of Massey Ferguson when Conrad Black and Argus Corporation walked away. Campeau, a development company, built Massey House as a home for Varity's final Massey Ferguson divisions, which were consolidated in a new company called Massey Combines. Varity announced that Massey Combines was part of a restructuring operation that would move two hundred positions from administrative and marketing offices in Toronto and Des Moines, Iowa, to downtown Brantford. The Massey House design was planned to accommodate the Massey Combines administrative offices in 5,000 square metres. The rest of the new office complex would be rented to other businesses. The project was heralded as a new beginning for agricultural manufacturing in Brantford.

In return for the Massey House project, the City of Brantford agreed to buy Massey Ferguson's former parts warehouse downtown, which was designated as the site of a new provincial telecommunications centre. This was the project that became the empty Icomm Centre that initially attracted Laurier to Brantford. As Massey House promised to revive agricultural manufacturing in Brantford, the Icomm Centre promised to revive its legacy as the city that gave the world the telephone. Massey House, the Icomm Centre, and the new Eaton's mall made up an ambitious three-pronged plan to create a revitalized downtown economy founded on the revival of Brantford's technological, industrial, and retail past.[2]

These three major developments fostered a celebratory mood in Brantford. The downtown mall opened with a forty-five-thousand-dollar party featuring seafood, elaborate desserts, and champagne. Speaking at the event, Mayor Neumann confidently noted that "Brantford's image and self-confidence had been affected by the deterioration in our core area. Current developments in the downtown will refocus our core as a vital thriving centre, indeed the heart of the community, one which will lead the way in reshaping a positive image for Brantford as a whole."[3] When Massey House was opened a short while later, Ian Porter, the president of the reorganized Massey Combines Corporation, concurred with the mayor, commending him for his "great understanding as to what is needed to bring industrial vitality back to Brantford," describing the building of Massey House as "a new start for Massey … here in Brantford."[4]

Like so many similar initiatives in other North American downtowns, the Eaton's mall and Massey House both faltered and then failed. Despite some forty million dollars' worth of construction being injected into the downtown, its spiral downward continued. The mall's attempt to re-establish the downtown as a retail district had a very temporary effect, shoppers preferring shopping malls closer to burgeoning suburbs and Highway 403. The promised restructuring of Massey did not bring hundreds of positions from elsewhere and Massey Combines went insolvent. The old warehouses the city bought from Varity became brownfield sites, and the location of the ill-fated Icomm Centre failed when Bell pulled out of the project. In downtown Brantford, it was three strikes and you're down and out again.

Bob Nixon, who helped arranged provincial support for the restructuring of Massey, described it as "a valiant attempt to keep the jobs and the prosperity not only of Brantford but of Ontario and to keep one of the major farm-machinery production companies of the world operating and productive."[5] Many years later, he told me that what had happened still made his blood boil. The collapse of Massey Combines was a dark and dispiriting moment, not only for Brantford, but for the history of Canadian business. Despite its rhetoric, the holding company that owned Massey Combines, Varity Corporation, had no real interest in helping turn Brantford's ailing downtown around. In hindsight, it is clear that they were after something else: the opportunity to hoodwink the city and a well-meaning mayor in order to secure local, provincial, and federal funding in a cold, calculated attempt to unload their fiscal issues. The strategy has been carefully, if disturbingly, described in a United States Supreme Court decision on Varity's liability in the wake of the Massey Combines collapse:

> In the mid 1980s, Varity became concerned that some of Massey Ferguson's divisions were losing too much money, and developed a business plan to deal with the problem. The business plan, which Varity called Project Sunshine, amounted to placing many of Varity's money-losing eggs in one financially rickety basket. It called for a transfer of Massey Ferguson's money-losing divisions, along with various other debts, to a newly created, separately incorporated subsidiary called Massey Combines. The plan foresaw the possibility that Massey Combines would fail. But it viewed such a failure, from Varity's business perspective, as closer to a victory than to a defeat. That is because Massey Combines' failure would not only eliminate several of Varity's poorly performing divisions, but it would also eradicate various debts that Varity would transfer to Massey Combines, and which, in the absence of the reorganization, Varity's more profitable subsidiaries or divisions might have to pay.[6]

Behind the scenes, in corporate boardrooms, Project Sunshine and Massey House were not what they were professed to be — an attempt to give Massey "a new start" in downtown Brantford. They were, rather, an attempt to offload Varity's debts to a Brantford company that was purposefully designed to fail. In the process, the company successfully manipulated three levels of Canadian government, which provided financial support for the restructuring. A cynic could say that Varity scored a double victory: precipitating the designed collapse of Massey Combines, at the same time profiting from the sale of the old Massey warehouses, which the city purchased to secure Massey House. There were no victories for downtown Brantford, where the new initiative went flat and the attempt to kick-start the economy failed.

In the end, after the demise of Massey, Massey House did manage to secure a new lease on life when it was purchased by another agricultural concern with a long historical tie to Brantford. Like Massey Ferguson, the Holstein Association of Canada was a symbol of the important role that Brant County played in the history of Canadian agriculture. Holstein cattle arrived in Canada in 1882 when they were imported from the United States (having been exported from Holland to the United States one year earlier). Two years later, the Holstein-Freisian Association was formed. Initially, its headquarters were established in the village of St. George, sixteen kilometres north of contemporary Brantford. In 1920, the association exchanged St. George for George Street in downtown Brantford, a block away from the Carnegie Library. As one of their advertisements in the 1952 *Expositor* put it, "Brant County is Our Cradle — Brantford Our Headquarters."[7]

Locally, the building the Holstein Association moved to on George Street was known as the Old Holstein Building. After seventy years on the same site, the association decided to move from downtown Brantford in 1989, in search of more modern offices. In the wake of the problems with Massey Combines, they changed their minds and purchased Massey House, turning it into their new headquarters. In its new incarnation, Massey House was known as the New Holstein Building. It served in this capacity for ten years, until the Association decided to leave.

It is easy to understand why the Holstein Association wanted to move. Its offices were mired in the middle of the worst section of the downtown, amidst the crumbling buildings on Brantford's original main street. This was not a positive place to bring its workers or the members. The association preferred a location in North Brantford, with easy access to Highway 403, where visitors from outside Brantford could easily come and go. In such a situation, Mayor Friel saw an opportunity to acquire one of the few Colborne buildings in a reasonable state of repair, and wanted to turn it into an opportunity to push the university into the heart of Brantford's problems on Colborne Street. What better way to bring life to the middle of a dead downtown? It was this thinking that prompted his proposal that the New Holstein Building become Laurier's new residence.

I resisted the idea. The Holstein building I wanted was the Old Holstein Building, the building the Association vacated when it moved to Colborne in 1989. It was located one block from the Carnegie Building and had the same kind of neo-classical grandeur, having begun its life as Brantford's 1880 post office. At a meeting in which one the campus's first professors Gary Warrick and I met with the mayor and other city officials, the conversation was heated. Voices rose to shouting levels as we debated the virtues of the "Old" versus the "New" Holstein Building. The Old Holstein was close to Victoria Square. The New Holstein was in better shape. The Old Holstein would allow us to extend the heritage restoration so successfully begun with the Carnegie Building. The New Holstein could be more easily acquired.

I was not willing to bend to the mayor's arguments and took the matter to the "Gang of Three" — the president and his vice-presidents. All of them, including the classically oriented Rowland Smith, sided with the mayor when we went on a tour of the New Holstein Building. As we went through rooms named in keeping with cow inspired themes — the "Cow-ncil Room," the "Cow-munications Room," and "Udder" Rooms, one had to concede that the Holstein Association had a sense of humour, and had maintained the building well. Faced with the choice between a residence in the building and no residence at all, I relented. Within Laurier, some grumbled about the wisdom of adding a building to a tiny campus that was having trouble attracting students, but the Gang of Three embraced the argument that a residence could help us solve the problem. When they tentatively agreed to the mayor's proposal, this initiated a series of complex transactions aimed at bringing the deal to completion.

In exchange for property the city owned close to the 403, the Holstein Association agreed to give the New Holstein Building to the city. The city secured the property and was ready to turn it over, but the university could not use an office building as a residence without extensive renovations. Given the campus's need for both a residence and an expansion of its academic programs, the university converted the top three floors into residence space and used the bottom two for administrative and faculty offices, classrooms, and a lounge. The city agreed to split the cost of the $3.8-million bill for renovations. The city secured its financing from monies paid annually to the city by the casino which had moved into the Icomm Centre. The renovations were designed and implemented by local firms.[8]

Most contemporary residences feel like a conglomeration of shoeboxes, arranged to maximize the number of students who can efficiently be housed. Not so the new Brantford residence, which was christened Grand River Hall. It required an imaginative reworking of an office complex, which

Courtesy of Kevin Klein

Laurier students (Zachary Mealia, Amanda Flanagan, and Kaitlin Reaume) stand on the lamppost in front of Grand River Hall, a residence and academic building, in 2009. Designed as Massey House, it began its life as an urban renewal project designed to house the headquarters of Massey Combines, the final remnant of the Massey Ferguson empire.

produced a refreshingly different residence with a unique feel and look. Individual residence rooms were designed around the large — for a residence, gigantic — office windows on the exterior of the building. This created spacious bedrooms, some first-class views (including, disconcertingly, some views of the casino), and living spaces of distinctive shapes and sizes. In comparison with the institutional look that characterizes new residences at most universities (the students on the Waterloo campus called the newest large residence The Hospital because it looked like one), the Grand River Hall accommodations were impressive. When the building finally opened in September 2001, President Rosehart, who had overseen residences in three different cities, described it as "the Taj Mahal" of residences.

In newspaper coverage that was a harbinger of things to come, an editorial in *The Expositor* supported the deal with the city, but was critical of the mayor. Its criticisms echoed the sentiments of councillors who complained that the mayor and the Planning Department had operated as an "in group" that made deals and arrangements behind the scenes, without properly consulting other members of city council: "Had all Councillors been kept informed right down the line, the questions could have been asked, and answers provided.... All 11 elected representatives would have played an equal role in the decision, precisely the way they should."[9]

Two years after opening, the deal provided the Brantford campus with the residence it was looking for. In many ways, the acquisition was a microcosm of the university's relationship to the downtown. In assuming ownership of a building that had housed the final remnants of the Massey Ferguson legacy and

the Holstein Association's last years downtown, the campus reasserted, even more than it was inclined to do so, its central role in the redevelopment of downtown. Instead of a new downtown built on a revival of its historic businesses — the kind of downtown the backers of Massey House and the 1989 mall had envisaged — the new downtown was emerging, in the middle of the squalor on Colborne Street, as a city centre with a new and different focus, founded on an experiment in post-secondary education.

THE MOHAWK CONNECTION

As we had hoped, the Grand River Hall residences quickly established themselves as a selling feature for the campus. Their impact was muted by their location in the middle of the urban decay on Colborne Street, but more than one parent said they looked like "high-end condos" rather than student residences. By September 2001, enrollment had reached two hundred. Laurier Brantford was still tiny and unsustainable, but five times larger than when it opened. I created a chart demonstrating that the entire population of Ontario would be attending Laurier Brantford in ten years if it continued to expand at this rate.

In a search for ways to expand the curriculum, I sought the advice of the local community. Almost everyone answered that they would like to see us partner with "Brantford's other post-secondary institution." Mohawk College had been in Brantford thirty years and was known for programs in policing, security, packaging, and design. I decided to take the desires of the local community seriously and pursued the partnership.

As fate would have it, the campus began its partnership with Mohawk at a time when the relationship between colleges and universities was in flux.

The distinctions between their offerings blurred as colleges pursued applied degrees and universities pursued technical, career-oriented programs. Colleges began developing alumni associations, development operations, research initiatives, and the trappings of a traditional university. Universities sought co-operative working arrangements with businesses and partnerships with industry. But like competitive siblings, colleges and universities still struggled with their relationships with each other. Universities would not let go of their superior attitude to colleges, which they saw as academically inferior. Colleges dismissed universities as ivory towers which were not in touch with the needs of their students and their communities.[1]

The Ontario Government was determined to change things. It wanted a system of "seamless" post-secondary education that allowed students to move back and forth between college and university programs. Students showed their preferences with their feet, as an ever-increasing number of college students moved on to university programs, and colleges developed "post-diploma/post-degree" programs. The fly in the ointment was the transfer credit issue — the question whether, and to what extent,

students who moved between colleges and universities would be granted credit for their work at their previous institution. Students from colleges fumed at their inability to secure credit for courses they had taken in college, sometimes being forced to cover the same material with the same textbook twice. I had one frustrated student — whom I sympathized with but could do nothing for — throw a final decision from the registrar's office onto the floor of my office before he stomped out the door. In comparison with other jurisdictions that regulated transfer credits to ensure that standards that were fair and clear — British Columbia and the United States for example — the Ontario government left decisions up to individual universities, producing a confusing patch work of inconsistent policies and standards.

University attitudes betrayed some contradictions in the way that universities saw themselves. We fancied ourselves as elite institutions where the brightest minds congregate. At the same time, we saw ourselves as the vanguard of social change, promoting diversity and the interests of the disadvantaged — single mothers, the poor, and the underprivileged. The resistance to college transfers reflected the first conceit but was very much at odds with the second. As it was sometimes put, universities tended to see college transfer students as "barbarians at the gate," and it was colleges, not universities, that provided access to higher education for the most diverse student population. It was colleges that provided the most opportunities for older students, students from visible minorities, and students from less advantaged socio-economic backgrounds. In resisting collaboration, universities resisted one of the most effective ways to promote opportunities for these groups.

The Harris government was not especially interested in diversity. It was interested in university-college collaboration, but for entirely different reasons — it wanted a system of higher education that emphasized job training. To push things in this direction, it established a College-University Consortium Council (CUCC) in 1996. It was mandated to facilitate, promote, and coordinate joint ventures between universities and colleges. Detailed negotiations produced the Port Hope Accord, which set general guidelines for student transfers between colleges and universities. The accord was endorsed by the provincial college and university associations in 1999, but this had little real effect. In a situation in which initiatives were voluntary and there were no fiscal incentives collaboration, little changed.

In an attempt to push collaboration further, the government provided hundreds of millions of dollars for building projects that crossed traditional college/university boundaries. One of them was the University of Ontario Institute of Technology.[2] They tried to blend the characteristics of university and college curricula. In many programs, students graduated with a degree and a diploma. These new programs crossed the traditional boundaries, but they did little to break down the silo mentality that characterized universities and colleges. Instead of eradicating the already existing silos, they created a third one that existed in the space between the other two. Concerns about transfer credits were not eradicated, but compounded, as this raised new questions about transfers between these new institutions and traditional universities and colleges.

Despite provincial rhetoric about the need to break down the barriers that separated universities and colleges, the attitudes that blocked collaboration persisted. In a 2003 overview, Wendy Stanyon concluded that, "Even though the calls for greater collaboration between colleges and universities in Ontario have intensified over the past several years, progress has been slow.... Considering the many initiatives and the amount of time that has been invested in promoting greater collaboration, the actual number of successfully negotiated agreements between colleges and universities in Ontario has been limited."[3]

This was the context in which the Brantford campus began working on a Laurier/Mohawk partnership. Our aim was an arrangement that would provide access to Laurier Brantford for qualified Mohawk graduates, and vice-versa. We saw the ability to combine our programming with college programming as a way to provide students with a useful mix of liberal arts and professional and applied education. The intent was to make this a draw that would bring more students to Brantford. It took months to get everyone on side. I negotiated the details of an agreement with Louise Bockner, a dean at Mohawk. Bockner and her colleagues were committed to the traditional college mandate, which emphasizes applied programming, but it was hard to see them as barbarians at our gates. They were too gentile and educated and fully appreciated the importance of the liberal arts and humanistic education. Having established one partnership with McMaster in the health studies area, they saw Brantford as a place where they could establish a second, this time with a focus on journalism, human resources, service, and education programs that could naturally be allied with our core program in Contemporary Studies.

At the university, the most difficult obstacle to a partnership was the need to change the rules about college transfer in order to make our agreements with Mohawk work. An old saying borrowed from milling says that the process of approving university programs grinds very slowly. This was true at Laurier and the situation created many opportunities for discussion and debate. In some quarters eyebrows were raised and noses were held as our plan for a partnership with Mohawk unfolded. The Registrar's Office was, in the words of a dean other than myself, "allergic" to change and frowned on the plan. Others saw us getting into bed with a college and worried about the progeny. The proposed changes to transfer credit rules were modest in the broader world of academe — an ambitious student could find richer transfer agreements elsewhere — but colleagues still turned up their noses at our initiatives, seeing them as a lowering of our standards. In the tussle of debate, I discovered that our ace-in-the-hole was the point that the relaxed rules would only be applied at Brantford, a feature that reassured the opposition, which was willing to accept the changes if they would be quarantined at Brantford.

In 2001, at the start of Laurier Brantford's third year of operation, the university Senate approved an agreement with Mohawk. It included ten "articulations" that allowed students to combine Contemporary Studies with a variety of Mohawk College programs — among them Graphic Design, Police Foundations, Human Resources Management, Public Relations, and Marketing. The new "Two By Four" programs allowed students to earn two credentials — a Contemporary Studies degree and a college diploma — in four years. In other ways the

The logo used in promoting Laurier-Mohawk programs.

agreement supported students who wanted to move between Laurier and Mohawk. It created a framework for college-university collaboration that propelled Laurier Brantford and Mohawk into the forefront of development in this area. Dean Bockner and I outlined our approach to other Ontario administrators at the province's College-University Consortium Council in March 2002.

Our partnership with Mohawk was not welcomed by everyone. Within our own institution, purists and traditionalists did not change their view of college collaboration. In Brantford this was a minor concern. Our target was not purists and traditionalists, but students, who welcomed a campus friendly to college transfers. On the campus itself, some college students struggled to adjust to a university setting. We decided that the problem with "transfer shock" was a problem of attitude — on our part. There were, after all, many high-school students who experienced another kind of transfer shock when they moved from high school to university. Because universities cater to these students, they have built support systems that aim to alleviate the social and academic challenges high-school students face as they adjust to university. In contrast, we were

ill-equipped to deal with the transitions college transfers had to negotiate in their transition to university life. The problems were exacerbated by the attitudes of college students themselves, who tended to assume that they were moving to an institution like the one that they had left. At Brantford, the campus learned to cope with these issues by developing an orientation program for incoming college students, and by developing protocols aimed at addressing the needs of transfer students.[4]

"O-week" was a particularly trying time for college transfers (the O stood for orientation). The week was geared to seventeen-year-olds who had recently graduated from high school, and arrived, fresh-eyed and bushy-tailed, to begin a new chapter of their life. But they were not just leaving high school. Most of them were living away from home for the first time. O-week was a time for them to learn how university operated, but it was more than that. It was a time for noisy packs of revved-up teenagers who hadn't slept to party, shout school chants, and roam around the campus and the city. The socializing and the introduction to the university were a helpful starting point for most students but had the hallmarks of a peculiar rite of passage for college transfer students who were considerably older, did not live in residence, and might have children of their own. The days when they could act like high-school students had long since come and gone. Not surprisingly, this meant they avoided O-week like the plague, often missing out on crucial things they needed to know about registering for courses, the expectations of professors, and the way to navigate one's way through the pathways of academe. Once we recognized the problem, the solution was relatively simple — a distinct orientation for college students — one which allowed them to learn what they needed to know in an atmosphere that worked for them.

At Brantford and in Waterloo the performance of the college transfers was debated. It was easy to find individual students who shone. Some of them came and thanked me when they graduated. I remember one single-mother who told me that she was afraid to go to university when she went back to school, so she went to Mohawk, where her teachers told her she should go to Laurier. She left, bound for a Ph.D. program at an established university. Needless to say, other college students did not perform well. It made it easy to back whichever side of the "pro" or "con" college-transfer debate one supported. To build a better basis to judge, I had Julie Sutherland, an administrative assistant, track the performance of every single transfer student over a three-year period. We compared their performance to that of a randomly selected group of high-school students. On balance, the results showed no significant difference. Students from some of the college programs we identified — journalism and some medical, social service, and business programs — achieved higher grades than the high-school students.

As a new campus which prided itself on thinking outside the box, Laurier Brantford was open-minded when it dealt with students who wanted to enter university without a traditional background. This included not only college students, but home-schooled students who had not studied at an accredited high school. Statistics cited by The Ontario Federation of Teaching Parents, the principal lobby group for home-schooling in the province, suggested that 1 to 2 per cent of the province's school-age children were home-schooled.[5] In Ontario, home-schooling was illegal, but some parents ignored the law, insisting on their right to educate their children. In April 2001, the Ontario Minister of Education, Janet Ecker, announced that the government "respects that some parents choose to educate their children at home," and promised that the government would "eliminate the institutional bias against home-schooling."[6] A year later, the Ministry of Education released *Policy/ Program Memorandum No. 131*, which made home-schooling legal in Ontario. The crux of the policy was a directive to school boards which dictated that they must "accept the written notification of the parents … as evidence that the parents are providing satisfactory instruction at home."[7]

In the wake of the new directive from the government, Robert Feagan, Holly Cox, and I decided to draft a policy that would allow the Brantford campus to admit home-schooled students. When Bruce Arai joined the campus as our first associate dean, he joined in the initiative. He and Feagan had chosen alternative schooling for their children, and had little patience with the prevailing myths about home-schooling. Our initial attempts to formulate an admissions policy for these students raised the ire of the managers in the university's Office of the Registrar, who were weary of Brantford's penchant for new initiatives. In a situation in which many high-school students who applied to Laurier were not accepted, it would not, they argued, be fair to admit home-schooled students unless we knew that they were better students than those rejected. But in the case of home-schooled students, who applied with no transcripts and no independent assessment of their abilities, there was no way to know if this was the case.

The issue was not resolved by Laurier Brantford, but by the Faculty of Music, which had already admitted one home-schooled student on the basis of her audition. When she went on to win a series of prestigious university scholarships, the dean of music orchestrated a change in the university's attitude to home-schooled students. When the registrar's office argued that home-schooled students applying to music were admitted on the basis of an audition that provided an independent assessment of their abilities, we devised a Brantford equivalent, creating a written admission test and an interview. With this in hand, the Brantford policy on home-schooled admissions was approved. In the aftermath, a string of such students came to Brantford. In many cases, they used us as a stepping stone to programs at other universities that were not open to home-schooled students, but accepted transfer students from other universities. By attracting media attention both inside and outside the university system — and wide ranging inquiries from home-schooling parents, organizations, and other universities — the Brantford policy pushed the university system to reconsider its attitude toward home-schooled students.[8]

By the end of its third year of operation, the doors of the Brantford campus were open to college transfers and home-schooled students. This was an important step forward, but it did not eliminate the major issues on a campus that continued to operate with a program mix that could not attract the enrollment the campus needed to sustain itself. We got by with "alternative offers" made to students who did not have the grades to gain admission to Waterloo. The downtown was still a desolate-state neighbourhood that was inhospitable to students. Despite these cold realities, the balance was shifting. A campus that many had doubted had acquired a residence and an elegant home in the Carnegie Building. It had discovered companion programming, which allowed it to balance its commitment to interdisciplinarity and the liberal arts with applied programs students sought. A ground-breaking partnership with Mohawk College extended their options. The admission process for home-schooled students underscored Brantford's unconventional approach to higher education. In celebration of its willingness to traverse new territory, the campus adopted a motto: NEW, INNOVATIVE, UNIQUE.

COURTING NIPISSING

Solving Brantford's enrollment problems required new programs. But developing them presented something of a paradox. In order to attract more students we needed new programs, but we could not develop new programs until we had more students, for we needed the larger enrollments that would pay for the new courses and professors the new programs required. This was Brantford's "chicken or egg" dilemma.

The Mohawk partnership illustrated one way out of the predicament. It allowed the campus to create new options for students by "piggy backing" on what was already available at Mohawk. In our continued search, we looked for another partner who would be interested in the idea that Brantford should provide teacher training, an idea that had been rejected by the university when it was proposed by Joe Rapai and the Grand Valley Education Society. The idea did not go away because it made good sense. We needed a program that would attract more students, and Ontario's established teachers colleges were inundated with applications for admission. Hundreds of students who were not admitted crossed the border and earned their credentials in expensive American programs. Laurier Brantford's

first graduate was one of them. In a university that did not have an education program, on a campus that already offered a program on children's education, we were well-positioned to provide these students with an Ontario alternative.

The BA/BEd program that came to Brantford was the fortuitous result of some divisive university politics. President Rosehart had come to Laurier from Lakehead University in Thunder Bay. Lakehead was a university built around professional programs. Rosehart believed that Laurier needed to move in this direction and saw teacher training and a Faculty of Education as a key move in this direction. Vice-President Smith saw the matter very differently. He was an academic with a healthy disdain for applied programming. He was furious when President Rosehart hired a faculty member in Science to compile a lengthy proposal for a Faculty of Education. Smith, who knew how to win at university politics, launched a quiet but determined campaign to block the initiative. In private conversations and in meetings with the existing Laurier faculties, he rallied opposition to the plan. The faculties came to see Rosehart's desire for a Faculty of Education as a top-down attempt to change the direction of the university: in a direction that led away from them. In public meetings, the faculty objected to the plan, arguing that the university should emphasize their own programming agendas rather than an entirely new faculty.

Rosehart knew when to back away from something and reluctantly gave up on the Faculty of Education he coveted. In resurrecting the idea that we should bring teacher training to Brantford, I appealed to both sides of this political antithesis. Rosehart saw a Brantford-based program in teacher training as a way to obtain an education program. Smith saw it as a way to keep a Faculty of Education away from the university's main campus. He was, he told me plainly, happy to "exile it to the perimeter," where he granted that we needed something to alleviate the issues with enrollment.[1]

When I discussed the possibilities with Rosehart in 2001, he was reluctant to revive his defeated attempt to create an education faculty at Laurier. But Bob the Builder was creative. In lieu of an attempt to build his own, he decided to look for a partner institution. He decided to call David Marshall, the president of Nipissing University, whom he had bunked with on a trade mission to China. When they talked, he proposed a radical idea — that Nipissing offer an education program in partnership with Laurier in Brantford.

The roots of Nipissing University were found in the North Bay Normal School, which became North Bay Teachers' College and later the Faculty of Education at the university. In 2009, Nipissing celebrated one hundred years of teacher training in North Bay. Some modest calculations suggest that some 12,750,000 students were taught by graduates

of the North Bay program.[2] David Marshall, who began his career at Nipissing as the dean of education, was interested in Rosehart's proposal. In particular he liked the idea of Nipissing establishing a foothold in southern Ontario. Ron Common, the Nipissing dean at the time, agreed, telling me that he thought that Nipissing would have doubled its number of applications if North Bay had only been named "South" Bay.

With the presidents on board, the universities negotiated a detailed proposal that would marry Laurier and Nipissing in Brantford. It was a complicated task that required two universities, which operated in very different ways, to jointly manage students in a manner that allowed them to attend two universities in one. A complex financial agreement was negotiated to determine how revenues would be collected and distributed, and expenses shared. Both sides wanted to maximize their share of the revenues and minimize their expenses and both favoured their own established regulations and their own computing systems. Negotiations alternated between Brantford and North Bay. The campus manager, Tracy Arabski, and I tried to arrange the meetings so we would meet in spring and summer in North Bay and in Brantford in the winter. Distance was not a problem on the Nipissing side as Dean Common was an avid pilot who flew south to come to Brantford meetings. (I took this as an opportunity to tell the president and Vice-President Smith that the negotiations would go more quickly if the dean of Brantford also had an airplane, but the idea never took off.)

The end result of all the negotiations was one of Ontario's first "concurrent" education programs. It combined Contemporary Studies with a Nipissing degree in Education. As the initial brochure announced, the program combined "Laurier's strengths in the liberal arts and sciences with Nipissing's long history of providing a rigorous teacher education program." Students could include traditional concentrations in English, History, and other "teachables." During each year of the program, students participated in a supervised teaching practicum in a local school. They graduated with significantly more classroom experience than their counterparts in the more common ("consecutive") one-year education programs students enrolled in after completing a B.A. or B.Sc.

The joint program began as a pilot project with thirty-five students in September 2002, with the city delighted to have the education program that earlier had been denied to them. Sandra Reid was appointed director. *The Expositor* wrote that "Everyone wins with the creation of a teacher education program operated by Wilfrid Laurier and Nipissing universities.[3] Laurier Brantford gains another jewel in its academic crown. Nipissing expands its outreach into southern Ontario without stepping on the toes of existing teachers colleges. The city gains postsecondary students, brings more life to downtown and adds credibility to its new image as a progressive community." As Joe Rapai, Brendan Ryan, and others had predicted, a teacher-training program attracted intense interest. As the program began and its students were placed in practicums throughout Brantford and Brant County, it became a key vehicle that solidified the link between the campus and the rest of the community.

When the joint program began, Nipissing's operations were housed in a suite of offices in Grand River Hall. As enrollment in the program expanded quickly, larger quarters were needed. Nipissing wanted a distinct building that would allow them to assert their own presence in downtown Brantford. In 2000, the largest-ever transaction between two Canadian financial institutions — the Toronto Dominion Bank's eight-billion-dollar purchase of Canada Trust — provided an opportunity. In the aftermath, the bank streamlined its operations and reorganized its branch offices. In downtown Brantford, it merged a TD and a Canada Trust branch located next to each other on the perimeter of Victoria Square.

At the end of the nineteenth century, the property that TD Canada Trust vacated was occupied by the Prince of Wales Livery Stable. In later years it was the location of the Grandview Flour and Feed Company, a butcher shop, a shoe repair, a baggage store, and finally a "messenger" service. In 1947, one of Canada's largest grocery chains, Dominion Grocery Stores, built a classic, if mundane, brick and steel-frame store on the site for seventy-five thousand dollars. The architects were Roy Bishop of Dominion Stores and F.C. Bodley, a significant Brantford architect. Bodley designed two of the city's architectural gems — the Land Registry Building downtown and the Glenhyrst Art Gallery, which he designed for Edmund Cockshutt, the fifth son of Ignatius Cockshutt, founder of the Cockshutt Plow fortune.[4] The Dominion store on Market Street was much less memorable, having been designed with a standard template that emphasized function over architectural imagination. In 1978, the building was converted into a branch of the Toronto Dominion Bank. In their 1991 *Victoria Park Square Study*, Alexander Temporale & Associates Ltd. wrote that

REINVENTING BRANTFORD

TOP: *The 1948 Dominion grocery store on Market Street became a Toronto Dominion Bank in 1978.* BOTTOM: *The TD Bank Building was converted into the Brantford home of Nipissing University's Faculty of Education in 2009.*

"the Bank represents a typical modern Toronto Dominion Bank of the modern 'International' style of the twentieth century. The rectangular, simple box form of architecture and the 'minimalist' detailing is typical of the style."[5]

When TD Canada Trust decided to vacate the building, it did not want its legacy to be another vacant building in an already ailing downtown, so it asked Mayor Friel how the building could be used to serve the community. Friel's first instinct was to acquire it for the city's own use, but the bank's guidelines for philanthropy did not allow gifts to cities. Because the guidelines did allow donations to educational institutions, he suggested, as a second choice, that the building be given to Laurier. The proposal was taken to the local employees in the building, who strongly supported it. Speaking at the official ceremony recognizing the gift in 2001, the bank's district vice-president, Harry Norton, remarked that "This really comes from our employees in Brantford, who are a big part of this community. When you look out [of the two branches across Victoria Park], that's what you see — Laurier Brantford."[6]

In a goodwill gesture, Laurier loaned the building to the city. The city and the university expected this arrangement to continue for five years or more, but the success of the Laurier/Nipissing partnership created a need for space much sooner than expected. In 2004, Laurier decided to support Nipissing's desire for its own building in downtown Brantford by leasing it the former bank for one dollar per year. Nipissing created a $1.2-million renovation plan that turned the building into seven classrooms, faculty and administrative offices, and common areas. The building opened in September 2005.

The aesthetics of the renovated bank branch reflect the city's values at a time when it was losing, without apology or regret, the heritage architecture around Victoria Square. As Temporale et al. put it: "The building does not appear to belong to the Square as the scale and use of materials is foreign to the majority of buildings in the … area. There is no apparent visual connection between the building and Victoria Park."[7] It is difficult to dispute this judgment. But it can still be said that the Nipissing building epitomizes the modernist architectural tendencies that characterized the development of downtown Brantford in the past forty years. Its plain looks notwithstanding, it successfully provided Nipissing with state of the art facilities on the perimeter of the square. Like the Grand River Hall renovation, it pushed the Brantford campus toward a broader conception of adaptive reuse, which incorporated buildings that represented later stages of downtown history.

| 17 |

WORKING WITH VICANO

In the spring of 2002, "Canada's magazine on higher education," *University Affairs*, recognized Brantford's innovative approach to curriculum in a cover article on the Contemporary Studies Program.[1] By the fall of 2002, enrollment had climbed to 340 students. The number of full-time professors and staff had climbed from five to almost twenty.

Brantford was passing milestones every month. One of them was the campus's first convocation, with a graduating class of twelve students. The university Registrar's Office took great exception to a convocation in Brantford, arguing that the students should come to Waterloo to graduate. *Everyone* in Brantford — the students, the faculty, staff, and everyone in the city — opposed the Waterloo plan and the university relented. The ceremony took place in Central Presbyterian Church, next door to the Carnegie Building. Chancellor John Cleghorn, the former CEO of the Royal Bank of Canada presided over the program, and James Hillier received an honorary degree. The pomp and pageantry of convocation, which at many campuses takes painful hours, was over in twenty minutes. Colleen Miller, one of the key people who brought Laurier to Brantford, told me that the convocation stood out

as the most memorable event in the history of the project — because a graduating class made it feel like a university had arrived for good.

Within the world of Canadian universities, the Brantford campus was still tiny, but the worst was over. At a time when other university campuses were growing their enrollments by 1 to 5 per cent a year, the number of students attending Brantford had increased 800 per cent in three years. Companion programming was taking off. The joint B.A./B.Ed. was a winner and looked able to provide the students needed to sustain the campus. By now, it was clear that the campus had the potential to grow, though growth required more facilities. In a situation in which we could not provide enough residence beds to meet the needs of our first-year students, the first priority was another residence. Though the idea had been vehemently rejected by Mayor Friel when we first discussed a residence, I took this as an opportunity to revive the notion that we should acquire the Old Holstein Building and turn it into a first-year residence. I told my Brantford colleagues that the New Holstein Building, now Grand River Hall, would be more valuable if we owned a full set of downtown Holstein buildings.

Photo by the author.

The graduates at Laurier Brantford's first convocation, June 2002. (Left to right) back row: Katie Fox, Darryl Sararas; middle row: Janice Alderson, Jesse Loncke, Nicole Payne, Katie McLaren; front row: Andrea Pearson, Kristian "Cricket" Donald, Christine Dzus, Peggy Weston, Kathleen Morningstar.

In the cache of historical buildings still found downtown, the Old Holstein Building stood out as one of the most significant. It had begun its life in 1880 as Brantford's Post Office and Customs and Inland Revenue House. A handsome example of the federal government's Second Empire style, it was designed by the chief architect in the federal Public Works Department, T.S. Scott. A celebrated landmark when first built, it lost its *raison d'être* when the federal government built a much larger beaux arts post office in 1913. In the aftermath, the Post House was acquired by the city, which searched unsuccessfully for a tenant. In 1920, the Holstein-Friesian Association of Canada expressed an interest in the building. The association had been a significant force in Brant County since 1884, three years after the first Holstein cow was exported to Canada from the United States. The first office was located at the farm of the association secretary, George W. Clemons, near the village of St. George. His son, W.A. Clemons, moved it into his house in St. George in 1912. In 1920, the association offered the City of Brantford twenty-five thousand dollars for its empty post office.

The offer provoked a spirited debate. Mayor Morrison Mann MacBride and a group of city councillors argued in favour of the sale. They pointed out that the building had produced no revenue for seven years. "The Holstein men would advertise Brantford and do a lot of good for the city,"[2] they claimed, predicting that farmers would come from western Canada to buy Holstein cattle. The councillors who opposed the sale argued that the building was worth as much as seventy thousand dollars, and worried about downtown cattle sales that would be conducted outside the building. They proposed an alternative — that the offer from the Holstein Association should be rejected and the Post House rented to the federal government or made into a city hall. Alderman J. Allen called the claim that there would only be "a few bulls" brought in by the Holstein Association "a cock and bull story." In a manner eerily similar to the criticisms of the city's purchase of the New Holstein Building some eighty years later, some councillors complained that the sale of the building was a deal that had been prearranged behind the scenes, without sufficient consultation.

In the end, the 1920 city council voted ten for and six opposed to sell the old post office to the Holstein Association for twenty-eight thousand dollars. It became The Holstein Building, serving as the association's national headquarters for almost seventy years. To accommodate growth (the organization employed six people in 1920; today it employs almost one hundred), the association secured an existing building on the north side of the old post office and attached them with an elegant art deco entranceway. Some small adjacent shops were acquired by the association and demolished. In 1977, the city presented the Holstein Association with a Downtown Improvement Award, in recognition of the work it did to maintain the appearance of the building. Twelve years later the building became the Old Holstein Building when the association moved to Colborne Street. Like the Carnegie Library after the public library left, the old post office languished without a major tenant. Over the next decade, a series of uses were considered. At one point, the site was proposed as a possible location for a downtown bus terminal; parts of the building housed law offices and a daycare; a developer proposed demolishing the building in order to make room for a mall. However, the building was neglected, and without a significant reason to be, it steadily deteriorated.

I had been disappointed when the city rejected my proposal to turn the Old Holstein Building into our first residence. The success of the Carnegie renovations, which impressed everyone who visited the campus, emboldened my conviction that this was an idea that I should continue to pursue. Prodded by a persistent real estate agent, I managed, in 2002, to convince the president and Ron Dupuis, the director of Laurier's building projects, to tour the building, with the hope that this would arouse their interest.

Some of Brantford's first letter carriers in front of the Post House, circa 1898.

The tour did not have the desired effect. As a real estate agent toured us through the dilapidated floors of the building, the president did his best to contain his irritation. When we reached the third floor, which was in particularly bad condition, he could not find his way out of the sagging interior quickly enough. In the course of working with him over many years, I found him to be someone who had a great deal of patience for my ideas, but this was an inauspicious day from that point of view. When we reached fresh outside air, he remonstrated with me about the condition of the "hopeless" building. His opinion about the Old Holstein Building was simple and direct — it should be demolished. In as conciliatory a way as he could manage, he told me not to waste his time on romantic notions about a hopeless old building. Dupuis echoed the assessment.

As I had done once before, I retreated. This was not because I was persuaded I was wrong. The Carnegie Library still stood witness to the advantages of adaptive reuse, and the Old Holstein Building could, despite its poor condition, contribute many positives to the campus. It was almost impossible to improve on its location — a one minute walk from the Carnegie; the building was a suitable size for a residence on a small campus; its architecture and its history were real assets; and its restoration would be a major contribution to the rebuilding of downtown. I would like to be able to claim that I convinced the president of this point of view, but it was someone else — Peter Vicano, the owner of a local construction company — who persuaded him. An animated and outspoken player in Brantford's construction industry, Vicano decided that the renovation of the Old Holstein Building was a perfect project for the university. He talked to Rosehart, then boldly bought the building.

Vicano created detailed plans for the renovations and took them to the president, who was impressed with the plans and Vicano's impeccable building credentials. As the discussion proceeded, our campus manager, Tracy Arabski, told me that the project would go forward. When I asked her how she knew, she told me she had seen a glint in the president's eye, and "When Bob has a glint in his eye, he makes a building happen." In this case, the crux of the making was the financial support of the city. The stars aligned in the right way when Mayor Friel cast off his earlier doubts and got behind the idea that the Old Holstein Building should be a residence — making it the fourth university building project he had supported. The total cost of the project was $2.7 million. To make it possible, the city forgave one hundred thousand dollars' worth of back taxes and contributed $1.5 million. The remainder came from Laurier.

In the course of the construction project, there were many bumps along the way. The existing building was in very poor repair. A great deal of design and construction work was done to upgrade the interior and the exterior. Cianfrone Architects Inc. of Hamilton developed a design that, in a very historically conscious way, turned the building into a contemporary student residence. A little drama ensued when building inspectors found asbestos in the walls and looked for someone to dress down. With the president off on a skiing trip, the director of Physical Plant and Planning in Waterloo, and no sign of the project manager, they had to be satisfied with me. They seemed disappointed not to find someone more

Courtesy of the Brant Museum and Archives, cat. no. 200214335.

Photo by Audrey Scott. Courtesy of the Brant Museum and Archives, 200431.

Courtesy of the Brantford Heritage Inventory.

significant than an academic dean, but in a pinch they put up with it and threatened to close the construction site. To make the financial operation of the building viable, the university looked for a way to add residence rooms. Cianfrone accomplished this by placing a new floor on top of the extension that had been added to the 1880 post office. In keeping with the character of the building, the floor was topped with a mansard roof designed to match the one on the original post office. In creating windows for some of the bedrooms, the construction workers cut holes through seventy-six centimetres of exterior wall.

At the end of the day, the Old Holstein Building was transformed into a one-of-a-kind sixty-eight bed residence with comfortable rooms, intriguing views, and unique floor plans. As the renovations neared completion there was some discussion about the name of the new residence. After the Carnegie, the university had decided to christen new buildings with the names of local rivers: Massey House became Grand River Hall; the TD Bank Building was named Nith Hall, after the Nith River. Extrapolating this system to the new building would have given it the unfortunate name of Brantford's one remaining river-like body

Views of the Post House (top to bottom): the original Post House and Customs Office circa 1912–15, where the original entrance can be seen at the front of the building; as the national headquarters of the Holstein-Friesian Association of Canada, the new front entrance is adorned by two miniature Holsteins; the Post House during the Vicano Construction renovation.

of water — White Man's Creek. The university
had no interest in a building called "White Man's
Residence" so it abandoned the system of river
nomenclature. In a bold step in a new direction,
the new residence was christened The Post House
Residence, a name that invoked its roots in the original 1880 Post House.

The *Toronto Star*'s architectural columnist, John
Blumenson, featured the Post House in one of his
columns, presenting it as a classic example of Second
Empire architecture.[3] He quoted Stephen Robinson,
a researcher for Brantford's heritage inventory, on the
significance of the university's presence downtown.
"Laurier's move into the downtown core may," he
said, "be a 'second empire' for the university but it is
truly a renaissance for Brantford."

| 18 |

BUILDING COMMUNITY

In directing the Brantford campus, I tried to build its progress on a shared vision of its intellectual and academic development. Thus, 2002 became a year of strategic planning. After months of meetings, conversations, and consultations in Brantford and in Waterloo, the finished plan proposed two options: Plan A envisaged a steady rate of enrollment of six hundred to eight hundred students; Plan B saw enrollment grow to fifteen hundred. Both plans required curriculum developments.

The development of new programs was not a trifling matter. The essence of a university is its academic programming, especially for professors who have deep convictions about such matters. Programming determines the identity of a university and to be successful, academic planning must chart a course through many deeply held — and often conflicting — convictions. But at Brantford this was not enough. At our stage of development, such planning also needed to guide us to new programs to attract more students. In practice this meant we would have to convince more students to come to us instead of our competitors. This was no small challenge on a campus surrounded by the campuses of some of Canada's most prominent universities (Brock, McMaster, York, Toronto, Waterloo,

Guelph, and Western Ontario), and made even more so as our choice of programs was constrained by the feelings of our colleagues on the Waterloo campus, who didn't want Brantford to develop programs they were already offering. Rather than compete with them, we decided to go in our own direction, even though this meant that we could not secure our future in the easy way — by offering popular programs like Business, Psychology, and History.

In looking for other opportunities, we decided to pursue interdisciplinary programs that would integrate well with our core program in Contemporary Studies. As the campus's strategic planning document described it, we wanted programs "that will attract students but also contribute to a clear Brantford identity built around a range of programs that are academically compatible, make up a coherent whole, and foster bridges between our local community, our students, and our faculty."[1] Indigenous Studies was an obvious choice, but it was clear that we would have to look elsewhere for the students we needed to achieve either Plan A or B.

Journalism emerged as the kind of program we were looking for. I was familiar with the world of journalism. My father was an editor of small-town weeklies in Alberta. One of the memorable moments in his career occurred when an RCMP investigation discovered that his name was included in a Church of Scientology blacklist, apparently because he had published a scathing exposé of their business dealings. I grew up in a household where newspapers were, like bread, a staple of survival. The options included everything from the *New York Times* to the *Catholic Worker* to whatever little paper my father had brought home from his travels somewhere or other. Journalism's emphasis on writing and contemporary issues struck me as a good fit for Brantford.

Many other faculty members saw things similarly. They identified with the skills that journalism required — the techniques of writing, television, videography, and web casting, and believed that the best journalism was, like the campus itself, founded on a commitment to critical investigation and an in-depth understanding of contemporary politics, culture, and world issues. At a time when some journalism programs were criticized for their emphasis on technique over substance, we concluded that a Brantford journalism program could contribute something worthwhile to the world of journalism education. Paired with our core program, it could inculcate in students an understanding of the form and content of good journalism. In downtown Brantford it would be surrounded by places of historical significance, by municipal government, the courts, and public and cultural events. It could take advantage of the fact that journalism had the highest applicant to entrant ratio amongst all university programs in Ontario — a sign that the two existing programs at Ryerson and Carleton could not meet student demand for journalism.[2]

Other positives we hoped to take advantage of were our proximity to the offices of the local newspaper, *The Expositor*, located a few blocks from the campus; a possible collaboration with Mohawk College's programs in Journalism and Public Relations; and Laurier Brantford's own student newspaper, *The Sputnik*. The latter had been initiated by one of the campus's first students, Adam German, and had struggled subsequent to his graduation. We expected a journalism program to invigorate, not only the campus, but also *The Sputnik*, providing student writers and editors who could turn it into the best of student newspapers. Six years later, we felt we had made great strides in this direction when one of the students in our first graduating class, Tara Hagan, won the Ontario Newspaper Association's Rob Austin Award, an award presented to Ontario's outstanding student journalist of the year. In our own convocation, we presented the national broadcaster Mike Duffy with an honorary degree, making him a part of our first class of graduates. After convocation, "Duff" regaled the journalism students in a pub, relating stories of Conrad Black and Pierre Trudeau and the ins and outs of Ottawa.

We did not expect a journalism program to generate all the students Brantford wanted, so the campus's strategic plans identified two other directions for program development. Like journalism, criminal justice seemed a "natural" for Brantford. Here I had another family connection, in this case a brother who taught human rights and criminology at St. Thomas University in Fredericton, New Brunswick. The idea that we should develop a program in criminal justice at Brantford was rooted in a conversation in which he told me that their program was struggling with too *many* students. This definitely caught my attention — why not at Brantford? When we investigated further, we discovered that criminology was one of the fastest-growing disciplines in Canada. When I asked the criminologists I knew why, they laughed. Students were, they said, beating down the doors of criminology programs because they loved popular television shows like *CSI*, which featured brainy and attractive forensic professionals solving difficult criminal cases. "*CSI* is," one said, "a big glossy advertisement for us."

The decision to develop a program in criminal justice drew some wry comments about the state of Brantford. When I joked in Waterloo about the possibility of taking over Brantford's downtown jail (suggesting that it could, with little renovation, be turned into a student pub which we could call "The Drunk Tank"), they smiled and said that the city needed the jail to house all the criminals in downtown Brantford. The Brantford image did not improve when *Maclean's* published a statistical analysis of 2006 crime data to determine a ranked list of "the most dangerous cities in Canada." Brantford came eleventh, a position that earned it the moniker of "the most dangerous city in Ontario."[3]

In downtown Brantford, it felt as though the crime issue was greatly exaggerated, though there were times when it spilled into the campus, usually in the form of some dubious characters pestering students or entering the buildings. The first instance occurred when the campus's first television set — a set that Art Read purchased for the Carnegie student lounge — disappeared. Read saved the replacement from an interloper who he ordered off the campus. But much too much was made of crime on the Brantford campus, which experienced many fewer criminal incidents than the Waterloo campus.

A program in criminal justice did make sense in Brantford but not because crime was rampant. Like journalism, an interdisciplinary study of crime could be usefully paired with a broader understanding of contemporary issues. Inevitably, issues of criminal justice were discussed in many Waterloo (and Brantford) courses, but there was no Laurier program in criminology or criminal justice. In Brantford, a program could take advantage of our proximity to the three courts and the jail downtown. One of the courts was a federal court with a significant legal history. Among other things, the jail attached to it had been the site of eight hangings: the cell used was still intact. When our students demonstrated an abiding interest in the macabre, and made a lecture course on multiple murder one of the most popular courses on the campus, I revived the idea that we should try and acquire the jail. Although it was not a possibility at the time, collaborative efforts with the courts were. These were initiated by the leader of Brantford's legal fraternity, the Honourable Justice Gethin Edward, who took me to lunch to discuss the possibilities. I passed him on to Lauren Eisler, a very capable professor who played the lead role growing our justice programs.

A third curriculum initiative rooted in the 2002 strategic plan was an honours B.A. in Leadership. The campus's local supporters had always wanted a Brantford business program. A number of them wanted it to be *the* focus of the curriculum at Brantford and did not understand why the university insisted on the liberal arts. They envisioned Business as an economic engine that would promote and develop Brantford. Whatever the merits of such an idea, this was a non-starter at Brantford because the School of Business and Economics, and especially its dean, were opposed to it. They saw their future in Waterloo and Toronto, and regarded Brantford as of little consequence. In discussions of the possibilities with senior administrators, I complained that the School of Business prided itself in teaching the free market but believed it had a monopoly on programs in business and management at Laurier. This, however, did not change the political realities, making it very difficult for Brantford to develop a business program.

The discussions that took place during the 2002 strategic plan were greatly influenced by a 1998 study on Arts and the Humanities graduates by a UBC economist. On the basis of an exhaustive survey of the statistical data on university graduates and employment, he concluded that the evidence did not support the popular prejudice that arts, humanities, and social science graduates fared poorly in the workforce. As Robert Allen put it: "the labour market experiences of humanities, social science, and education graduates are generally quite favourable. They readily find jobs. A majority are also employed in managerial and professional occupations. Very few graduates work as waiters, bar maids, or the like. Humanities, social science, and education graduates generally earn high incomes."[4]

Allen's research convinced us that we should develop programming at Brantford that recognized the connection between the study of the liberal arts and careers in management. We envisioned a program that combined the traditional liberal arts skills — the ability to think critically, to communicate well, to solve problems, to analyze data, to place things in a broader societal, cultural, and historical context — with some study of businesses, organizations, management, and leadership. We wanted a program with the word *business* or *management* in the title but the School of Business objected. In a spirit of good citizenship, we relented and aimed for a program in Organizational Leadership that would marry the liberal arts with a growing literature on the sociology and psychology of organizations, and the study of leadership from a historical, sociological, and political point of view. The program would prepare students for leadership positions in any kind of organization. Like Criminology and Journalism, we believed that it would combine well with Contemporary Studies, and with downtown Brantford, which could afford professors and students connections to local government, business, and social service organizations.

The development of new programs is a laborious and often thankless task. In the wake of Brantford's 2002 strategic plan, the campus began to assemble the key ingredients for our new programs. By the end of 2004, we had hired professors to develop programs in Criminology, Journalism, and Organizational Leadership. Our first associate dean, Bruce Arai, was a key catalyst in the development of these detailed program proposals. I had known him from my years on the Waterloo campus, where he was a well-respected member of the Sociology Department. When we advertised for an associate dean, I was not willing to stand by and hope that good candidates applied. To ensure an excellent pool of candidates, I encouraged three Waterloo faculty members to apply with an emphasis on professors widely known for their administrative smarts. Arai was one of them. He had decided not to apply until I accidentally met him at 1:00 in the morning at an all-night grocery store, and took the opportunity to enthuse about what was happening at Brantford.

The work that Arai and the rest of us did in shepherding our program proposals through multifarious levels of approval pulled the campus together. When a new faculty member from the University of British Columbia, Andrew Robinson, proposed a program in Human Rights and Diversity, I added it to our menu of new initiatives.

The sense of community that we were trying to build among students, faculty, and staff was reinforced by many shared experiences. During a period of severe weather in January of 2004, a pipe burst in the lobby of Grand River Hall, flooding the building. During the clean up, a sprinkler in the lobby burst, bringing a second flood. Like Greek mythology, we were destined to have three floods, the third and final deluge arriving the next day, when another pipe burst. In the final case, five thousand gallons of water spilled into the building, causing water damage that cost three hundred thousand dollars to repair. In the aftermath, we were forced to close Grand River Hall and remove thirty students from their residence rooms. They enjoyed the misfortune when we lodged them in the Holiday Inn. Weeks later they emerged wearing T-shirts emblazoned with the biblical slogan I SURVIVED THE FLOOD.

Though they could be a source of great frustration, the tensions that sometimes characterized relations between Brantford and Waterloo fostered, in their own backhanded way, Brantford's sense of solidarity. Anyone who has studied "satellite" campuses knows that this is one of the hallmarks of life on

a secondary campus. At Brantford, everyone appreciated the interest of Laurier's most senior administrators — President Rosehart and Vice-President Smith — but Brantford still felt misunderstood and constrained by the policies and priorities of the university's "main" campus. When Rowland Smith and I participated in a session at the Association of American Colleges and Universities, I met a series of administrators from satellite campuses who all talked about their difficulty managing relations between the central campuses at their institutions. I was struck by the thought: "We are not alone."

Many of the managers in Waterloo supported Brantford, but it still felt that Waterloo interests trumped those of the Brantford campus. In creating policies, the university was driven by a view of things at Waterloo, sometimes leaving Brantford with the feeling that it was a lesser partner in the broader scheme of things. Though the Brantford campus was unable to pursue management programs that might impinge on offerings in the School of Business, Waterloo zealously pursued a Waterloo Faculty of Education after Brantford's education programs took off. Instead of welcoming all the initiatives at Brantford, the Registrar's Office resisted them. The dean of arts once told me that *all* the faculty appointments at Brantford should be part-time, and that full-time appointments should be reserved for Waterloo. In an effort to reinforce and foster a more equal partnership, I stopped referring to Waterloo as "the main campus" and to Brantford as a "satellite." At Brantford we talked of Laurier Brantford and Laurier Waterloo, but Waterloo talked of Laurier and Laurier Brantford.

From the point of view of some managers in Waterloo, Brantford must have been a headache, as

Bruce Arai, the Brantford campus's first associate dean (and subsequently, its third dean) with one of the paintings collected in the Laurier Brantford art drive — a painting of Emily Carr's home by Dolores Appleton.

One of the campus's community art projects, designed and created with the assistance of Rose Risi and Smak Dab Pottery. More than four hundred individual clay tiles were created by students, staff, and faculty, some of whom are pictured here: (left to right) Tony Araujo, Holly Cox, Kevin Klein, Penny Barnett, Dave Prang, Jennifer Brickman, Kate Carter, the artist Rose Risi, Leo Groarke, and Sherri Bocchini.

it strove to be an exception to so many rules and policies — on residences, college transfers, and everything and sundry. When the president, who was a zealous anti-smoker, got approval for a rule prohibiting smoking within ten metres of any building, Brantford had to have an exception, because the property ten metres beside some of our buildings did not belong to us.

In many ways, Brantford did not fit the mould. One of the most irritating situations occurred when the university's Office of Cultural Affairs decided that the Brantford campus could not, for insurance reasons, display original works from the university's art collection. This was an issue in my own office because it was adorned with some original pieces I had brought from Waterloo. If they belonged to Laurier, I argued, and we were Laurier, how could this be a problem? Cultural Affairs fuelled the Brantford discontentment when they said that we could, like Western or McMaster or another university, apply for a special loan. "But we are not another university," was the heart of my reply. In protest, I told my staff to ignore the requests that I return pieces I had brought to the campus from Waterloo. Cultural Affairs could come and get them, but I was not going to help with their removal. Things came to a head when they sent staff (which my office dubbed "The Art Police") to remove an original painting from my office.

In the aftermath, I tried to tackle the issue in a more positive way, by launching a campaign to collect art for the Brantford campus. It aimed to build a Brantford collection emphasizing works donated by local artists and members of the university community. A press release and donations from the local artists garnered extensive publicity for the campus. In a spirit of community, the collection contains projects designed by local artists that incorporate the work of faculty, staff, and students. The result was a growing art collection that now provides public display space for pieces by a number of significant local artists — among them Rose Hirano, Michael Swanson, Nico Kuilboer, Marguerite Larmand, and Hendrik Lenis.

Hendrik Lenis's painting of Lorne Bridge presents the bridge from the banks of the Grand River, close to Brant's Ford, reaching out toward the buildings on the far south side. Visually, it captures the spirit of the Laurier Brantford art collection (and, more deeply, the campus's attitude to development), which is founded on a determined attempt to build bridges to the community that surrounds it.

| 19 |

THE ODEON

As Laurier Brantford found its footing on the enrollment front, it still struggled with its location in the middle of downtown. In an effort to give visitors a good first impression of the campus, our recruitment office designed a tour that navigated them away from the worst of the downtown's buildings. But they were unable to remove a walk past a large derelict theatre on Market Street. The Odeon was located right there on the way from the Carnegie Library to Grand River Hall.

As Laurier was preparing its move to downtown Brantford in January 1999, Cineplex Odeon closed the theatre, which was no longer able to attract the audience needed to keep it viable. When I arrived, I was captivated by the thought that it might be turned into a lecture theatre for the university. Stuart Parkinson, Vyrt Sisson, and other members of the Grand Valley Education Society told me that it was an "obvious" project for the university — it would be cheap to buy and could function as a large classroom. Ted Donald, who regularly commented on Brantford goings-on via letters to *The Expositor*, argued that the Odeon should be donated to the city, refurbished and given to WLU "in the hopes of moving music, drama, and fine arts programs to the Brantford campus."[1]

Moving Music and Fine Arts programs from Waterloo to Brantford was not possible, but Rowland Smith and I toyed with some possibilities. Something seemed right about the idea of a film studies program housed in a classic Odeon theatre, but the equipment costs were prohibitive, and it would have competed with existing programming at Laurier Waterloo. Even if we could find a way around these issues, we had no funding for such a project.

As the Odeon sat empty, Laurier took root and began to grow around it. The opening of Grand River Hall placed the theatre halfway between the campus's north and south ends. Pushed by a relentless real estate agent and the thought that a renovated Odeon could help us build a more unified, less disjointed campus, I talked to the president, who agreed to have a look. He and Ron Dupuis, who oversaw all of the university's building projects, joined me for a tour of the building in 2002. The size of the interior — built to house an audience of eight hundred — was impressive, but the building was in a serious state of disrepair, much of it ruined by plumbing problems and a fire that had consumed ten rows of seats in 1979. It was difficult to imagine it as usable academic space. The president concluded that the Odeon would be too costly to repair. Dupuis agreed. Like every other potential buyer, we shunned the former theatre, leaving the building to deteriorate in the middle of downtown.

One might contrast the lack of interest shown in the Odeon at the end of the twentieth century with its reception half a century earlier. When the theatre was first proposed, at the end of the Second World War, its construction was opposed by four different Market Street businesses — a bakery, a fruit and grocery store, a tea room, and a hair salon. All of them were unhappy when they were evicted to make way for the new theatre. In an effort to stop the project, they launched a complaint with the Wartime Prices and Trade Board, a government agency established to regulate prices and supply during and after the war. Lawyers on the two sides of the complaint debated a variety of questions. One point of contention was the suggestion that the construction of the Odeon would use materials that should, in the aftermath of a war, be used to address a shortage of housing for veterans.

The Odeon lawyers prevailed. Cineplex spent $120,000 building its new theatre, which opened with much fanfare on December 17, 1948. An article in *The Expositor* announced that "Imaginative planning, the untiring efforts of skilled Canadian craftsmen, and the finest of equipment have resulted in a theatre that is the last word in attractiveness, restful environment and luxurious comfort."[2] At a time when the normal price for a ticket to the movies was thirty-five cents, the many state-of-the-art amenities included: air conditioning, a smoking lounge with a separate air circulation system, in-house hearing aids for moviegoers who had

"difficulty in following dialogue or music accompanying the films," "scientifically planned" and acoustically engineered walls and ceiling, exquisite pile carpeting manufactured by Brantford's own Harding Carpets, and other lavish details.

The projection and sound equipment were a special point of pride:

> Under the sponsorship of the J. Arthur Rank organization, one of the most extensive and far-reaching programs in the history of the film industry was already in full swing before the end of the war. Co-operating in it, along with the film industry's own technical leaders, were a co-operating group of British manufacturers of precision instruments, scientists who had aided in the discovery of radar and other wartime devices but who are now applying these advances to peacetime uses as well as skilled European technicians who had fled to the United Kingdom for refuge and are now remaining there.
>
> Through its link with the J. Arthur Rank interests overseas, the results of these advances are already becoming evident in the new Odeon Theatre here. One of the specific projects launched in Britain was that of producing the finest machine for the projection of sound-film used in theatres. The result, known as Gumont-Kalee 20, went into service

One of the design drawings for Blanche Fury, *the first film shown at the Odeon. The artist was John Bryan, an Oscar-winning British film producer/production designer. From Edward Carrick,* Art and Design in the British Film, *1948.*

The Odeon in its first heyday. Both the theatre and the Dominion grocery store have now been turned into post-secondary buildings.

about a year ago after two years of testing. The Odeon will be equipped with Gaumont-Kalee machines.[3]

The initial advertisements for the Odeon promised "the finest" in British and Hollywood films, but it was popular demand, not refined tastes, that determined its choice of movies. The first attraction was *Blanche Fury*, a Gothic blockbuster still known as a masterpiece of melodrama, featuring a torrid romance, a murder, and lurid, or, in today's vernacular, "hot" visuals. The Odeon promised "more fine films" to follow. The offerings included *Oliver Twist*, *Blue Lagoon*, *Woman Hater*, *Scott of the Antarctic*, and *The Bad Lord Byron*. For fifty years, the theatre offered an annual series of "major motion pictures" that were an essential staple of popular entertainment in Brant County.

A half century after it opened, the Odeon sat unused and unwanted. On both sides of it, Laurier continued to evolve. As enrollment began to increase dramatically, the university was in need of more classroom space, the most difficult problem being our lack of large lecture halls. Inclusion in the Grand River Hall renovation was not possible as the building's support pillars interfered with the sightlines required. When one of the larger lecture halls we tried to insert into the building was denounced by students and faculty, we cut it into two separate classrooms. This created better teaching space but exacerbated the need for lecture theatres elsewhere. Investigation of the possibility of using the vacant theatres in the empty downtown mall only revealed another set of negative issues. As we canvassed the options, one thing was clear — one way or another,

the campus would have to find lecture halls or curtail its plans for growth.

A key variable in our considerations was the president's approach to buildings. Bob the Builder was an engineer who favoured function over form. He was not greatly moved by the history or the aesthetics of old buildings, and once told me that the right way to construct a building was with steel and glass and concrete. Drywall could define the interior. Above all else, he wanted to avoid the headaches of asbestos removal, outdated HVAC systems, and old configurations of space that matched another era's needs. Even after the roundly praised renovation of the Carnegie Library, his ideal was new construction. It was not easy for him to give up the idea that we should leave the downtown and move to a greenfield site, but the development of the Brantford campus made him think twice. Grand River Hall and the Post House project proved that renovation could turn old buildings into imaginative, first-class space. At the official opening of the Post House Residence, he joked that Brantford was forcing him to rethink his aversion to older buildings.

In the wake of the Post House project, a success for both the university and Vicano Construction, it was Peter Vicano who revived the idea that the empty Odeon Theatre could be a viable building for the university. Peter Vicano's son Paul took the initiative, and convinced his father that they should buy the building. If the university was not interested, Plan B would have it converted into private residences or downtown condominiums. While the alternative plan was talked about, it was not pursued, as the president, in the glow of the Post House renovations, was interested in the other possibility.

In consultation with Ron Dupuis, he agreed that Vicano could make the Odeon viable. Vicano began preparing an imaginative design that would turn the theatre into university space.

Like all of the Brantford projects, the Odeon project could not proceed without some creative financing. In the overall scheme of things, residence projects were the easiest to finance because one could use the residence fees one charged students to offset a mortgage. Financing was more complex when it came to academic buildings. Student tuition paid the cost of operating the university — the salaries of faculty and other staff; the cost of equipment, maintenance, and so on — which left little for capital projects. Universities expected the provincial government to bear the cost of new buildings, but the government continued to reject requests for capital support in Brantford. In lieu of such support, President Rosehart turned to the Brantford mayor and city council for support. The city was reluctant. It had supported a number of Laurier projects and felt that the province was abdicating its responsibilities. President Rosehart felt the same frustration, but this did not alter his bottom line. He was adamant that Laurier could not proceed without some government support. In the absence of provincial support, the city was the only option. He refused to pursue the project unless some funding was forthcoming.

After much discussion and hand-wringing, the city agreed to contribute six hundred thousand dollars toward a project that would cost $2.4 million. This was progress but the president was not satisfied. He threatened to cancel the project. In conversations at the university he frequently declared that the university was "the only thing working in downtown Brantford" and would not pay more than half of the project's cost. An equally determined new mayor was determined to keep the city's contribution to 25 per cent — the percentage it used to calculate its support for other projects that qualified for city grants.

At Brantford, we felt caught in the middle of the standoff. When I pushed the president, he relented slightly. He told me that he would proceed with the Odeon purchase and renovation if we could find a way to raise another five hundred thousand dollars for the project. The first stop in the campaign we launched was another visit with the mayor and the city. They remained adamant that they could not contribute any more funding to the project. My second stop was a meeting with Dave Levac, the MPP for Brant County. He was deeply committed to the future of the university and said, frankly, that he saw half a million dollars as "loose change" in a government budget that totalled billions of dollars. Despite his pushing and prodding at Queen's Park, money was not made available, and Levac apologetically suggested we look for a private donor to make the Odeon a go. We began looking. As some intriguing architectural drawings took shape, the project hung in the balance.

Like other attempts to secure the five-hundred-thousand-dollar gap in funding for the project, my attempt to find a private donor failed. Though we were growing desperate for space to serve our growing student body, it looked as though financing for the Odeon was a bust. In a last-ditch effort, I met with Doug Baker, the dean of Mohawk College's Brantford campus. In working through a series of articulation agreements, we had established a positive working relationship and met regularly to discuss post-secondary issues. Baker was the first of a series of deans who began to see co-operation with the university as one of the cornerstones of their Brantford operations. In a situation in which the college's campus was located in an industrial neighbourhood, I asked him if he and Mohawk would be interested in collaborating on the Odeon project. If they could provide the five hundred thousand dollars the project needed to proceed, they could make their interest in the building the basis of their own downtown campus.

Baker welcomed the idea. We agreed to see if we could convince our presidents. The ultimate result was a Hamilton meeting two weeks later with both sides of a potential Mohawk-Laurier alliance. Bob Rosehart, who was in his element when negotiating any deal, proposed the details of a partnership in the Odeon. Laurier and Mohawk would co-own the building, with the college owning a share equal to its relative contribution to the total project cost. The money provided by the city would be split between the two institutions. The agreement would include a clause that allowed the university to purchase Mohawk's share of the building in the future. An administrative office would be included in Mohawk's designated space. Baker and I contributed our thoughts on the programming initiatives that the building would make possible.

President West-Moynes was guarded in her response. There were many things for Mohawk to consider. Though it had welcomed Laurier's arrival in Brantford, it felt that the city took the college for granted when supporting a series of Laurier projects. At one public meeting I was put on the spot when someone said: "Mohawk has been in this city

for thirty years. Why does the city give so much to Laurier and so little to Mohawk?" I answered that the city gave Laurier what it asked for because we asked it for what it wanted to give. When we asked for something, it was to help us bring some beaten-up old building — or a whole neighbourhood that nobody would have anything to do with — back to life. Although the Odeon project would give Mohawk a chance to claim a share of the money the City of Brantford was willing to provide for post-secondary projects, West-Moynes had competing priorities to contend with.

One of these realities was the interests of her campuses outside Brantford. Even in Brantford, her first priority was Mohawk's existing Elgin Street campus. She wondered about a new start-up when the current campus was not fully utilized. We left the Hamilton meeting unsure what she would decide. My impression from afar was that Baker was relentless and eventually prevailed. West-Moynes agreed to join the project, subject to an agreement on a great many financial and operational details, all of which were ironed out in a series of meetings that included deans, managers, and Mohawk's and Laurier's chief financial officers, Dick Raha and Jim Butler.

In a race with growing enrollment, work on the building proceeded quickly. Because the interior of the original theatre was a large hall built to hold eight hundred seats, the builders had a great deal of flexibility as they rearranged the space for a new use. In their final design they almost doubled the useable space by inserting a second floor, created by extending the original balcony to the end of the building that housed the movie screen. On the first floor, the design featured two 150- to 180-seat lecture halls

The Odeon Theatre as a Laurier/Mohawk building, after the renovations were completed in 2004.

Courtesy of Kevin Klein.

that were the front sections of the original theatre. The lobby of the building was expanded to include common space and offices for managers, professors, and staff. The second floor and the basement housed a computer lab, a student lounge, a production room for Mohawk classes, and various small and mid-size classrooms. The old projection booth, hidden behind second-floor classrooms, was transformed into one-of-a-kind faculty offices.

Like the original Odeon Theatre, the new version of the building opened to much acclaim. At the opening ceremony in October 2004, it was hailed as a unique partnership including Laurier, the city, and Mohawk College. For Laurier, the building dramatically increased our academic space, allowing our expansion to continue without the threatening constraints of a looming "space crunch." The Odeon location, beside the Nipissing Building and roughly halfway between the Carnegie and Grand River Hall, was a major step toward a more contiguous campus in the middle of downtown. In another way, the building strengthened the campus's connection to Brantford history, reinvigorating yet another abandoned building in the middle of the city's downtown.

| 20 |

A CHANGE OF STATUS

There is no dull moment in Brantford city politics. For five years, the university enjoyed a productive working relationship with the city's "boy mayor." His three terms as mayor were a turning point for the city, and especially its downtown. Although I did not always agree with him, no one ever doubted his commitment to the university's role in the new Brantford.

His Worship Chris Friel was an intriguing figure. His detractors resented his leadership style, which was not consultative. Profoundly committed to Brantford, he sometimes cut political corners, not doing the work required to get everyone (or at least as many councillors as possible) on board with his ideas and initiatives. This was interpreted as arrogance by those who criticized him. When he told me, in a deferential tone, that he wanted to write a biography of Joseph Brant, I wondered whether their styles might be compared. For Brant, too, was accused of having a haughty, arrogant style of leadership.[1]

In personal conversation, Friel was a more complex figure than the media allowed. He had achieved political success at a young age and struggled with his role in life. He did not see himself as the permanent mayor of Brantford and was not sure what he wanted to do next. On a morning when we met for a walk along the Grand River — a walk interrupted by continual phone calls from his office — he told me that he was "tired" of being mayor, that the job had lost its verve, that he was stuck in a rut. He toyed with the idea that he would run another corporation; that he would enter a different kind of politics; that he would write his book on Massey Ferguson or Joseph Brant; that he would not run for another term. His existential doubts were real, but his name was on the ballot when the next municipal election rolled around. In a situation in which the success of the university depended on a positive relationship with the mayor and the city, I wondered what would happen.

It was a difficult time for Friel at city hall. The charm of his status as "the boy mayor" had worn thin and after three terms many councillors saw him as "the old boy mayor." Increasingly city hall was characterized by ever-growing tensions among the young mayor, the press, and city councillors who felt that Friel did not properly consult with them. In the fall of 2003, these tensions boiled up in an acrimonious election campaign. I watched from the sidelines. When a number of would-be politicians pushed me for support, I maintained a strictly non-partisan stance. The official Laurier position was the bland, but truthful, statement that "We will commit ourselves to working hard with whoever is elected by the citizens of Brantford. We will work with them to ensure the continued redevelopment of the downtown."

Aristotle described the human species as "a political animal." This description applied to no one more than President Rosehart, who was continually enmeshed in, and intrigued by, politics. He called election time "the silly season" and warned me to make sure that none of our goings-on became "a political football" in the middle of the campaign. I withstood the continual attempts to draw us into the election debate. From where I sat, what struck me was the vehemence of the attacks on Friel in the media and, even more so, his half-hearted response to them. Friel could be a commanding speaker but this seemed to be an election in which he was "going through the motions" instead of fighting for re-election. When the ballots were finally counted, he lost the election by fifteen votes. A recount that reversed eight of twenty-four thousand votes would have overturned the result, but Friel decided not to request one. It was a surprising decision, but it fit with his angst about his career.

At city hall, Friel was replaced with a popular and self-effacing veteran of city council, Mike Hancock. Having worked on local employment issues for the federal government, and as executive director of the Brant Skills Development Group, Hancock had a long history with the city and had seen Brantford at its worst. He had served as councillor for five terms. The election ushered in a city council with five new

faces: the mayor and four new councillors. A key ally of Friel's, councillor Vince Bucci, went down to defeat. The re-elected councillors who sat with the new faces were those who had opposed Friel. This new council was defined by its fiery opposition to all things Friel. Even the ex-mayor's chief administrative officer, Hans Loewig, who had worked on many of the Laurier projects, quickly fell out of favour. He saw the writing on the wall, announced his retirement, and left in October 2004. In a symbolic, if somewhat bitter, move that underscored its disenchantment with the way that Loewig and Friel had worked together, city council eliminated the position he had occupied, restructuring city hall to create an alternative position.

The new political realities posed some challenges for the university. Friel, Bucci, and Loewig had been key supporters of the Laurier initiative. With the three of them deposed, in a situation in which Laurier was so closely associated with the old regime, we had had to negotiate a testy transition to a new order caught up in its rejection of the one that had preceded it. On the new council, Mayor Hancock and councillors Kings, Ceschi-Smith, and Starkey were significant supporters of the move to make post-secondary education a key component of the downtown, but our relationship to the city was in question at a time when three issues were straining relations between the university and the city.

Issue number one was the university's decision to demolish a Victorian home-turned-law-office on the southeast corner of Victoria Square. The Wyatt-Purcell Building was in a state of poor repair when the university purchased it, and deteriorated further when an upstairs pipe froze and burst, flooding the building. The property it sat on — on the border of the square — remained a prime location, but the building itself was a health hazard and an eyesore. Tensions arose when the local heritage committee, backed by councillor John Starkey and others active in heritage issues, objected to the university's plan to demolish an 1875 residence in the city's most significant heritage district. It did not help when they pointed out that the residence had once served as the home of E.L. Goold, an important manufacturer of hardware, industrial supplies, and agricultural equipment in the heyday of industrial Brantford.

Issue number two was the university's decision to give the TD Bank Building we had loaned the city to Nipissing University. We had no other practical way to accommodate Nipissing's desire for its own identity in downtown Brantford and no one doubted our right to dispose of the building as we wanted. But this could not change the fact that our decision to do so was not in keeping with what we told the city when we acquired the building. At that point, we informally agreed to let the city use the building for five years. On the basis of this agreement, it had undertaken an expensive renovation project turning the building into a downtown Business Resource Centre that they planned to operate for this five-year period. Our change of plans meant that they had to abruptly change their strategy and find a new location for their resource centre after having gone to considerable expense to create one in the old TD Bank.

Issue number three was an agreement we had arranged with Mayor Friel, who had agreed to support a project that would turn another city-owned building — the Old Hydro Building on Wellington Street — into The Brantford Centre, a Laurier/Mohawk initiative. The project would boost post-secondary initiatives downtown, but it would displace city workers. Friel and Loewig had an ambitious solution to this problem: the city would purchase the almost empty downtown mall and move the workers there. Their plan was tied to a broader vision that would see the mall house a number of municipal departments. It was an intriguing concept that would have addressed the issues in the mall as well as the university and college, but it was one that the new council rejected in its move to distance itself from the previous administration. At Laurier and Mohawk, the fallout was an end to the agreement on The Brantford Centre that we had painstakingly worked out.

In some minds, Laurier's relationship with the past mayor and the issues that characterized its relationship with the city raised deep questions concerning Laurier's intentions. In local conversations, some of them with city councillors, I was questioned about Laurier's commitment to Brantford. How, I was asked, could the city be sure that Laurier would not pack up and move back to Waterloo? At times, the urgency of such questions left me speechless. Not because the asker had stumbled on a Laurier conspiracy, as they sometimes supposed, but because the suggestion made no sense at all. One might as well have asked me how I could assure them that Laurier would remain a university. In a situation in which Laurier Brantford had acquired four buildings, an enrollment on its way to eight hundred, a unique set of programs, and local partnerships with Mohawk and Nipissing, we could not move its operations to Waterloo even if we wanted to. And we did not want to. No one on the Brantford campus thought, even for a second, that our campus would ever move from Brantford. In such a situation it was eerie to deal with persistent local worries, some of them raised by prominent Brantford figures, that Laurier might leave.

On a campus built upon a partnership with the city, the sensitivities that characterized the university's relationship with city council were troublesome. In an effort to promote its understanding of post-secondary issues, Doug Baker, the dean of Mohawk College, and I met with each of the elected councillors individually. This helped build some positive relations, but failed to end the tough questions being asked about the university and its plans in Brantford. Councillor Starkey took the lead in public, calling for a Laurier plan that could help the city do a planning exercise of its own. His call was backed by Councillor Ceschi-Smith. Their sentiments were echoed in an *Expositor* column at the end of 2003, in which Michael-Allan Marion asked that Laurier "open its heart to the city and give council a more complete understanding of its long-term plans."[2]

On the campus, it seemed that our "honeymoon" with the city was over. To build a more positive long-term relationship, we began working on a new strategic plan to answer all the questions being raised about the direction of the campus. Work on the plan coincided with the approval of the campus's journalism program, the last major initiative proposed in the 2002 plan. During the course of a year, we struggled to find the time for more than forty meetings on the different issues the campus faced. There were times when it felt that we were being strategic-planned to death, but we persisted

and finally emerged with a new plan. Like the previous one, it proposed two scenarios for growth at Brantford. One envisioned a campus of 1,500 to 1,600 students, the other 2,000 to 2,500. Both scenarios envisaged a major reorganization of the campus that would incorporate enrollments that exceeded anything that had been imagined a few years earlier. Here was our answer to the persistent questions about Laurier's plans in Brantford.

Earlier strategic planning had emphasized new academic programs. The new plan reaffirmed a liberal arts mission now manifest in a core program and a mix of applied and professional programs built around it. On an interdisciplinary campus, much discussion was devoted to the question of how we could ensure that Brantford did not break up into the departmental silos that characterize most universities.

One of the most pressing issues that arose was student life. On a small campus in a still inhospitable location, classroom needs were taken care of, but students lacked many of the services and opportunities they took for granted on more established campuses. These included health services, counselling, special needs, career services, athletics and recreation, a writing centre, learning support services, student union activities, and much more. In attempting to rectify this situation after the plan, I had already focused on a Brantford student service fee. It was paid by all of our students, but the revenue it produced was lodged in a budget envelope in Waterloo, where it was not reserved for Brantford initiatives. This became a sore point on the campus.

With the help of Laurier's dean of students, David McMurray (who the students embraced as "Daddy Mac"), I had arranged a budget for some modest student services. But Brantford wanted more — in particular an agreement that would ensure that the monies the campus's students paid for student services would be used for services on the Brantford campus. Lobbying for such an agreement was complicated. An existing contract between the university and the student union — a contract that never mentioned Brantford — governed the use of the student service fee. McMurray was sympathetic but one could not establish a Brantford-specific budget without negotiating a change to this contract that involved lawyers and detailed bargaining on both sides. I was frustrated with our lack of progress until fate shone down on us — Laurier's student body elected a president who had grown up in Brantford.

Dave Prang, known by all as "Pranger," was a student union president who was not shy about saying what was on his mind. This did not always endear him to the university's other president, but it helped him build a strong team of student advocates. When I met with him, I discovered that he was excited about Laurier's move to his hometown. It was not difficult to convince him of the need to reserve Brantford student fees for Brantford student services. Fuelled by his enthusiasm for Brantford on the other side of the table, the two Davids — Daddy Mac and Pranger — and I negotiated a Brantford amendment to the university's contract with the students. Because student union presidents have a very short shelf life — serving for an impossibly brief one-year term — I rushed to have the agreement ratified before Prang's term ended. In recognition of his work, I wanted to ensure that he was the student president who signed the agreement we

Katie Reaume and Jessie Olsen at a Laurier Students for Literacy "Franklin" event in the Brantford Public Library. Photo by Jessica Grimes.

Courtesy of Wilfrid Laurier University Students' Union.

had negotiated. We made it, just barely, signing the agreement on April 30, 2002, the last day of his term of office.

With a budget in place, the campus expanded Brantford Student Services. An early priority was the development of a residence life program. The

Brantford residences were tame in comparison to larger residences elsewhere (the residence one of my children attended at the University of Western Ontario was known as "the Zoo" — its occupants were delighted when *Late Night* host David Letterman included it in a list of the "Top 10 Party Locations" in North America). But issues are inevitable whenever hundreds of young students live together. In Brantford's early days, the most memorable occurred when Graham Hawkins, the campus's first residence life co-coordinator, evicted a student for possessing marijuana. He responded to the charges by yelling and accusing other students, including his residence don, of lying. When I would not overturn the decision to evict him, he went home and brought back reinforcements.

Every university struggles with "helicopter" parents. They hover over their sons and daughters, trying to intervene in and manage their affairs. In many cases, they are more difficult to deal with than students themselves. This was a case in point. When the student who had been evicted brought his parents to a meeting with Hawkins and myself, they refused to believe that their progeny could be guilty of mischief. When I explained that their son was caught with a bag of marijuana, the father did not flinch. The residence don was lying, he said, scheming against his son. In an aggressive manner that reminded us of his son's behaviour a week earlier, he raised his voice and accused us of being part of the conspiracy. By the end of the session he was pounding his fist on the table. When the angry father went to see Vice-President Smith to try and overturn my decision, Smith decided to send a message and had one of our security police posted outside his door.

A week later, his son phoned and told me that he was going to host a press conference on Colborne Street if we did not readmit him to the residences. He wanted me to know that he was going to say that Laurier Brantford was selling drugs in its residences and had framed and evicted him because he was trying to stop it. I told him I would not reverse my decision and that he should do what he had to do. In my mind, I imagined a newspaper headline that read CAMPUS DEAN ACCUSED OF DOPE SCHEME. It did not appear.

When Graham Hawkins left to become a police officer, he assured me that it was not because of incidents like this. Following in his stead, the student union president who had negotiated a student services budget for Brantford, David Prang, became the campus's second residence coordinator. In the 2004–05 strategic plan, "Pranger" and the director of Brantford Student Services proposed new building acquisitions, better recreational facilities, more residence beds, and expanded student services. Within the plan, these and other changes were proposed in the context of a major reorganization of the structure of the campus. It had operated like an academic faculty, like the Faculty of Arts or the Faculty of Science, though the campus encompassed much broader responsibilities, operating its own buildings, residences, library, and student services, with everything founded on a unique relationship with the city and the local community. The significance of these differences grew as the campus grew in size and complexity.

In a search for a new structure that would recognize the unique nature of the Brantford operation, the campus struggled with the competing desires for more autonomy and an identity that tied it to a well-respected Ontario university. Many of the campus's local backers — key members of the Grand Valley Education Society, prominent politicians, and others — wanted the campus to become an independent college with a Brantford Board of Governors. They saw this as a major step toward a truly *Brantford* institution and interpreted some of the things that President Rosehart had said as a promise that the campus would move in this direction. But Rosehart did not want Brantford to have too much autonomy, a move he saw as a way to fragment the university.

In the midst of all the differences of opinion, the strategic plan attempted a compromise: that the Brantford campus would become an affiliated college of Wilfrid Laurier University. An old adage in the law of contracts has it that good judges make compromises — they know they have made the right decision when "Everyone is unhappy." Compromises make everyone unhappy because nobody gets what they want. So it was with the Brantford proposal. It did not give the city an independent college with its own Board, but it did recognize the campus as something more than the Waterloo faculties and departments. The details of the plan proposed a system of coordinators that would manage the academic programs on the campus. When the president reviewed the plan, he proposed that the campus's senior administrator be a "principal" who reported directly to the president. To ensure that Brantford had a presence at the highest levels of administration in the university, he added a proposal that one position on the university Board of Governors be reserved for a Brantford representative.

University decision-making is a cumbersome process that requires many levels of approval. After the strategic plan was approved by the campus, the proposed changes to its structure went to the Senate Academic Planning Committee, from there to Senate, and then to the Board of Governors. On April 26, 2006, the Board unanimously made Laurier Brantford an affiliated "university-college." By the time the change was approved the campus had more than sixty full-time faculty and staff — more staff than it had students in its first year and a new structure that featured a principal, a dean, directors, managers, coordinators and advisers, and departments. The doubts about the viability of the campus were gone. The question that remained was how it would achieve the lofty enrollment targets set in the new strategic plan.

| 21 |

FINDING A MIDDLE WAY

One of the key drivers behind Laurier Brantford's second strategic plan was a desire to ease the city's doubts about Laurier's intentions. One of the prime priorities the plan identified was the need for space devoted to student life. Acquiring such space should have been another positive step in the rehabilitation of downtown. But this was not the way that things played out. As fate would have it, the attempt to secure such space priority was about to collide with the desire to appease local concerns that raised the question of whether Laurier could be trusted.

The development of the Brantford campus was guided by the principle of "adaptive reuse." Instead of building new buildings, we grew by restoring and renovating existing downtown buildings. Though it was not the approach the president favoured, a series of successful — in some cases, spectacularly successful — building projects convinced him that a great deal could be done with old buildings that no one else was interested in. On the ground in Brantford, adaptive reuse was a key component of our good relations with the city, making us a campus that embraced the old streets and buildings that had fallen on hard times. From an architectural and historical point of view, this made us

a more interesting campus than the shopping-mall-like buildings that are found on most new university sites.

The Brantford campus was proud of its commitment to the old downtown. When asked about green initiatives I always said that we were committed to recycling but took it one step further — we recycled buildings. This was a new approach to the redevelopment of downtown. When the new city hall and adjacent courthouse were built in 1967, the architecture set off in a new, modernist direction. In the 1980s, Mayor Neumann and Phil Gillies made a determined attempt to resurrect the downtown's industrial, mercantile, and telecommunications significance, but did so with modernist, newly constructed buildings: Massey House, the Eaton's mall, and the Icomm Centre. In sharp contrast, the university headed in the opposite direction, exchanging the downtown's old activities for new ones focused on education, but placed these new activities in the built architecture already found downtown.

Before Laurier, some Brantford visionaries had argued against "progressive" architectural endeavours. At the 1978 meetings of the Architectural Conservancy of Ontario, the Brantford branch of the Conservancy expressed its concerns about a proposal from a development company that wanted to demolish a series of historical buildings on Dalhousie Street. The buildings on the list included the Commercial Hotel, which dated from the 1850s. Audrey Scott, who spent much of her life lovingly compiling a photographic record of Brantford architecture, criticized the plan, noting that other cities had chosen to restore rather than reconstruct their downtown core. She pointed to Hamilton's Hess Village as a good example. "Something has to be done," she conceded, "but these old buildings do not have to be destroyed in the process."[1] The Brantford lawyer who represented the development company was Richard "Dick" Waterous. He was destined to become a prominent proponent of the downtown who spearheaded a number of refurbishing projects, but he disagreed with Scott in 1978, arguing that "It has been the unprofitability of the stores in the downtown area that has allowed the core to deteriorate in the first place." A new development would change this and "the newer buildings would themselves become an integral part of Brantford's heritage."[2]

The perspective Waterous defended was a sign of the times. Across North America, the standard approach to urban revitalization was the removal of old buildings in a state of poor repair and the consequent alteration of the neighbourhoods in which they were located. In downtown Brantford, this produced a kind of "modernist creep," as contemporary architecture eradicated old spaces: the original city hall, the YWCA on Victoria Square, the farmers' market. In the wake of these developments, much of the city's most significant architecture — the Sanderson Centre, Brant Community Church, the Carnegie Building, and the Post House — was on the endangered list.

Governments spent large sums on this attempt to modernize downtown — much more than they spent on later university developments — but it failed to reverse its decline. Sadly, the adventures in modernization systematically eroded an impressive architectural tradition that could be traced from Brantford's glory days at the end of the nineteenth and the beginning of the twentieth century.

The move in a new, but old, direction began when the city decided to restore the Sanderson Centre. The heritage committee scored a victory for old buildings when it managed to save Park Church from the wrecking ball. The university followed with its renovations of the Carnegie, the Post House, and the Odeon. Under the leadership of Cindy MacDonald-Kreuger, councillor John Starkey, and others, these developments energized and emboldened the heritage committee. It advocated a model of redevelopment that would preserve what remained of Brantford's architectural heritage. The committee members were especially concerned about the buildings on the perimeter of Victoria Square. By coincidence, these were the buildings that interested the university the most.

By any measure, Laurier Brantford's first building projects provided it with an impressive record of adaptive reuse — a much better record than the city, which had been at the forefront of the dismantling of many of the downtown's heritage spaces. When city officials pushed the university in this regard, the university's attitude tended to be "People in concrete houses shouldn't cast heritage aspersions." This did not stop heritage issues from coming to a boil, however, when the university decided that it wanted to demolish the Wyatt-Purcell Law Office on the southeast corner of the square.

Public domain image, Chas. Shober & Co., Chicago.

The Goold House on the 1875 "Bird's Eye View" map of Brantford. St. Andrew's Church is item 24 on the map; the Commercial Hotel is item 31. Clockwise from St. Andrew's one crosses Darling Street to Victoria Square; then George Street to the future location of the Carnegie Building and Park Church; then Darling Street (again) to the original Goold House. The provenance of the house is not entirely clear, but the original owner is listed as M. Lyman, who was the wife of F.P. Goold, the father of E.L. Goold.

The law office, located at 103 Darling, was a once grand home known as The Goold House. Built before 1875, it was designed by John Turner, Brantford's most acclaimed architect.[3] The house was one quadrant of "Turner's Corner," an intersection of four Turner creations: the Goold House;

Victoria Square, which he designed in 1861; Park Church; and St. Andrew's (originally Zion) Church. The house was built for one of the city's first physicians, Henry Allen, who came to Brantford from Chicago in the year of Confederation, 1867. Selina Louise Goold married him later that year. In addition to his medical practice, Allen pursued business interests. He and Selina moved to Detroit in 1875. After they left Brantford, 103 Darling was occupied by Alex Robertson, the manager of the Brantford branch of the Bank of British North America.

City directories list 103 Darling as the residence of Edward L. Goold from 1896–1907. Like his father, F.P., Edward played a key role in the rise of industrial Brantford. In 1883 he was described as "yet a young man, of a modest and retiring disposition, but among the energetic and pushing business men of the city."[4] In keeping with this assessment, he was active in many of the firms that epitomized Brantford's strength in manufacturing. These included Goold & Agnew, stove and hardware merchants; J.O. Wisner, Son & Co.; and Goold & Co., manufacturers of refrigerators and beekeepers' supplies. He was a founding partner and president of Goold, Shapley & Muir, which operated the largest windmill factory in Canada and produced grinders, pumps, and engines sold under the brand The Brantford Ideal. In 1899, one of Goold's other enterprises, the Goold Bicycle Company, joined forces with Massey-Harris and four other bicycle manufacturers and formed the Canada Cycle and Motor Company Limited. More than a century later, CCM has evolved into one of the world's leading suppliers of hockey equipment.

In Brantford, Goold was widely respected for his active business interests, his work with the Brantford Board of Trade, and his commitment to public good. After leaving 103 Darling, he moved to a magnificent home on Chestnut Avenue, but his name was still associated with the Victoria Square building the university acquired in 2002. By then, the building's ties to Brantford's emergence as a wealthy manufacturing centre were obscured by sagging walls, a paved yard, and a bland and architecturally inappropriate concrete-block extension. Inside, the basement and the extension were dank and dingy, the first floor was in desperate need of maintenance, the second storey was the victim of a major plumbing accident, and the third floor and the stairs leading to it swayed when one walked on them. The president and Ron Dupuis, who managed all of Laurier's buildings, were not impressed, but granted that the building's location, half a block from the Carnegie Building, was an ideal place for future campus expansion. After much discussion, the president agreed to purchase it for a small sum.

In a situation in which we lacked the offices needed for an expanding cadre of professors, the president suggested that the Goold House be converted into offices for faculty. When it appeared that renovations would be costly, John Wilson of the Grand Valley Education Society spearheaded a plan to turn the building into a fifteen-bed residence. The economics of such a tiny residence were a problem and the president put the development of the property on hold. The once-grand home sat on the corner of the square, dilapidated and forlorn.

In the winter of 2004, Ed House, who managed campus student services, decided to store some equipment in the empty house, looked in the window, and discovered that the ceiling had collapsed. He informed me and we explored the house together.

Courtesy of the Brant Museum and Archives, cat. no. x2006317.

When the Goold House, pictured here in the 1960s, suffered serious water damage and the university decided to take it down, a major controversy arose.

It was an eerie experience. House, who had spent time in the military, said he felt as though he was enlisted once again, being sent on a reconnaissance mission to inspect a bombed-out building.

When we gained entry, we made our way through the debris from the collapsed ceiling, up a rickety staircase, and found a broken pipe leaking a steady stream of water on the second floor. The result was soaked and bloated walls, with water dripping everywhere. Because it was evening and the basement and the extension attached to it had no windows, we had to return to the Carnegie and find a flashlight before we could explore them. We proceeded down the basement stairs with some trepidation, into ankle-deep cold water, then sloshed through the dark, looking for the main water valve and the power box. In an old building in poor repair, the bouncing beam of the flashlight revealed exposed wires intermingled with water dripping from the plumbing pipes. When we turned what looked to be the main valve off, the only change was that water began dripping from a different set of pipes. We did what we could to ensure that the power in the building was turned off, then retreated to my office to make a series of emergency phone calls.

The water must have been dripping water for weeks, possibly for months. The pipe froze and burst because the pipes were not drained when the heat in the building was shut off. This raised some uncomfortable questions about the university's maintenance of the building. Whatever its cause, the flood put an end, once and for all, to any thoughts of renovation. The university applied to the city's Planning Department for a demolition permit, noting that the building was a safety hazard and an eyesore. A letter to the planning department explained that a rupture of the plumbing and substantial flooding left the building in "complete disrepair and unsafe."[5] Laurier promised to erect a new building on the site at some point in the future, when provincial funding was secured. In the meantime, the university planned to use the property as a parking lot, to address a shortage of parking spaces on the Brantford campus.

Sitting in my office on Victoria Square, half a block away, I wondered how the city would react. It came as no surprise that the idea that one of the historic buildings around Victoria Square should be taken down to create a parking lot was not enthusiastically received. The rumour mill in Brantford went into high gear, accusing the university of purposely letting the pipes of the Goold House freeze because it wanted a pretext to justify its demolition. It was not easy to respond to these accusations. One could not deny that the president never liked the Goold House and it was peculiar that an institution that oversaw the operation of a hundred buildings seemed not to know that it should turn the water off in a building it decided not to heat. I said that mistakes happen and I knew of no plot to purposely damage the Goold House, but I could readily see why rumours to the contrary flourished. The committed conspiracy theorists told me that the university would not have shared a real conspiracy with me.

Whatever was true about the causes of the damage in the Goold House, the university's request for a demolition permit launched a storm of criticism. When the application went to city council, it was rejected it by a vote of 6–5. The most vocal critic of the university, Councillor Starkey, maintained that we could restore the devastated building and were obliged to do so, but the argument that carried the day was the heritage committee's claim that the university's plans violated the spirit of the city's bylaws, which allowed the demolition of a heritage building only when it was replaced by another building.

The council vote raised the ire of President Rosehart, who was not going to be pushed into a rescue mission and decided to board the building and leave it empty. In a stand-off in which he and Dupuis were unwilling to give in to political pressure, this had unhappy consequences, meaning that one corner of Victoria Square, the most prominent block for both the campus and downtown Brantford, was occupied by an unsightly, decaying, boarded-up old house.

The stalemate between the city and the university persisted for a year. Everyone turned a blind eye to the Goold House until the work on the new strategic plan identified the need for another building to improve student life. Ever inventive, President Rosehart, in discussions with the president of the Students' Union, Steve Welker, proposed a solution to the problem that would replace the Goold House with another building, one that would provide space for the student union and Brantford Student Services. This would address a real need in a manner that would also answer the reasons given for the rejection of the earlier application for a demolition permit. According to a complex plan that Rosehart and Welker devised, the university would lease 103 Darling to the Students' Union, which would demolish the Goold House and construct a student-owned centre that would include space for Brantford Student Services. The university would rent this space from the Students' Union. The result would be a student centre that provided space for student services, student government, and student life activities.

To finance the new centre, the Students' Union proposed an annual thirty-dollar student building fee, which was put to a student referendum. Sara Neziol, the commissioner for the Students' Union in Brantford, told me it was "easy" to get students on board, in part because the campus was small and she was able to talk to almost every student individually. When the referendum passed, the design of the centre raised some new controversy. In the wake of the previous debates about the demolition of the Goold House, the idea that it should come down to make way for a new Student Centre was not well-received in every corner. Some councillors and some members of the heritage committee still argued that the house should be saved. It did not matter to them that the building had become a project of the Students' Union rather than the university. No one should be allowed to demolish a heritage building on the square. A standoff materialized when the leadership in the Students' Union adamantly rejected any attempt to resurrect a building in the devastated shape that characterized the Goold House.

Members of the heritage committee proposed a compromise. It would not require a restoration of the house but would require incorporation of some existing parts of the building into the new construction. The Students' Union rejected this approach as well, arguing that a design of this sort would unduly constrain the development of the building. When Mike McMahon, the Students' Union manager, came to talk to me, I told him that the members of the heritage committee were approachable and he should talk to them. To his credit, he decided to be proactive. He and Cianfrone Architects (the architects who had designed the Post House renovations) met with the members of the heritage committee and listened to their concerns.

The Students' Union continued to reject any attempt to save the Goold House, but agreed they would replace it with a building designed to match the architectural features of the original house and the heritage themes around the square. As a result, the final design featured many details one does not expect in contemporary architecture. Such details included keystoned windows, a raised tower facing Victoria Park, arched windows on the second floor, a mansard roof, and a decorative cornice that replicated aspects of the original Goold House. One of the fireplaces from the house was preserved and installed in a lounge on the first floor of the Student Centre.

In August 2004, the city approved the design. Some heritage supporters were still unhappy but city councillors viewed it as a worthy compromise that made a serious attempt to address heritage concerns. The Students' Union could not replace the Goold House with a nineteenth-century building, but it had created a design that promised to add rather than detract from the character of the nineteenth-century district around the square. From an architectural point of view, the building was a key precedent that initiated a new "Brantford Revival" style of architecture. Some argued that it captured the traditional Brantford style more effectively than the version of the Goold House it replaced — a version which had been altered on a number of occasions and was suffering from wear. No one could deny that the downtown would have greatly benefited if a similar architectural compromise had informed the construction of other contemporary buildings (notably, the city hall and two modern bank buildings) on the perimeter of Victoria Square.

The new Student Centre. Many of the architectural details were modelled on the existing architecture around Victoria Square.

Photos by Darragh Christie.

The new nineteenth-century look on George Street — a renovated Carnegie Library, the Brant Community Church, the new Student Centre, and the refurbished Post House.

In the construction of the Student Centre, one final battle over heritage was sidestepped when the Goold house was prepared for demolition. In order to raise funds for the project, some suggested that we should auction off the first swing of the wrecker's ball. The highest bidder would push a button that would initiate the destruction of the Goold house and the building of the new Student Centre. This was a popular fundraising strategy that was used to initiate, with much fanfare, new capital projects at American universities. It was a creative suggestion but I nixed the idea, imagining that a heritage advocate, probably the formidable Councillor Starkey, would outbid everyone so that he could refuse to push the button, stall the party, and delay the launch of the wrecking ball. When we crossed paths in the Brant Archives some months later, I told Starkey what I thought. He looked at me, smiled an enigmatic smile, and nodded in agreement. By then the battle over the Goold House was over. The demolition had proceeded — without fanfare, but also without incident.

From the students' point of view, the Student Centre was a great step forward. At a time when the campus was growing rapidly, it provided desperately needed study and social space; two lounges with commanding views of the park; a computer lab and copy centre; student union offices with an impressive boardroom; space for clubs and foot patrol; and areas designed specifically for health services, counselling, special needs, and academic services. In time, one hoped, the benefits would prevail. We counted on them, and on the Brantford Revival architecture the Students' Union incorporated in the building, to heal the bruises left by the loss of one of downtown Brantford's historically significant houses.

| *22* |

THE WILKES HOUSE

The Student Centre provided key space for student life in Brantford. But it did not address all the campus's requirements. The need for recreational and athletic space, more residences, and expanded library operations stood out. In attempting to address the first of these, we began thinking about the Wilkes House, a run-down old mansion half a block from the square. Even in downtown Brantford, its shabbiness stood out. On a dark night its weed-infested grounds, broken windows, and decrepit walls looked like the backdrop of a murder mystery. When Laurier first arrived in Brantford, it was impossible to imagine the rehabilitation of the Wilkes House, but we were, six years later, emboldened by our successes and by opportunities that began to align in the right way. Little did we know, when we began to move in this direction, that the Wilkes House would be a project that, more than any other, would bring to the fore the tensions and competing interests inherent in the building of a campus in a seedy but historically significant downtown.

In part, the issues with the Wilkes House arose because it was, even more than the Goold House, a building that had significant ties to the history of Brantford. In this case, the ties that bind connected it to three different epochs in the history of the downtown. In an indirect and circumlocutious way, the house could claim a distant connection to the world's most infamous Wilkes — John Wilkes Booth — who murdered Abraham Lincoln in 1865. Booth was named after a famous distant relative, John "Liberty" Wilkes. In the course of a tumultuous career, Liberty Wilkes was famous for radical journalism, and for his polemics against King George III and the British Parliament, which saw him convicted of obscene and seditious libel, and made him famous as the father of freedom of the press in Britain. Wilkes was known as something of a scoundrel, but this did not prevent him from pursuing a successful political career that saw him elected to the British House of Commons, then becoming alderman, sheriff, and lord mayor of London.[1]

In 1820, the Wilkeses came to Ontario. One of Liberty Wilkes's grandsons, John Aston Wilkes and his wife Susan Philips Wilkes, emigrated from Birmingham to "Little York" (Toronto). In 1823, they sent two sons, James and John, to establish a branch of the family's general store in a tiny settlement known as Grand River Ferry. Their parents,

John Aston and Susan, followed, joining their sons in the village destined to become Brantford. When the Wilkeses arrived, it had a resident population of less than one hundred people. They lived amidst a scattering of frame buildings, log houses, and taverns along Colborne Street, where James and John established one of the area's three trading posts. Their early clientele were villagers, settlers in the adjacent areas, customers from Six Nations, and travellers on the road to Detroit and elsewhere. The "chief article of trade" was whisky.[2]

The family store prospered. Over the next fifty years, it moved up and down Colborne Street, occupying a series of buildings. In 1830, John Aston established Brantford's first distillery. The land destined to become much of Brantford was farmland belonging to Chief John Hill, whose sister was married to Joseph Brant's eldest son. John Aston Wilkes and his wife would purchase a significant portion of this farm. A sign of the Wilkes's success was an imposing house on Colborne that featured a semi-circular driveway sweeping from the street to its front entrance. William Mathews, the mayor of Brantford from 1855–56, described it as a "most ambitious residence," comparing it to a "Baronial Hall."[3] On September 25, 1855, when John Aston was seventy-three, his prominence in the city made him a featured speaker when Brantford celebrated British victories in the Crimean War. In newspaper coverage he was described as the "aged patriarch" "John Aston Wilkes, Esq." His speech provided what the crowd was looking for, manifesting "a [great] deal of patriotism" as he explained how "he would have the canker-worm of despotism eaten by piecemeal."[4]

John Aston and Susan Philips Wilkes's major contribution to Brantford was not their successful store, but a large family of thirteen children and many more grandchildren. The clan played a profound role in the evolution of the city and beyond. Henry became an important leader of the Congregational Church in Montreal. John Aston Jr. took a leading role in the formation of the Brantford branch and was known for his close relations with Six Nations and his knowledge of the Mohawk language. James was city treasurer, alderman, and reeve of the city, and was commonly regarded as Brantford's most distinguished citizen in his elder years. His daughter Clara died as a missionary and was recognized as "Canada's first missionary to fall in the service of the Master in the wilds of Africa."[5] James's son, George S., who built the Wilkes Dam across the Grand River, served as Brantford's mayor. George H. was reeve and deputy reeve and a series of Wilkes served as town or city councillors. In Brantford, the Wilkes family was involved in the churches, public events, charity, the courts, children's issues, property development, business, transportation, education, health, the fire brigade, the military, and the Ladies' Aid Society.

In this rich tapestry of Wilkeses, three stand out in the public record: James, George H., and Alfred J. James was fifteen when he became one of the first two Wilkeses to arrive in Brantford, and the city's oldest citizen when he died at the age of ninety-six. He was elected to Brantford's first town council, served as city treasurer for fifteen years, held the post of chairperson of the School Board, and was a deacon and the librarian at the local Congregational Church. His son George H. began his working life as the purser on *The Queen*, a stylish paddleboat that ferried passengers to Buffalo. He later turned to business enterprises, and played a key role in railways, an electric light company, and the Waterous Engine Works. Like his father, he was active in the political affairs of the city and the county, serving as reeve, deputy reeve, and city councillor. His brother Alfred J. was born in 1847, the same year as his friend Alexander Graham Bell. He practised law with Arthur Sturgis Hardy, who became the premier of Ontario, and was appointed crown attorney and king's council. He helped found the Brantford Dragoons, a local military regiment, was chairperson of the School Board, president of the Brantford Opera Company, a member of the Boards of the Ladies' College and the Brantford Trust Company, and the Master of Doric Lodge 121.

During the second half of the nineteenth century, James, George H., and Alfred J. were active in the key events in Brantford. In a disastrous epidemic of "ship fever" in 1847–48, it was James who moved that the Board of Health should find a building that could be used as a hospital and take measures to fight the epidemic. When the Board of Trade was disbanded in the 1880s, George H. became "the life of the Board," worked through legal problems, secured a charter, and became secretary-treasurer and then president.[6] Alfred J. served on the committee that oversaw the creation of the Joseph Brant statue in Victoria Square, was a member of the Brantford Golf Club in its first year (1879), and was, with his father James, one of the fifteen guests who witnessed Alexander Graham Bell's demonstration of the telephone at his home in Tutela Heights in August of 1876.[7] Many years

later, Alfred J. served as one of the directors for the Bell Memorial project.

When the university began discussing ways to turn the Wilkes House on Darling Street into a university building, it had no knowledge of the history of the house that sat on a piece of property that John Aston and Susan Philips acquired in 1852. Over the next fifty years, the ownership of the property passed through many hands, belonging, at different times, to James, George H., and Alfred J. Other notable local figures who owned the property included Ignatius Cockshutt, the founder of the Cockshutt Plow Company; Jesse Wisner, whose manufacturing company was absorbed by Massey-Harris; and Magistrate Henry Moyle. In 1853, Moyle submitted a petition to the federal government, lamenting "the increasing demoralization of the Indians" in the area and "the statistics of crime, the results of drunkenness, bigamy, prostitution and indolence."[8]

According to popular lore, the Wilkes House was built in 1870, but the restoration work done after the university acquired the property showed that the house began as a one-storey Brantford cottage, common in the 1840s and 50s, and was later expanded by the addition of a second floor. It is pictured as a one-storey building on Brantford's 1875 Birdseye View Map, a time when it served as the home of James Wilkes and his third wife, Matilda.

The earliest known photograph[9] of the Wilkes House, sent to me by one of the family's descendants, Liz Rhodes, presents a portrait of the expanded house with the Wilkes family. It dates from around 1880. A rumour I accidentally began erroneously identifies the men at the front of the house as Alexander Graham Bell and Alfred J.

Courtesy of Brant Museum and Archives, cat. no. 937101.

A.J. Wilkes, with his long, white handlebar moustache, is pictured with the Brantford Bicycle Club in 1897.

Wilkes.[10] Bell was a close friend of Alfred's, but this is a family photo with Alfred and his father, James. The women on the verandah at the side of the house are James's wife, Matilda, and Alfred's future wife,

Esther Haycock. A note on the back of the photograph states that it was prepared for Miss Haycock by Park & Brothers' Brantford Studio. The photograph is a visual counterpart of a report in *The*

Courtesy of the author.

The Wilkes House and the Wilkes family, circa 1880. James and A.J. are seen at the front of the house, Matilda and Esther Haycock at the side. The photo highlights the distinctive John Turner chimneys, the new second floor, and the house's French windows and decorative wrought iron.

Expositor of December 7, 1877, which noted that "James Wilkes, Esq. has transformed his brick cottage, on the corner of Charlotte and Darling Street, into one of the many pretentious residences of our city. The work has been done at a cost of $2,500."[11] This seems to be the work that turned an ordinary one-storey house into a fashionable two-storey residence. In the process, the Wilkeses employed John

Turner, Brantford's most distinguished architect, whose work included the Goold House, just two doors down the street.

In 1887, Alfred J. married Esther Haycock and purchased the Wilkes House from James and Matilda for six thousand dollars. The house served as their family home for many years, and was widely known as the Alfred J. Wilkes House. The house's ties to one of the city's most significant pioneering families made it an important symbol of the earliest days of Brantford, but this was only the first chapter in its history. One cannot understand the historical significance of the building — and the sensitivities raised by the university's plan to renovate it — without understanding its role in two other periods of downtown history.

| 23 |

A TEMPLE AND A CLUBHOUSE

Though their influence is not as evident as it once was, fraternal societies have played a profound role in the evolution of North America. In the popular imagination, these "secret societies" are intertwined with ideals of brotherhood and sometimes sisterhood that stem from ancient origins and secret initiations associated with the Knights Templar and the search for the Holy Grail. In the development of cities, such societies played a more important but less esoteric role than this suggests, functioning as engines of social good that brought people together to perform good works. Like the Rotarians and Kiwanians of today, charitable work helping the poor and disadvantaged was an important part of their activities.

In early Brantford, the International Order of Odd Fellows — the IOOF — was very active. Its origins can be traced to seventeenth-century England, where it was established as an organization "to improve and elevate the character of man." Members were deemed "Odd Fellows" because it was thought odd to find people "organized for the purpose of giving aid to those in need," and "pursuing projects for the benefit of all mankind."[1] In North America, the IOOF's first continuing lodge was established in

Baltimore, Maryland, on April 26, 1819. The society came to Brantford in 1844, when Brant (Manchester Unity) Lodge was founded. Five years later, its popularity gave birth to another lodge, Gore Lodge, probably named after the local gore, a triangular piece of land annexed to Burford Township. By 1873, the popularity of this lodge spawned yet another lodge, named Harmony Lodge No. 115.[2]

The growth of the Odd Fellows movement forced its lodges to continually expand their premises, and in 1895, in an attempt to accommodate growing memberships, Harmony and Gore lodges moved to the upper floor of *The Expositor*. In 1918, at the end of the First World War, the Odd Fellows moved once more, procuring two floors of the Cockshutt Building on Market Street. The Lodge records declared that "with a splendid Lodge room, a commodious club room, committee and paraphernalia rooms, large banquet hall with completely furnished kitchen, Brantford Odd Fellows hold a place second to none in the jurisdiction."[3] But still the facilities proved too small. To accommodate expansion yet again, the International Order of Odd Fellows purchased the A.J. Wilkes House sometime around 1930, after it ceased to be a private residence.

Courtesy of the Brantford Heritage Inventory.

The Wilkes House as the International Order of Oddfellows Temple, with the back hall added in 1932. Photo by Audrey Scott.

By the time that the IOOF acquired it, the house that Alfred J. and Ester lived in had been altered a number of times. The society continued this evolution, rearranging the interior to create a "temple" for lodge meetings and other rooms for meetings and social gatherings. A major addition constructed in 1932 added a three-storey addition on the back of the house, to add space for formal dances and other social and charitable events. The exterior of the addition featured impressive brick buttresses and elegantly designed brickwork. In its earlier role as an important private home, the house had hosted the key early families in Brantford. In its new role as a lodge house, it became a vital location for important meetings and social events. The influence of the Odd Fellows ensured its significance and the quality of the renovations the society undertook made it even more elegant and impressive.

As an Odd Fellows Temple, the Wilkes House flourished until the popularity of fraternal societies began to wane in the twentieth century. The expensive dues that the society charged could no longer be afforded, especially during the Great Depression, and many balked at the commitment required. As service organizations like the Rotary and Kiwanis began to supplant them, the popularity, influence, and prosperity of the Odd Fellows slipped away throughout North America. In Brantford, the IOOF could no longer maintain the Wilkes House in a manner that sustained its stylish elegance. Sometime around 1965, their fading financial resources forced them to leave the building. In a situation in which no buyers were interested in a once-grand building clearly headed downward, the Wilkes House was purchased by the City of Brantford, then stood empty, waiting for a purpose.

In 1972, the Wilkes House was sold to one of the successors of the popular fraternal lodges, the Rotary Club. This act initiated a third phase of the house's history, turning it into the home of the Brantford Boys' and Girls' Club. The building's rooms became offices, meeting rooms, and space dedicated to play and recreational activities. The hall at the back of the building, which had served as a ballroom, was turned into a gymnasium. Six years later, the Boys' and Girls' Club constructed a fourth addition to the original building.[4] In the process they removed the two-storey verandah on the east side of the home and attached two large, nondescript rooms. From an aesthetic point of view, the new addition was a major disappointment that detracted from the grace and style of the building. As one comment has described it, "This construction was unfortunately not sympathetic to the style of either the original house or the IOOF Hall."[5]

As the Brantford Boys' and Girls' Club, the Wilkes House lost its status as a stylish place for Brantford's movers and shakers to congregate, but its new role made it an important centre for children and teenagers, especially those from families with limited means. In a manner that foreshadowed what was to come, the club turned the building into a magnificent haunted house every year at Halloween. In 1980, after his first year in the National Hockey League, one of Brantford's most famous offspring, Wayne Gretzky, played floor hockey with the boys and girls in the gymnasium. Many of Brantford's children grew up with fond memories of the time they spent in the Wilkes House, but its unrelenting use during a fifteen-year tenure as the Boys' and Girls' Club took its toll. With limited resources at its disposal, the Club's upkeep of the building did not match the high standards maintained by its former owners. In the end, the deteriorating quality of the building and the growth of the club culminated in a Rotary campaign to raise funds for a new facility. In 1989, the Club left the downtown, leaving a depleted Wilkes House in its wake.

Despite a century as a notable Brantford building, the Wilkes House entered a period of serious decline. For ten years, the house sat vacant, deteriorating further. In a situation in which no one else was interested, it was purchased by a local developer, Steve Kun. In 2000, he leased it to another developer, Adam Stelmaszynski, who attempted to turn the building into downtown condominiums. He tried to sell a future condo to me and to one of Brantford's first professors, Gary Warrick. The idea had some appeal, but a prescient local member of the Grand Valley Education Society told me to be wary of any financial dealings with Stelmaszynski. Whatever his credibility, he was imbued with enthusiasm about the future of the Wilkes House. While he was trying to peddle his ideas for downtown condominiums, he lived in primitive conditions inside the house, sawing through walls and readjusting the interior.

When Stelmaszynski failed to find buyers for his condominiums, he switched gears and looked to turning the building into student housing. The owner, Steve Kun, lost patience with the failure to move either project forward and applied for a permit to demolish the building. When the Brantford Heritage Committee objected to Kun's plans, he appeared before the city's Community Development Committee and pointed out that the building had been vacant for more than ten years and was no longer fit for use.[6] The argument did not convince the committee. The motion to grant a demolition permit was defeated, in part because Stelmaszynski appeared before it and talked about his plans to renovate the building. However, his plans were never realized, and the local gossip about his trustworthiness was confirmed at Victoria Square two years later, when the Superior Court found him guilty of fraudulently collecting seven hundred thousand dollars in GST rebates. He had collected them in the course of his attempts to convert Hamilton warehouse space into loft-style condominiums.

In Brantford, Stelmaszynski's plans for the Wilkes House evaporated, and the building joined the ranks of Brantford's derelict downtown buildings. Its prime location, adjacent to Victoria Square, its Turner architecture, and its rich history were not enough to prevent it from becoming another casualty in Brantford's downward spiral.

THE WILKES HOUSE REBORN

In the early days of Laurier Brantford, I often wished we could do something with the Wilkes House. Its location — around the corner from the Carnegie Building — and its historical demeanor were attractive but we needed projects that were more manageable. The president's doubts about older buildings meant that he had little interest in the Wilkes House until he was pushed by a fervent Laurier supporter, Shawkey Fahel.

Fahel was a Palestinian who moved to Waterloo from Israel to escape the turmoil in the Mideast. He brought with him a commitment to hospitality that often turned into lunch or a glass of wine in his Waterloo office. It was adorned with souvenirs of his projects, and with photos of him with the Pope, with Prime Minister Paul Martin, and with Yasser Arafat. Scott Hayter, who ran Laurier's development operations, told me that Fahel's office had the most remarkable cashews he had ever tasted — "as big as your thumb." When I asked Fahel about them, he said he imported them in bulk from the Middle East, and took out a sack and filled all the bowls around us.

Fahel was not a wallflower. He liked his status as a mover and a shaker, and did what he did with gusto, creating both admirers and detractors in the process. Sometimes the same person would vacillate back and forth in their opinion. When I mentioned Fahel in a conversation with an architect, he perked up: "Shawkey Fahel," he smiled, "we've worked with him. We say that he can be Shawkey from heaven or Shawkey from hell." In Brantford, Fahel was a big supporter of the Laurier initiative and was keen on participating in some way. His first Brantford initiative was the renovation of a derelict 1869 Masonic building on Colborne Street, a building he turned into a private residence — a daring move on the wrong end of Colborne, mired in the midst of urban decay. After the residence was completed, he looked for other possibilities. In the end, he purchased an option on the Wilkes House, envisaging a plan that would convert the original home into residence suites and the hall at the back of the building into a recreational complex for the campus.

Fahel's proposal was attractive. At a location close to the square and the Carnegie Building, it would address some of the unmet needs identified in the 2005 strategic plan. As appealing as it was, however, there was no way to make the project work without government funding. In a situation in which the province continued to reject capital funds for Brantford,

THE WILKES HOUSE REBORN

Courtesy of the Brantford Heritage Inventory.

The Wilkes House from the east in 2001, showing the out-of-character Boys and Girls Club additions. The sign advertises Stelmaszynski's unrealized plan for loft condominiums.

we once again approached the city. With each successive approach, the voices of those who opposed city spending for the university grew louder, so the president went to great pains to prepare our case. Armed with architectural drawings prepared by Fahel's architect, Ryszard Gancewski, the president took Sherri Bocchini, Scott Hayter, Jim Butler, and me to a meeting with the city's Post-Secondary Committee. Having learned from the ruckus that erupted when the university decided to take down the Goold House, the president decided to approach the Wilkes House in a way that would make heritage concerns a reason to support, rather than oppose, university development. To this end, he proposed a renovation of the Wilkes House that would be the first step toward a Heritage Block composed of heritage buildings operated by the university. The Post House and the Student Centre had already secured one end of the block. A renovated Wilkes House would secure another.

The Post-Secondary Committee wanted to see the university continue its expansion. In the wake of the previous projects downtown, it was captivated by the idea that it could be done in a manner that expanded the heritage architecture around Victoria Square — precisely what the city failed to do for most of the twentieth century. Finally, the city was waking up to the value of heritage architecture. To ensure the proposed refurbishing of the Wilkes House would preserve the heritage aspects of the building, the committee asked for changes to the details of the renovation plans. The university amended the plans to highlight heritage details, and the members of the committee — Mayor Hancock and councillors John Starkey and Marguerite Ceschi-Smith — agreed to take the project to city council for approval. The final proposal asked the city to contribute, depending on the cost, up to $1.2 million to the project, approximately 20 per cent of the total price tag.

On March 29, 2005, the university proposal was presented to councillors at a public forum held in the council chambers. Within Laurier Brantford, Sherri Bocchini sent an email encouraging students and members of the campus community to come

Students showing their support for the Wilkes House project at City Council Chambers. Among them, Sara Neziol, Nicole Kaufman, Jenn Diniz, Meghan Sneek, Lauren Zakaib, Kristi Edwards, Fred Laliberte, Matt Elliott, Brad Murray, Andrew Mistry, Kas Alyea, Steven Hicks, Kelly Street, Dan Schell, Jeff Moggach, Ian Gillies, Bianca Moos, and Natalie Briski.

Courtesy of Sherri Bocchini

and demonstrate their support. Nearly a hundred did. The university presentation was orchestrated by the president, who was in fine form. In a lively discussion, he responded to questions posed by councillors, explaining university finances, emphasizing the positive impact the growth of the university was having on the city, noting that other municipalities (in particular Kitchener and Cambridge) were providing financial support to encourage the development of satellite campuses. He told city council that he could not take the proposal to renovate the Wilkes House to the university's Board of Governors without a commitment from the city.

A week later, council voted on a motion to approve the university's request for financial support. Two of the councillors argued against it. Higher education was, they said, a provincial responsibility, and it was time for the provincial government to "step up to the plate" and fund Laurier Brantford buildings.

Every councillor was frustrated with the provincial government, but most argued that the province's lack of leadership should not hinder downtown redevelopment. Four Laurier representatives — Butler, Bocchini, Hayter, and myself — watched the debate unfold. In the early hours of the morning on April 5, the motion to support the renovation of the Wilkes House passed by a vote of eight to two. Our group of four wanted to celebrate but it was difficult, at 2:00 a.m., to find a place to mark the occasion. We made our way to the restaurant at the Charity Casino, which was open seven days a week, twenty-four hours a day. It seemed fitting, but also ironic, to be celebrating the occasion in the building that had attracted Laurier to Brantford, but had done so because it seemed to be a site that would allow us to avoid decrepit downtown buildings like the Wilkes House.

With the city's financial support secured, the president took the Wilkes House proposal to the university Board of Governors, which approved the project. The refurbishing of the Wilkes House could now begin. But the politics were just beginning. In the course of its work on the house, Fahel's company, JG Group, removed some historical details from its exterior walls. Councillor John Starkey, who had been a key supporter of the project, felt that the university was not living up to the spirit of its agreement with the city, and notified the heritage committee. It was dismayed to learn that the original brick walls of the house would be covered with a white stucco finish. They protested to both the university and the city. In the exchanges that followed, the decision to cover the brick walls of the 1870 house was said to betray the university's repeated assertion that the Wilkes House renovation was a heritage project.

President Rosehart and a feisty Shawkey Fahel would not back down. Without the use of the stucco finish, they claimed that the renovation would be too costly. An equally adamant Councillor Starkey, backed by the heritage committee, maintained that the brick must be cleaned, repointed, and stained in a historically appropriate manner. Much was made of the city's decision to support the refurbishing of the Wilkes House because it was a heritage project. As the debate intensified, the resolve grew on both sides. When it was clear that the university would not reverse its decision on the stucco, Councillor Starkey warned that he was preparing a motion to have the Wilkes House declared an official heritage site. If he was successful, it would force the university to cease its work on the building immediately. Even if permission to stucco could eventually be secured, a heritage

designation would mean that the university would have to secure it through a lengthy process, making it impossible to keep the project on schedule, adding significantly to the cost.

Starkey's warning came at a time when heritage issues were a sore point with the president. In Waterloo, he was exasperated with a heritage house owned by the university. On one occasion, he told me that it took more than a year to paint its porch because of debates about historically appropriate paint. His impatience with heritage committees was fuelled by the university's experience with the demolition of the Goold House, and headaches that arose in Kitchener when the university turned an old high school into the home of Laurier's Faculty of Social Work. At times it seemed that the president was fighting heritage battles on all fronts. In his opening remarks at a Waterloo conference entitled "Re.think, Re.invent, Re.urbanize," Rosehart went public with his concerns, warning his audience that the revitalization of downtowns could be hampered by zealous heritage committees. Their decisions could, he argued, seriously interfere with urban redevelopment, creating obstacles for developers and prohibitively increasing the cost of building projects.[1]

The president's frustration with heritage committees did not leave him in a conciliatory mood when questions arose about the treatment of the bricks on the Wilkes House. In an atmosphere in which he and Councillor Starkey looked to be headed for a collision course that could derail the project, Ron Dupuis, Scott Hayter, and I met with Mayor Hancock and councillors Ceschi-Smith and Starkey. With helpful pushing by Hancock and Dupuis, we agreed to a tentative compromise: that the university would support Starkey's motion for a heritage designation so long as the designation applied, not to the entire Wilkes House, but only to the front facade of the original building. This meant that the building's 1870 bricks and mouldings would be saved from the stucco finish. In return, Starkey agreed that he would not seek a heritage designation for the entire building. He, Ceschi-Smith, and Mayor Hancock agreed to ask city council to share with the university the additional cost this would add to the Wilkes House project (a cost estimated, and probably over-estimated, at $150,000). Like peace negotiators, we took the compromise back to our respective sides. With some grumbling, both the city

and the university agreed to compromise. The heritage details were re-attached to the 1870 brick walls, which were cleaned and stained instead of stuccoed. The Wilkes House project was back on track.

In some ways, the struggle over the bricks on the Wilkes House unfortunately overshadowed a largely successful renovation of a decrepit building — a building that JG Group brought back to life. After more than a hundred years of wear and tear, and ten

TOP: *Before its renovation, the Wilkes House was a shambles. One of the prestigious Brantford residences when it was renovated in 1880, it had degenerated into a dilapidated eyesore a century later.* BOTTOM: *During the Wilkes House renovation the removal of paint from the bricks revealed two sets of bricks (one red, the other yellow) used for the first and second floor, a sign of their different origins. The second set must have been added in the extensive renovations carried out by James Wilkes between 1875 and 1880. Today the former Wilkes House is the Wilkes House Residence and Recreation Centre.*

Photo by the author.

Courtesy of JG Group of Companies.

years without a tenant, the house was in poor condition when Stelmaszynski tried to convert it into downtown loft condominiums. He made the condition even worse when he sawed through the majestic inner staircase at the front of the house, filled the gymnasium with garbage, and dismantled much of the interior in a helter-skelter fashion that was difficult to understand. By the time that Fahel and Gancewski began their work, water damage and eroding or collapsed walls and floors were a problem throughout the house. The interior was a rabbit warren of odd-shaped rooms, floors that did not abut properly, awkward additions, and unexpected passageways. Truckloads of garbage had to be removed from the gymnasium before the renovations could begin.

In tackling the challenges, JG Group transformed the Wilkes House into a one-of-a-kind university building that combined unique residences and recreational facilities. The former home of A.J. Wilkes and Esther Haycock became a residence for forty-one first-year students. The Odd Fellows temple, which boasted four-metre-high ceilings, was turned into a series of multi-room, two-floor suites with cathedral ceilings. The recreational complex incorporated a refurbished version of the Odd Fellows Hall that had been added in 1932, a hall the Boys' and Girls' Club had used as a gymnasium. To provide additional space for recreational and athletic purposes and for practices for the Laurier Brantford dance team — which became, under Jill Orpen, the campus's first team to win an inter-university athletic award[2] — an extension was added to the exterior of the gymnasium. The new renovation continued the process of evolution and expansion that had characterized the history of the house for more than a century.

The final work on the Wilkes House project spilled over into an 1880 home adjacent to it. This house had been included in the land the university acquired when it purchased the Wilkes House and began building the Heritage Block. The house was built for Jesse O. Wisner, a Brantford industrialist whose companies built seed drills, ploughs, bicycles, and farm implements. Early in his career, E.L. Goold worked for J.O. Wisner & Son. In 1891, the house was bought by the Harris family. In contemporary times, it served as the home of the Prison Arts Foundation of Canada. The foundation began its work in 1969, when members of the Colborne Street United Church, in collaboration with the city's St. Leonard's Society, decided to work in support of a halfway house for federal inmates. Under the leadership of Marnie Knechtel, well-known for her charitable work in the community, they looked for a way to raise funds for the project. Because they knew that high-quality artwork was being created by prisoners in Canadian prisons, they decided to raise funds by selling Christmas cards designed by Canadian prisoners. When a competition, held to generate card designs from inmates, attracted many more entries than anticipated, they established the Prison Arts Foundation to promote art programs and the art that inmates created. In 2000 it celebrated its 29th Annual Awards for art created in Canadian prisons.

In the wake of the Wilkes House project, the university hired JG Group to turn it into offices and student space. As part of Laurier, the Wisner House first functioned as Faculty House — a conglomeration of faculty offices and student space. Because I wanted a more focused space, I convinced others that we should change the name to Journalism House and

In 1985, Journalism House housed a dentist's office, the office of the Ontario Legal Aid Plan, the headquarters of the Prison Arts Foundation, and the offices of the Brantford Regional Arts Council.

make it a space dedicated to the campus's fledgling journalism program. It now houses offices for journalism faculty, a student newsroom, a journalism seminar room, and the offices of *The Sputnik*, the campus's student newspaper. Following on the heels of the Wilkes House renovation, its restoration contributed to the building of the Heritage Block. The two houses provided key space for the university at the same time that they renewed yet another element of downtown heritage, in a manner that reflected its former lustre.

THE BPL — A BRANTFORD ICON

No campus is complete without a library. In a much-cited essay entitled "Why You Should Fall to Your Knees and Worship a Librarian," Erica Olsen takes the world to task for its "preconceived notions about librarians and what they do.... Many people think of librarians as diminutive civil servants, scuttling about 'Sssh-ing' people and stamping things."[1] A library is a storehouse for learning that catalogues everything we know. As for librarians: "Librarians have degrees. They go to graduate school for Information Science and become masters of data systems and human/computer interaction. Librarians can catalogue anything from an onion to a dog's ear. They could catalogue you.... People become librarians because they know too much. Their knowledge extends beyond mere categories. They cannot be confined to disciplines. Librarians are all-knowing and all-seeing. They bring order to chaos. They bring wisdom and culture to the masses. They preserve every aspect of human knowledge. Librarians rule."[2]

When I first arrived in Brantford, I discovered that there was no budget for the library. This was not intentional, but the result of poor planning. The first year of library operations were funded out of "one-time" money included in a donation from the Grand Valley Education Society. For some things — a new building, the purchase of equipment, a special event — it makes sense to pay for something with money that is not a part of annual revenue. It makes little sense when one is funding an annual activity like the running of a library. One year later, the result was that we had no money to pay for library operations. In a situation in which it was never easy to squeeze new money from the central finances, I was able to report that we took pride in our ability to run an efficient operation, but the university librarian and I could not run a library on zero dollars. In return, we were given sheepish and apologetic looks, and a small operating budget.

The need for a library was a major concern. As the university could not provide an independent library for forty students, it depended on a partnership with the Brantford Public Library, known locally as the BPL. The partnership was rooted in the proposal to develop a private university in Brantford, which first put forth the idea that a university could utilize BPL. Once the idea was proposed, the driving force behind it was Wendy Newman, the CEO of the Brantford Public Library.

Newman was proud of the history of the library, which began as a Brantford "Mechanics' Institute" in 1835, but was determined to push it forward. She arrived in 1994, a few years after the BPL moved from the Carnegie Library to a retro-fitted Woolco Store on Colborne Street. In 1995, the library won the Ontario Library Association's Angus Mowat Award for its Public Internet Access Program. In 1996, it received the first Ontario Library Association Building Award for the Best Public Library. In 2000, it became the first North American public library to be invited to join UNESCO's model library network. In September 2002, Newman became president of the Canadian Library Association, and the first North American meeting of the UNESCO network was held in Brantford. Delegates came from Zimbabwe, Spain, Malaysia, Sweden, Portugal, and Estonia.

When Newman was asked if the BPL would be willing to provide library services to students and professors at a new private university in Brantford, she did not hesitate. The library was already engaged in the redevelopment of the downtown. The post-modern exterior of its renovated building could not compete with the elegance of the old Carnegie Library, but the decision to move into an empty store on Colborne was an important precedent. It placed the library in the middle of the worst street in Brantford — a street that was populated, when it wasn't empty, primarily by vagrants — but gave an early indication of the possibilities downtown, dem-onstrating how existing buildings might be adapted for uses that would attract people to the downtown core. When approached about a partnership with a university, Newman worked with the Grand Valley Education Society and outlined an arrangement that was included in the plan for a private "Brant University" — the plan that laid the groundwork for Laurier's Brantford campus.

A partnership between the university and the library seemed a "no-brainer" to everyone in Brantford, but it went against the grain in the world of libraries. For the world of libraries is not one world but two — one made up of public libraries, the other made up of their university counterparts. The relationship between these worlds is complex and contentious. According to one view, they have different missions — the one providing information, material, and resources for the general public; the other providing specialized teaching and research resources for students and professors. According to an opposing view, the differences between pub-lic and university libraries are greatly exaggerated, and have more to do with academic snobbery than substantive issues. Within library scholarship, some have argued that academic librarians treat public librarians as though they are marked with a scarlet *P* — like the scarlet *A* (for adultery that Nathaniel Hawthorne's protagonist is forced to wear in *The Scarlet Letter*).[3] Whatever the reason — whether snobbery or real differences in purpose — the worlds of academic and public library rarely meld, making partnerships between university and public libraries very rare.[4] Here, as elsewhere, Laurier and Brantford were treading on new turf.

When the Laurier library and BPL began imple-menting joint services, there were other contentious issues afoot in the world of libraries. It is not too much to say that the nature and the very existence of libraries were a matter of debate. Traditionalists

The new BPL, formerly a 1970 Woolco store on Colborne Street. In 2007, the vacant second floor was converted into an "information commons" that significantly expanded services for the university's and the public's use.

Photo by the author.

celebrated the library as a temple dedicated to the book. Others dismissed this picture as hopelessly romantic. In a digital age, they did not emphasize the reading of books, but quick, convenient, usually electronic, access to information. The future of the book was itself a matter of debate. The massive collections of books (or scrolls) that were the apex of library development from the time of the Great Library in Alexandria to the founding of Carnegie's libraries were, some argued, increasingly less relevant.

In its own operations, Laurier struggled with the relative importance of the book and electronic information. The undergraduate calendar, the annual book that defined the university, persisted long after prospective students gleaned their knowledge of universities through their websites. I watched, with some feelings of nostalgia, as my own children chose universities without ever looking at their calendars. At Laurier, the web calendar eventually became the "official" calendar because it could be changed immediately when the university changed rules and regulations. The publication of the print version persisted

for some years, but with a steadily decreasing print run. Eventually it ceased completely. In the Laurier library, it was clear that books would not be obsolete soon, but the evolution of the library was characterized by a growing demand for electronic access to data of all sorts. The broader understanding of a library collection that gained currency was nowhere more evident than in the grand opening of the New Library of Alexandria in 2002. An attempt to reconnect with the heritage of the ancient Alexandrian library, its contemporary counterpart incorporated not only millions of books, but a vast internet archive, three museums, a planetarium, a nine-projector cinema, a virtual reality environment, and nine art galleries.

The new electronic possibilities evolving in the world of libraries were a key component of the WLU/BPL partnership, for they provided access to the Laurier collection for students studying at Brantford. Already in 1995, Laurier, the University of Waterloo, and the University of Guelph had established TUG — the Tri University Group of Libraries. It merged the collections of all three universities, turning them into one large collection that was electronically available at each. At Brantford, connecting BPL to the already established TUG system made one of the country's best university collections available to Brantford students and professors. Material requested at BPL was delivered through a service that shuttled between the campuses of all three universities. This access to TUG, along with on-site databases, a small collection of books, and co-operation between BPL and the WLU library provided our library service. The details of the collaboration were worked out by Wendy Newman, Laurier's University librarian, Virginia Gilham, and Angela Madden, the Brantford campus librarian. In the process they had to negotiate their way through the two different sets of cataloguing systems, loan systems, circulation software, loan policies, security systems, and systems of reserve.[5] In recognition of the partnership and the Memorandum of Agreement it was based on, BPL was awarded the 2003 Angus Mowat Award of Excellence at the one hundredth annual conference of the Ontario Library Association.

In a number of ways the partnership with Laurier enhanced the BPL. The access to university collections that Laurier made available to students was available to the library's other users, and the fee that Laurier paid for the use of the BPL contributed to its budget. Calculated on a per student basis, the fee rose substantially as student numbers grew. But the most inspiring products of the partnership occurred on occasions when Laurier and Nipissing students worked with the BPL on particular projects. Laurier Students for Literacy, an association that helps children learn to read, met with their "reading buddies" in the children's section of the BPL.

During a week designed to promote reading, student volunteers occupied the display window at the front entrance of the BPL, reading books and doing homework. They were there to inspire younger readers and bring attention to the university and the library, something they accomplished with élan when the display caught the attention of the media, which interviewed the participating students. A member of the GVES told me that they were "the best looking mannequins" she had ever seen.

In the discussion leading up to the 2004–05 strategic plan, some faculty pushed for a separate university library. They wanted a library that was more clearly a part of the Laurier campus, with more space for a university book collection. I was skeptical but the new university librarian, Sharon Brown, and I looked into the possibilities. At one point, it seemed that a donor might provide a suitable building, but this possibility did not materialize. In lieu of new premises and a new relationship with BPL, we looked for other ways to provide Brantford students and professors with stronger library services. As we did so, the campus debated library services. Students were blasé — more blasé than one would like — but it became something of a sore point with some faculty who circulated a letter pointing out that Algoma University, an eight-hundred-student campus in Sault

Ste. Marie, had a bigger book collection than Laurier Brantford. On a liberal arts campus where libraries were venerated, this was meant to be an anathema, but it was not as shocking as it seemed. Algoma had more books for a simple reason: it had been collecting books since 1964, thirty-five years before Laurier Brantford existed. On more important measures, professors and students at Brantford had access to many more resources than their counterparts at Algoma. It included access to a Laurier library many times the size of the library at Algoma, and the even larger libraries at the University of Guelph and the University of Waterloo.

The building of a university book collection housed inside the BPL began as soon as the university arrived. Because there was no way to rapidly acquire a significant number of volumes, Laurier Brantford leaned in a different direction, emphasizing access to electronic databases. Within the Contemporary Studies Program, the Laurier Brantford librarian, Angela Madden, taught students how to access information in "information literacy" tutorials. Given the limits on stack space available, we tried to emphasize increasingly available electronic resources as we pushed forward with plans to expand Brantford's library operations. After an engaging visit to the library at the University of Edinburgh, Sharon Brown proposed the development of an "information commons" that would make books, articles, and data available through electronic databases.

The discussions within Laurier fortuitously coincided with developments in the BPL itself. In view of the city's expanding population and increased post-secondary enrollments, Rose Vespa, the library CEO replacing Wendy Newman when she retired, proposed the development of the library's empty third floor.[6] It was not load-bearing, and had been left vacant when the library moved in. Although it could not accommodate book stacks, this was not a problem for an emerging consensus that emphasized the need for public spaces and an information commons. Vespa's proposal was strongly supported by the chair of the Library Board, Bruce Hodgson, who had played a key role when a nascent Laurier campus came to Brantford.

The councillors on the board, Larry Kings and John Starkey, took the proposal to city council, which provided three million dollars for the renovations. Canon Design, the architectural firm that had worked on the 1992 retrofit of the Woolco store, was hired to design and direct the new third floor. Opened in the spring of 2007, it incorporated a new back entrance designed for students, an office for university librarians, meeting rooms for both the university and the public, and an information commons. The Board chair, Bruce Hodgson described the renovations as "a very exciting addition to the Main Library ... that will build on other recent improvements in the downtown.... We are looking forward to the opportunity to create an area that will benefit both the public and post-secondary users."[7] From the point of view of downtown Brantford, the BPL renovation reinvigorated the earlier decision to convert an empty Woolco store to a new use designed to attract people downtown. The university partnership with the library was a key catalyst.

However the partnership with BPL evolves in the future, its inception was one of the prerequisites that made the arrival of Laurier possible. In establishing the partnership, the university reached outside campus boundaries in a way that helped spur on an expansion of another institution on Colborne Street, thus contributing to the revitalization of Brantford's downtown core in a way that reached beyond the campus. In this and a number of other cases, Laurier Brantford was one element within a larger project that consolidated and extended the effects of the university's arrival. In Brantford, Laurier's ability to reach its full potential both supported and depended on the success of the rest of the downtown.

A UNIVERSITY PRECINCT

Before the renovation of the Wilkes House, Laurier students and staff used the recreational and athletic facilities available at the downtown YMCA. At one point it became a YM/YWCA, and then became a YM again.[1] In Brantford it was simply called "The Y" and the building it operated was called "The Old Y," with the emphasis on *old*. For some time their executive director (pronounced, sometimes intentionally, as the "Wise" executive director) was Terry Jones, one of Brantford's unsung downtown heroes. For more than twenty years he worked tirelessly on behalf of the YMCA and the city core. As the downtown declined, he found ways to sustain the association and its building. For two long years, he worked with the Downtown Renewal Group and Mohawk College on the plan that would have moved it to the empty Eaton's mall. When that fell through, he supported an alternative proposal that would have combined the Y with a condominium development at the river end of Colborne Street. When Laurier arrived, he dedicated himself to a partnership with the university, then pushed the Y in the direction of a new building before he retired in 2004. When I saw him in retirement, he looked relieved, as though someone had lifted a large weight from his shoulders.

The condition of the Old Y building was a microcosm of the condition of downtown Brantford. In the early twentieth century, it had begun its life as an architectural tour de force. Designed by Burke, Horwood & White and Lloyd Barber, and built by Shultz Construction in 1912, it was welcomed as an outstanding example of the Renaissance Revival style. Its details included an imposing pillared entrance, elaborate brickwork, and finely worked limestone trim. The graceful lines and looks were not sullied until 1977, when the Y decided to add an ugly concrete block extension to provide racquetball and squash courts. In the years that Jones was working to promote the Y, the building slowly deteriorated around him. By the time the university arrived, it had been used for ninety years and was showing signs of age, the problems going beyond cosmetic issues created by sagging doors and floors. For Jones and his managers, overseeing a building with constant heating, cooling, and plumbing concerns was a headache. In the winter months, I attended meetings in Spartan rooms with plastic taped over the windows to keep the drafts at bay.

The YMCA's problems were closely linked to the decline of the downtown. As the core of Brantford spiralled downward, residents fled to the suburbs. This was especially true of the Y's core membership, which consisted of families wanting to raise their children away from the troubles downtown. As the suburbs pulled families away, the age and the deteriorating condition of the Old Y made it difficult to attract new members. The kinds of members that kept YMCAs and YWCAs successful in other cities saw Brantford's Old Y as an out-of-the-way location that did not provide the space and amenities they expected in a modern recreational facility. To keep the Y afloat, Jones and his managers were busy developing new kinds of programming, but revenue from memberships waned as the cost of maintenance increased, creating a rising imbalance between revenues and costs.

When I went to Brantford, I liked the quaint old track in the Old Y. Running on it felt like a trip to an earlier, less complicated time — a time when an indoor mile meant seventeen laps around a wooden track. As an institution, Laurier had a different view. It was not interested in an antiquated exercise club and felt, like the new members the Y struggled to attract, frustrated with the facilities in Brantford. It was disconcerting to compare them to athletic and recreational services in Waterloo, where the university took state-of-the-art facilities for granted. In a situation where there was no significant alternative, the location of the Old Y — a few blocks from the Carnegie Library — still convinced it that a partnership with the Y was the best way to provide recreational facilities for Brantford faculty and students.

Terry Jones was committed to the Laurier partnership, but some of his managers felt differently,

generally irked because they didn't like the price the university paid for access to their facilities. In a situation in which the YMCA was strapped for revenue, they thought that students should pay regular membership dues. The university saw it differently. It argued that students used the facilities less frequently than members and believed that the university was entitled to a discount because it purchased memberships in bulk, hundreds at a time. The managers in the university, myself amongst them, struggled to work within very limited budget constraints, and were frustrated with the position of their counterparts in the Y. Like a difficult anniversary, the disagreement came up annually, when it was time to negotiate a contract for another year. On a few occasions, an impasse had to be resolved in a meeting between Terry Jones and myself. Despite this irritation, we always managed, during the campus's first five years of operation, to find a compromise that allowed the Old Y to function as Laurier's recreational facility.

The advent of university programming in Brantford provided the Y with new revenue, but the low enrollment during the first years of Laurier operations meant that this new revenue was limited. Though it improved the financial health of the Y, it was not enough to eliminate pressing questions about its future. Each and every year the association struggled to sustain itself, teetering on the brink of closing. In a year when I served on the board, one of the questions that was very seriously discussed was the liability of board members if, as looked possible, the association went bankrupt. The problems with finances were exacerbated by the condition of the Old Y, which cost more and more to maintain. Under Jones's leadership, the association decided that the key to a better future was a new building that would attract new members and eliminate the constant problems with the upkeep of the building. This precipitated a debate over the location of a new building within the association, at city hall, and throughout the community. The two alternatives pitted two different views of Brantford development against each other — a downtown location that would continue the revitalization of the core, or a location on the outskirts of the city where the Y could serve suburban families, as it did in many other cities.

The thought that the Y might move troubled the supporters of downtown renewal. It might help the Y from a financial point of view, but it would rob the core of one of the few enterprises that had managed, despite its issues, to attract people downtown. Some potential donors and the city declared that they would provide support for a new Y building only if it was built downtown. The university maintained an interest in a partnership, but only if the Y chose a location close to the campus. The city offered a site beside the river, but a health and environmental assessment concluded that it was not suitable for construction.

While the debate over the location of a new building proceeded, the YMCA decided to raise money for the new venture by selling the Old Y. In a situation where its poor condition and a prevailing lack of interest in property downtown made it difficult to find a buyer, the building was sold to a Y subsidiary called Y Homes, which already owned and operated a number of affordable housing projects in Brantford. After the sale, it separated from the Y and became Your Homes, a non-profit organization dedicated to "the provision of affordable homes to students, families, singles and seniors." With financial support from the City of Brantford, the Old Y's new owners converted it into subsidized apartments.[2] Renovations of the building began with the removal of the gym and the pool and the unsightly concrete block extension. The 1912 exterior was cleaned and repaired, creating a new version of the Old Y that was renamed Heritage House.

To expand the rental capacity of the new project, Y Homes attached a newly constructed six-floor red-brick tower designed to provide housing for more than one hundred students. The new tower was named Lucy Marco Place, in honour of a distinguished Brantford resident known for her work on immigrant settlement services and as a participant on more than thirty volunteer boards. She had a reputation for being determined and persistent in her approach to volunteering. Heritage House and Lucy Marco Place were widely seen as a sign of Brantford's equally determined commitment to the rehabilitation of its old downtown. At a time when it was no longer clear whether the YMCA would stay, Brantford took some solace in the thought that an updated version of the Old Y would be a viable part of the new downtown. It was especially significant that its rebirth was executed by an organization other than the university. This was, it seemed, a welcome sign that the downtown revival was spreading beyond the campus.

But downtown Brantford was never easy on attempts at new development. When the newly renovated Old Y opened, Your Homes quickly rented its subsidized apartments in Heritage House, but not the units in Lucy Marco Place. Dave Prang, Laurier's housing manager, estimated that there were

Courtesy of the Brantford Heritage Inventory.

Courtesy of MMMC Architects

LEFT: *The "Old Y" building in Brantford viewed from the south, a view that emphasizes the aesthetically unsuccessful 1977 extension. The extension was removed in the 2006 renovation.* RIGHT: *The MMMC renovation of the "Old Y" in 2006 restored the 1912 exterior on the building. A second tower designed to accommodate student residences, Lucy Marco Place, was added.*

seven hundred students living downtown when the building opened, but Your Homes seemed unable to attract them. As its financial situation went from good to marginal to bad to worse, it became clear that the financing of the building was founded on an unrealistic business plan. The rents were not competitive, the plan assumed an unrealistic occupancy rate, students were required to rent in groups of four, parents were required to co-sign rental agreements, and the building earned a reputation as unresponsive

to student inquiries. At a meeting with one of the private landlords who filled his downtown apartments with students, I asked why Your Homes was so unsuccessful. He scoffed and told me that they operated like a charity, full of red tape, without the business instincts of private landlords. He told me he wished that all of his competitors were charities who didn't know how to run a business.

In an attempt to avert a growing financial crisis, Your Homes turned to the university, and then to Lucy Marco herself. I soon discovered that her reputation for commitment to a cause was well-deserved. In an attempt to help alleviate the problems at Your Homes, we recommended it to students looking for apartments. When this had little effect, Lucy spearheaded a drive to have us sublet the empty units. We welcomed the proposal, but Your Homes wanted rents that we found unacceptable. As the negotiations went back and forth, I felt a sense of déjà vu. Like the YMCA managers we had haggled with about the same building, the managers at Your Homes wanted rates that would solve their financial crisis. What our managers needed were rents comparable to those in other residences. In a situation with no Terry Jones to resolve the impasse, the pressure mounted. Caught in an impossible situation, Lucy did her best, trying by force of will to convince my managers and then me. One day the mayor called to say that she had phoned him. In the most delicate of ways, he went on to say that the city had contributed more than a million dollars to the Your Homes project and would be disappointed if it failed. He hoped that we could help. But we could not accept the terms that we were offered.

From the university's perspective, it was by now obvious that the financing of the Old Y renovation did not work. In a situation in which Your Homes had assumed an occupancy rate of more than 90 per cent, the rate in Lucy Marco Place languished at less than 25 per cent. At a time when many locals were still touting the success of the Old Y renovation, things were going sour behind the scenes. The inevitable came to pass when Your Homes began defaulting on its mortgage payments. This continued for more than a year, until the mortgager seized the building and tried to sell it. But no buyer could be found. One potential owner called me to say that he would like to purchase the building and lease it to the university, but there was no way to make this work. The price of the building would have forced him, like Your Homes, to charge rents we could not pay. The bottom line was simple — no one was interested in a building that could not generate the income needed to cover the mortgage. The new Old Y would not be a viable business operation until "someone took a haircut."

What followed was a long drama with many acts and scenes. The list of characters included Brantford managers; a new Laurier president; Laurier's senior executive; the City of Brantford; the mortgager for Your Homes; lawyers for Laurier, the city, and the mortgager — the latter with a penchant for surly behaviour; an earnest local MPP; the mortgage insurer, Canada Housing and Mortgage Corporation; the provincial and federal governments; and a contractor who had helped fund the Your Homes retrofit. In a situation in which there were no other options, the mortgager agreed, after lengthy negotiations, to a lease that turned Lucy Marco Place into a Laurier residence that charged fees competitive with those at other universities. Heritage House became a city-run affordable housing complex. By the start of the 2008–09 academic year, both were full. The new Old Y was a productive, thriving downtown building, but the transition had been anything but easy.

In comparison with Your Homes, private developers were more successful launching downtown housing projects. They were not motivated by charitable intentions but by an opportunity to turn a profit in a neighbourhood where property was cheap. The city was willing to contribute to new developments and the market for housing was headed in the right direction. Already in the 1990s, the city tried to entice developers to the core with "downtown performance grants," but it could find few takers. A key turning point was a fire set by arsonists in 2002. It destroyed a historic building owned by Nick Rizzo, a local developer. Originally it had been a 1929 Kresge's department store that, in turn, became a retail hardware store, a theatre for silent "moving pictures," an Eaton's mail-order warehouse, Foster's Jewellers, and eventually Rizzo's own shoe store. One of the few things that survived the fire was a blackened sign from one of the building's last tenants — ironically declaring: SMOKER'S HAVEN.

The Rizzo building was across the street from Grand River Hall. The fire that burnt it down was reported by Laurier Brantford students who saw the blaze from their bedroom windows, then arranged chairs on Colborne Street and sat and watched the blaze and the firefighters. "It was better than a movie," one of them told me.

In a bold move, Rizzo decided that he would redevelop his property as a private residence for students. He pieced together a $1.2-million business plan and took it to the city, which awarded him a $240,000 performance grant. The damage from the fire was so extensive that the contractors he hired, Lanca Contracting, had to dig through the basement floor and set the foundation on new footings. They maintained some historical continuity by embedding five stone blocks from the original building in the new construction — four stones etched with a rose pattern, and a blank stone on which they carved 2003, the year of the construction.

Photo by the author.

The Rizzo Residence, at the end of its construction in 2003, initiated a series of residence projects financed by private developers.

The success of the Rizzo Residence initiated a series of downtown projects by other developers who saw that one could turn a profit building student residences. In the wake of its success, the Dost and Rana families purchased other historical buildings destroyed by the same fire that burned down the original Rizzo building. The most notable dated from the birth of Confederation (1867–68), when it was erected as an outlet for George Watt, a prominent Brantford merchant. In later years, it served as the Stedman Bookstore and a popular Tamblyn's Drugstore. The new owners erected a residence similar to the one that Rizzo had built next door. On the ground floor they built a pharmacy that re-established, at the site of the former Tamblyn's, a working downtown drugstore.

Gabriel Kirchberger was a developer who had worked on revitalization projects in Germany

Colborne Street, Brantford, Canada.

TOP: *Lawyer's Hall in a turn of the century photograph of Colborne Street. Lawyer's Hall is the cream-coloured building with the pediment.*
BOTTOM: *The newly renovated Lawyer's Hall — one can still see vacant buildings on both sides of it.*

Courtesy of the Brantford Heritage Inventory.

after the dismantling of the Berlin Wall. In 2002, he brought his company, G.K. York, to Brantford. Specializing in the refurbishing of neglected properties, with a special interest in heritage buildings, it initiated a series of downtown projects. Harold Mannen, a downtown restaurant owner, converted a series of vintage houses into student accommodation. Peter Vicano followed suit. Shawky Fahel, the developer who restored the Wilkes House, bought and restored an 1869 hall built by T.G. Tisdale, a local stove manufacturer. He gutted the interior of Tisdale's Masonic Hall and rebuilt it as a set of apartment-style student residences. He named his new residence Lawyer's Hall, the popular name of the building in the nineteenth century, when its first floor housed a series of lawyers' offices.

The first private developments downtown were housing projects. Taken in conjunction with the building of the university and the expansion of BPL, they began to reorient downtown around the new post-secondary developments. In 2002, while Chris Friel was mayor, the City of Brantford advocated such moves in a "General Implementation Plan for Downtown" that proposed a University District downtown.[3] In 2006, Councillor Starkey wrote to me proposing a University Precinct that would "define the boundaries of an area in which we would like the university/college and its associated uses (residences, et cetera) to become established and grow."[4] In keeping with a vision shared by many, Victoria Square would become the centre of the proposed "Precinct," which would incorporate adjoining blocks that were directly or indirectly involved in university activities.

To an outsider, the impact the university had on downtown Brantford was most directly evident in the buildings Laurier acquired, built, and restored. But the university's arrival had a much broader impact. In a situation in which a fledgling campus could not provide all of the services students and professors needed, it reached out to the community. The partnership with the public library was one step in this direction. The partnership with the YMCA was another. The decision to convert the Old Y into a housing project with student apartments highlighted a different way in which the arrival of the university spurred downtown redevelopment. The project faltered, then rectified itself as the same demand for housing produced a series of private downtown residences. As the post-secondary operations grew, a variety of developments motivated by the university's activities began to congeal in a manner that of their own accord began to establish the precinct that Mayor Friel, Councillor Starkey, and others had envisaged.

A NEW SQUARE

As the effects of the university pushed downtown Brantford in a positive direction, the fly in the ointment was Brantford's original main street. The renovation of Lawyers Hall was a bold attempt to establish a viable building on the end of Colborne Street that most resisted attempts at renewal — the wrong end. It could not single-handedly remediate blocks of boarded-up buildings that stretched all the way from the river to Grand River Hall and the Rizzo Residence. This was Brantford's no-man's land — a stretch of blocks that might easily be compared to the worst streets in Detroit, New York, or Montreal.

The ramshackle buildings that lined Colborne Street showed many signs of Georgian, Victorian, and modernist architectural influences. An educated eye might identify some elegant commercial buildings from the 1860s. A person who knew local history might recognize Grafton's Clothing Store, which sold its wares for more than a hundred years; the Stedman Bookstore that gave rise to one of Canada's largest retail chains; and a row of shops that were built for Arunah Huntington, Brantford's mayor in 1852. The most significant of the lot was a building that once housed the 1876 telegraph office where Alexander Graham Bell made the world's first long-distance phone call.

Some of the buildings on the bad stretch of Colborne were owned by Nick Rizzo, but most had been acquired by another local developer, Steve Kun. He purchased them as the street declined. In local circles Kun was sometimes, unfairly, treated as a scapegoat when people talked about the decline of the downtown. In a search for someone to blame for what had happened, people ignored the complex causes of the problems in the core and said that Kun acquired blocks of buildings, let them decay, and drove everyone away. In reality, it was the other way around. Over a long period of time, Kun acquired his buildings because other businesses and developers fled. He purchased them when no one else was interested. In business dealings with the university, Kun and his wife, Helen — who continued to manage the business into her eighties — were eminently reasonable and fair. He did not apologize for being a businessman and we knew him as a straightforward negotiator who looked for a fair market price. On one occasion I expressly sought his advice, asking what he thought of a price that someone else wanted us to pay for a downtown building. He and Helen were steeped in the history of Brantford and welcomed the improvements downtown.

In the end, Kun's success assembling a long row of dilapidated buildings helped turn the street around, allowing the city to acquire a row of twelve buildings for $1.5 million. They became a focus of urban renewal when the city announced, in 2004, that it would replace them with a new civic square. To make way for the square it had to demolish the buildings it had purchased. Some questioned the demolition of historically significant buildings, suggesting a heritage designation, but the city moved swiftly. Concerns about heritage issues were drowned out by the rumble of bull dozers and the kinds of sentiments voiced in an editorial in *The Expositor*:

> Mayor Friel touched a nerve when he pronounced our downtown the worst in Canada. But he was right. There is no use pointing fingers. The rot set in decades ago and took hold despite city council's best efforts. Everyone is sick and tired of looking at a block of boarded-up buildings. It's an embarrassment for the city of Alexander Graham Bell, Pauline Johnson, James Hillier, Wayne Gretzky, Debra Brown and Phil Hartman. So let the buildings come down. The wreckers started on the first three buildings this week. Nine more buildings will be felled in September. The public agrees the time has arrived to get moving.[1]

In conversation, Mayor Friel told me he was determined to move quickly to avoid heritage battles over demolition. This was something he accomplished. In the process, however, Brantford lost one of its most significant heritage sites — the building that had contained the telegraph office that carried the world's first long-distance phone call from Brantford to Paris, Ontario. After the buildings were bulldozed, Friel and city council held public hearings on the new square. After much discussion, the city invited proposals for a development that would include private businesses on the perimeter of a public square area of approximately an acre; a stage; a water fountain in a pool that could become a skating rink in winter; and, as a nod to heritage concerns, a display highlighting the world's first long-distance phone call. Groups submitting bids for construction were asked to include plans for public and private financing.

City council debated the bids in closed-door meetings. Key stakeholders, among them the university, were invited to city council discussions. The public was asked to vote on the three proposals selected as finalists in the competition. The attempt to open the process to public input was welcomed but precipitated controversy when city hall was deluged with six hundred paper ballots and 125 email messages in the last weekend of voting, all of them favouring one proposal. With growing acrimony and much debate, city council approved a contract with G.K. York, the firm that Gabriel Kirchberger had moved to Brantford. It proposed a $22–24-million development that required a $5.5-million contribution from the city. Bell Canada donated $150,000 to sponsor the square's public stage, in celebration of

A few of the boarded-up buildings and storefronts removed to make way for the new Civic Square. On the left side of the top photo is the Total Hearing Clinic, which is reputed to be the building that contained the Colborne Street Telegraph Office where the world's first long-distance call was made.

its longstanding ties to Brantford. The city agreed to name it The Bell Heritage Stage.

Even before G.K. York won the civic square contract, Kirchberger had established it as a key player in Brantford's redevelopment. Kirchberger, a tall,

handsome man with a pleasant, charming demeanour, brought a wealth of business experience to Brantford. The first time he dropped by the university I mistook him for a very polite father who had come by to inquire about a student. On one occasion

Courtesy of Steve Colwill.

At one point the city attempted to inspire developers and others to reinvigorate Colborne Street by painting scenes on its boarded-up buildings, to show what Colborne Street could be if it was redeveloped. In this series of shops, the artists imagined vacant buildings as a photography studio, a bank, a bakery and delicatessen, and an art gallery. Steve Colwill has commented on these murals in a photo blog entitled "The Saddest Street in Ontario." As he aptly comments, the downtown in Brantford created "a classic 'doughnut city,' meaning that while the suburbs eventually rebounded from the industrial decline, the downtown became a hollowed-out shell of its former self. I've witnessed similar scenes in many Ontario towns I have visited, but none sadder or more pronounced than the shock I got seeing Colborne Street on a recent trip. Basically the entire street is either boarded up, for sale, or gutted. It is one of the highest-crime areas in all of Ontario. Perhaps the bleakest symbol of all, however, is that they have painted hopeful scenes of the life that once thrived in this beautiful old street on the boarded up windows, much like they did in the South Bronx of New York back in the 80s."

"Gabe" told me how much he had enjoyed owning a professional hockey team in Germany. He had come to Canada after working on modernization projects in the reunified East and West Germany. Creating G.K. York Management in 2001, he recruited other German investors to help him expand the Canadian holdings he had already acquired. Under Kirchberger's leadership, G.K. York specialized in the refurbishing of neglected and abandoned properties he found in Brant and Norfolk counties. Its holding included nine buildings in downtown Brantford. When the former Market Square Mall was put up for sale, G.K. York acquired it and leased it to businesses and municipal government departments.

Some G.K. projects were significant heritage initiatives. The Commercial Hotel (originally known as the Pepper House) was an 1861 hotel in poor repair when the company acquired it and the 1881 building that sat next to it — a John Turner designed office and apartment complex called Royal Victoria Place. York turned the top floors of both buildings into apartments after the university arrived. Their location, across the street from the Post House Residence, one block from the Carnegie Building, made them ideal for students, who could walk to classes in the Carnegie through a nineteenth-century streetscape. The buildings they passed along the way included St. Andrew's Church, formerly Zion Presbyterian, the home church of George Brown, one of the fathers of Confederation. Built in 1859, it was severely damaged in a fire set by an arsonist in 2005, but rebuilt in a historically conscious manner that accommodated Laurier offices in the church hall. Across the street, the students passed Brant Community Church, built as Park Baptist in the 1880s. One hundred and

twenty-five years later, the result was a remarkable cluster of nineteenth-century buildings.

For Brantford, a key York project was the Temple Building adjacent to the Sanderson Centre, on the north side of the proposed civic square. In 1844, it was the site of Van Brocklin, a foundry which became the Waterous Engine Works, one of the key concerns that established Brantford as a prosperous industrial town. In 1909, the foundry was replaced with the Temple Building. It was designed as a Masonic structure that housed commercial businesses and offices and, from 1911 to 1945, a lodge of the Order of Ancient Free and Accepted Masons. After he saw a 1915 Brant Museum and Archives photo of an elephant parade making its way up Dalhousie Street, Kirchberger decided to recreate the storefronts, awnings, and brick and tile work in the photo.[2] In a prominent location nestled between the Sanderson Centre on the one side and Brantford's stately 1913 post office on the other, the renovated Temple Building asserted Brantford's impressive architectural past on the border of a block destined to become a new public square.

Gabriel Kirchberger's work on the Temple Building, and on other Brantford projects, won him some acclaim and great goodwill in the community. Many admired his willingness to invest in Brantford projects at a time when few were interested. They proclaimed him a downtown hero. But Brantford never tends toward consensus and others saw him in a very different light — as a shrewd businessman who took advantage of Brantford properties that were available for a song. They complained that city council was too generous in supporting his endeavours and worried about the

Courtesy of Brant Museum and Archives, X9774741.

Photo by the author.

TOP: *The Commercial Hotel on Dalhousie Street, as it appeared* circa *1880. Royal Victoria Place is the building to the right of the hotel.* BOTTOM: *The Commercial Hotel and Royal Victoria Place today, after the renovations by G.K. York. The building on the far right is the Post House Residence.*

Elephants from a visiting circus march down Dalhousie Street by the Temple Building on June 16, 1912.

number of downtown properties he owned and controlled. When city council awarded G.K. York the civic square project, they accused city hall of favouritism. Two Brantford icons, Kirchberger and John Starkey, one of Brantford's most devoted and most vocal city councillors, clashed when Starkey came out on the anti-G.K. York side of the debate.

The criticisms of council's decisions reached a new intensity in February 2006, when Laura Starr of Windcorp Developments, the Toronto development company which had lost the Civic Square contract to G.K. York, wrote a letter to the mayor

Courtesy of Kevin Klein.

The newly renovated Temple Building on the perimeter of Harmony Square. The windows that overlooked the elephant parade in 1912 now overlook the downtown's new public square.

and Brantford councillors. In it she claimed that city council had flouted the laws on tendering and acted in bad faith when it reviewed the Windcorp proposal. In view of the issues, Windcorp announced that it would consider its legal options if the city did not pay damages that amounted to more than five million dollars. John Starkey broke ranks with the rest of city council when he refused to keep the letter confidential, publishing it on a web blog. On the same blog he included a column by David Sharpe

that criticized a "marriage of convenience" between
G.K. York and some members of city council — a
column that had been rejected by *The Expositor*.[3]
A forensic audit undertaken by the city concluded
that there was no wrongdoing in the Civic Centre
deal, but Starkey persisted with his allegations, criti-
cizing council and the press. When his criticisms
went nowhere he announced that he would not
seek another term on council because he had more
important work to do exposing the "trend towards
corruption at City Halls of all sizes."[4]

The debate about the politics of the new civic
square did not stop the work on it from proceed-
ing. Two years after the decision to go with the
York plan, in June of 2008, the square was officially
opened. Ironically, in view of all the politics, acrimony, and debate that swirled around its birth, it
was named Harmony Square. As the city had hoped,
it created a new public space that turned a block of
decrepit buildings into a focal point for public activities downtown: for family skating, cultural events,
concerts, movie festivals, drama, and restaurants
and commercial activities all year round. From an
architectural point of view, the square's most notable
feature was a heritage-style hotel, The Bodega, which
G.K. York constructed on its east side. Designed by
Cianfrone Architects, it was named after a century-
old hotel that had occupied the site until 1962, when
it burned down. Like other examples of Brantford
Revival architecture, the hotel successfully recreated
the forms and shapes that characterized the best of
Brantford's architecture in the glory days of the city
at the end of the nineteenth century.

| 28 |

THE BRANTFORD CENTRE

In Ontario, the province builds university campuses. But not in the case of Brantford, where it was the city, not the provincial government, that provided the capital funds to make a downtown campus possible. This was not for lack of asking. During the campus's first years, the provincial ministry in charge of universities was repeatedly asked to fund a series of building projects. Nothing happened until the run-up to a provincial election in 2007, when the province finally provided two million dollars for post-secondary downtown projects — one million to Laurier and one million to Nipissing. This was a small grant in a multi-billion-dollar provincial budget, but a major breakthrough in a province that did not welcome, and in many ways resisted, the idea that Laurier should establish a campus in downtown Brantford.

The key figure in provincial politics in Brantford was Dave Levac, the local MPP elected to the legislature in 1999 — the same year that Laurier Brantford was born. He was not invited to the opening of the campus but came anyway, raising the ire of some Laurier representatives when he spoke of a bright future with an independent Brantford university. These separatist inclinations did not prevent him, in three successive provincial governments, from trying to arrange provincial funding for Laurier Brantford building projects. When Laurier and Nipissing finally received the two million dollars, the minister of universities joked that this was because Levac sat beside him in the House and it was the only way that he could stop Levac from harassing him. I knew from my own experiences working with Levac, that this was only half a joke. A series of ministers quickly learned that Levac did not miss any opportunity to push the cause of post-secondary education in downtown Brantford.

On the institutional side, President Rosehart was the campus's central link to government. From the earliest days of the Brantford project, he pursued provincial funding. In communications with the Ministry, he compared the campus to the new University of Ontario Institute of Technology (UOIT) in Oshawa, which received tens of millions of dollars in capital funding. But the province paid no attention to his requests. In 2002, an opportunity arose when the Ontario minister of universities, Dianne Cunningham, announced a "Superbuild" program that would fund the expansion of Ontario's universities. It was designed to provide the additional spaces needed to accommodate the "double cohort" students expected to arrive at Ontario universities in September 2003, when the province's elimination of grade thirteen produced twice the usual number of high-school graduates — one group graduating from grade thirteen in the old system, the other from grade twelve in the new one.

Rosehart wanted to submit two applications to this 2002 fund — one for the Waterloo campus and one for Brantford — but stewed about the provincial requirement that he rank the projects he submitted, a requirement that would force him to choose between his two campuses. Brantford was tiny, but its enrollment was growing at 70 to 100 per cent a year in a system in which most university enrollments were growing at less than 5 per cent. In Waterloo, the percentage gains were smaller, but the increase in student numbers much larger. Both Waterloo and Brantford were among the fastest-growing campuses in Ontario. To avoid having to choose between them, Rosehart incorporated both in one Superbuild application. It presented projects at Waterloo and Brantford as two parts of a one-growth plan. He referred to Brantford as the university's "south" campus.

Rosehart, however, was forced to abandon his strategy when the Ministry balked, refusing to accept the Superbuild application he submitted. It directed him to submit two proposals, one for each campus, and to rank them in importance. Forced to choose, he ranked Waterloo first and Brantford second. Many months later, the funding came through, but the Brantford application was not supported — the Ministry was unwilling to fund two Laurier projects. When I phoned officials inside the Ministry, I was told that our proposal was "very seriously considered," but the government had in the end decided that it wanted to "spread the money around" to different universities in the province.

In the wake of Brantford's failed Superbuild application, the president agreed to let the campus ask the Ministry for one-time funding for a building. At a time when the government had a special interest in college-university collaboration, we decided to design a project that would emphasize our partnership with Mohawk. In co-operation with the GVES, Mohawk College, and the City of Brantford, we put together a working group that began working on a plan to build a centre for university-college collaboration in the middle of downtown. This high-spirited, and at times unruly, group decided to approach the province with a significant contribution to our centre in hand, so we began by asking the city for a building that could house the new centre. We saw the plan unfolding in two stages — the first would secure a building for the project, the second would secure provincial funding that would allow us to convert it into a post-secondary building.

When the city was approached, Mayor Friel offered the Hydro Building, a modernist edifice built for the Public Utilities Commission in 1957. When I brought the president down for an inspection, he declared it "a pig of a building" and lost his enthusiasm for the project. The city was not willing to entertain other options, so we soldiered on, hoping to make a silk purse out of our pig's ear. Through the mayor's office, we successfully negotiated a letter that formalized a commitment to provide the university and the college with the building. Because one of the issues the president had raised in his inspection of the building was the out-of-date heating and ventilation system, the city agreed to contribute five hundred thousand dollars toward the cost of a new system.

With city support in hand, the working group began meeting in an old, empty house on Nelson Street, adjacent to the Hydro Building. The GVES assistant who arranged the meetings filled the table with food — pastries, fruit, cakes, muffins, and baked goods of all kinds. However the discussion went, the group's sugar levels never faltered. We met in the living room, which had dark, oddly patterned wallpaper that someone must have chosen fifty years before. I tried to imagine, without success, what kind of family could have chosen such an odd design, and took solace in the thought that they, whoever *they* were, could not have imagined the gaggle of interested citizens, city officials, and university and college administrators who sat in their living room fifty years later, eating pastries, trying to save Brantford.

A well-fed working group turned its attention to Dave Levac and the provincial government. Levac said that he would try to arrange a meeting with the minister of universities and colleges. As a member of Her Majesty's Loyal Opposition, this was not an easy task, but he eventually succeeded. On the appointed day (July 17, 2003), Mayor Friel, Betty Anne Jackson from the Grand Valley Education Society, dean Doug Baker from Mohawk College, and I went to Toronto to meet with Dianne Cunningham, the minister of universities and colleges. Her handlers allotted us twenty minutes. On a pleasant summer Friday we arrived at an empty Queen's Park, on a day that did not seem an auspicious day for a meeting. Levac ushered us into another building, through a maze of identical-looking hallways, up an elevator, and into an anterior

office, where we waited for Minister Cunningham. When she arrived, he introduced us, and cordially left the room, determined to make sure that partisan politics did not interfere with the discussion.

In a small boardroom, we dimmed the lights and showed a video presentation prepared by Mohawk College students. Mayor Friel, looking his dapper best, followed with an eloquent history of the City of Brantford's decision to make post-secondary education a priority. Baker and I explained the academic side of the project, and Jackson relayed the broad community support for what was happening downtown. A benign Cunningham listened, was interested, intrigued, and finally enthusiastic. Our allotted twenty minutes turned into half an hour, then an hour, and finally an hour and a half of questions, answers, and discussion. By the time the meeting ended, the minister promised, "We will make this happen." To pave the way for funding, she asked us to prepare a detailed proposal outlining the details of the project and the contributions from its different partners. Friel, Baker, Jackson, and I emerged from a rabbit warren of ministry offices into bright sunshine, feeling that we had hit a home run.

We returned to Brantford thinking that The Brantford Centre would soon be a reality. In the ensuing weeks, we put our group of stakeholders to work, ironing out the details of the formal proposal as requested. It required letters from presidents making this a high priority, an official commitment from the city, and a detailed explanation of the centre. We raced, wanting to submit the proposal as soon as possible, while the afterglow of our meeting lingered, before anything disrupted our momentum. As was often the case in Brantford, events did not unfold as planned. The first hint of trouble arrived on September 2, when premier Ernie Eves called a provincial election. Wanting to make the most of the support of the current minister, we pushed our work into high gear and delivered a proposal for The Brantford Centre for Community, Communications and Design two weeks later. It envisaged a post-secondary centre housed in a renovated and expanded Hydro Building. The project partners — Laurier, Mohawk, and the City of Brantford— agreed to provide three million dollars. We asked the Ministry for $5.25 million.

Things took a turn for the worse on October 2nd, when the Conservative government went down to a crushing defeat. In the riding of London North Centre, our backer, Minister Cunningham, lost her seat. The people on the Brantford working group were profoundly disappointed. One of them told me that it was the first time she was sorry to see a Conservative defeat. I wondered how she had voted. Without the support of the minister who had invited our proposal, the political landscape suddenly looked dismal. As we looked for a way to keep The Brantford Centre alive, it suffered another blow at the beginning of November, when its most important local backer, Mayor Friel, was defeated in an acrimonious municipal election. As a new mayor and council were ushered in, it was not clear whether a council that rebuked Friel's legacy would uphold the commitment he had made to the Centre project. The new uncertainties extinguished anything that remained of the elation felt when we had met with the minister four months earlier.

In an effort to shore up municipal support for the Centre, Dean Baker and I decided to meet with Mayor Hancock and each of the recently elected councillors, to talk about higher education. He selected some names, I selected others, and we flipped a coin to decide who would meet with each of the councillors who were left. In the wake of our political setbacks, our proposal seemed to right itself and things began to move in the right direction. Baker and I emerged from our meetings with a more positive feeling about support at city council. The Grand Valley Education Society was awarded $250,000 in federal infrastructure funding to cover architectural designs that would convert the Hydro Building into a post-secondary centre. We discovered that some of the senior staff in the Ministry of Training, Colleges and Universities continued to support our proposal. Best of all, Premier McGuinty appointed our local MPP, Dave Levac, the whip of the Liberal party, a position that gave him access to the provincial cabinet and the new minister of universities, Mary Anne Chambers.

Levac wasted no time inviting Chambers to Brantford. She agreed to come, but resisted after a visit to Kitchener where she was publicly criticized for her government's failure to support its post-secondary initiatives downtown. The Brantford Centre working group badgered Levac about thin-skinned politicians who ran from their critics, but it badly wanted the minister to visit, and promised to be on its best behaviour. When Levac returned to Queen's Park, he resumed his attempt to court Chambers, promising her that he would ensure that a local visit did not become another Kitchener. Privately, he told me he was exasperated by her reluctance, but by sheer persistence, he finally succeeded.

Despite all of the anxieties that almost prevented it, the January 2005 visit went well. Chambers

Courtesy of Dave Levac.

Dave Levac stands at the entrance of the Carnegie Building in 2008. He served as the provincial member of Parliament for the first decade of Laurier Brantford's existence. He was always supportive of the campus but it took a decade for the provincial government to throw its weight behind the project.

seemed impressed by the renaissance that greeted her downtown. Two students she stopped at random said just what we hoped they'd say about their professors and their classes. The visit ended with a lunch in the boardroom of the Hydro Building, a grand room with oak panelling on the walls and a magnificent board table. In a closing interview with reporters, Chambers congratulated Brantford on its work in higher education, but made no commitments when they asked her when the provincial government would start funding the building of the Brantford campus.

On February 25, the Brantford working group sent the minister an updated proposal for The Brantford Centre. It included an introductory letter from the Mohawk and Laurier deans, letters of support from our presidents, a letter from the city clerk confirming a vote to support the project, and detailed architectural drawings by Ventin Architects who had been hired with federal infrastructure funding. With renewed confidence premised on the feeling that we had rebounded from the setbacks experienced in the provincial and municipal elections, we submitted an updated request for $6.35 million in fuding. Because Chambers had suggested that Brantford developments should interest other ministries, the working group sent the new proposal to four more ministers on March 14: the minister of finance, the minister of municipal affairs and housing, the minister of economic development and trade, and the minister of public infrastructure renewal.

We waited on tenterhooks for Chambers' response to the new proposal. Nothing happened. In a situation in which "No news is good news" was not a good rule of thumb, she ignored a series of enquiries. The normally placid Mayor Hancock, who was waiting to see what would happen to his building, finally decided that his office would end the "cat and mouse game." When he contacted Chambers' office she refused to come to another meeting, but agreed to a conference call. A few weeks later, I sat with the mayor, Dave Levac, representatives from the GVES, and Dean Baker in the mayor's office, waiting for her

to call. The presidents of Laurier and Mohawk joined us by phone. When Chambers called, she struggled to deliver a simple message — the government would not fund The Brantford Centre. At one point in the discussion, a frustrated President Rosehart, who had unsuccessfully pushed three subsequent ministers to fund an increasingly successful Brantford campus, lost his patience. In a tone that said what everyone in Brantford felt, he asked Chambers how many students would have to attend university in Brantford before the province would finally fund its buildings. A manifestly upset Chambers answered that the government was doing great things for post-secondary education. The most uncomfortable person in the room was Dave Levac. Caught between his own minister and a Brantford project he supported, he stared down at his shoes.

After the meeting with Chambers, the Brantford working group retreated to its lair on Nelson Street and stewed. Amidst coffee, tea, candy, grapes, and lemon poppy-seed muffins, it analyzed and re-analyzed, discussed and debated the province's failure to support The Brantford Centre. Some of the more frustrated members proposed marches to Queen's Park and a new MPP for Brantford. At a time when it was difficult to keep the project a priority for the university, the college, and the city, President Rosehart told me that he would let us have one more go at provincial funding. If we were not successful, he would have to switch his support to other priorities. Putting the past behind it, the working group decided that its next move would be a submission to a provincial review of post-secondary education in Ontario. The review was headed by Bob Rae, the former NDP premier, who happened to be Laurier's chancellor. In a situation in which he was close to the premier, and the government was very tightly controlled by the premier's office, university administrators joked that Rae was the "real" minister of universities and colleges.

Rae used his profile effectively to stimulate a stirring discussion of higher education across the province. To gather input for his review, his commission created a discussion paper: "Higher Expectations for Higher Education," and invited responses to it. Like many colleges, universities, and interested groups across the province, the working group on The Brantford Centre decided to treat the request for input as an opportunity to have our arguments heard. In November 2004, it submitted a brief to the commission, which outlined the goals of The Brantford Centre in light of broader issues in post-secondary education.[1] It argued, in a manner that drew President Rosehart's approval, that the government should back its call for college-university partnerships with incentives that rewarded institutions committed to joint projects, and that it should tie its post-secondary developments to community development. We pushed the idea that satellite campuses could, as Brantford demonstrated, promote community development and enhance post-secondary opportunities where they were needed most.

Rae had visited Brantford on a number of occasions in his role as chancellor of Wilfrid Laurier University. He was a beguiling public speaker who elevated formal university events to a standard few could compete with. In his speeches, he was funny, entertaining, and never at a loss for words. On an occasion when he came to speak to a Brantford conference we organized on universities and city development, I escorted him to the conference room. Along the way we stopped in the men's room. "What is happening in Brantford?" he asked casually. Ten minutes later, I was treated to an evening speech structured around our conversation in the washroom. In the buzz of talk at the reception afterward, everyone was impressed. "Who," they said admiringly, "could have imagined that Bob Rae knew so much about what is happening in Brantford?"

On his formal visits to Laurier Brantford, Rae was interested in the campus and what it was trying to accomplish. As a social activist, he could not fail to see the good in the transformation of downtown. He was always supportive, but the Brantford working group was disappointed when his commission's final report, released on February 7, 2005, did not push the government in the direction we had hoped. It spoke highly of university-college partnerships but failed to propose any financial commitment to them. Our suggestion that the province tie university expansion to community development by establishing satellite campuses seemed to have fallen on deaf ears. On the heels of the commission's report, the government chose to emphasize two aspects of post-secondary education — Health and Medicine, and Graduate Studies — which left Brantford in the cold. On the campus, the increases in enrollment continued unabated, but did so without any capital funding from the province.

In circumstances in which the working group was debating whether to give up on The Brantford Centre, Chris Bentley replaced Mary Anne Chambers as the minister of training, colleges and universities in June 2005. One morning a month later, Dave Levac called with a tip — Minister Bentley was participating in a local golf tournament. After a round of frantic phone calls, Betty Anne Jackson, Dean Baker, myself, and others drove out to the golf course and intercepted him at the end of his game. On a sweltering day, he joked about an ambush, but was cordial, promising that he would return to Brantford to talk with us. When his office resisted our attempts to arrange a meeting, it felt like a convenient brush off, but an ever-persistent Levac would not give up. In December, he managed to have Bentley stop in Brantford on a trip from London to Toronto. A moody and flustered Bentley showed up in body, but not in spirit. He cut his tour short and was anxious to be gone. It was hard to avoid the conclusion that he was there for one reason — because his party whip had made him do it.

Before he left, Bentley came to a meeting around a crowded table at the old house on Nelson Street. With the living room's outdated wallpaper as his backdrop, he told the Brantford working group that his government would not provide funding for The Brantford Centre. When asked why it would not support Brantford building projects, he shifted the blame to Laurier and Mohawk, saying that they had decided to use their capital funds on projects in other cities. I answered that the province had turned down a Brantford application in the Superbuild competition, and forced Laurier to choose when it restricted its support to a single campus. Why shouldn't the government support two campuses? In the testy conversation that followed, Bentley defended the province. "Every student and every professor on this campus has a *P* for province on their back," he insisted, "because they are supported by provincial operating dollars." His argument missed the point,

which was an issue about capital, not operating, dollars. He left the meeting as the fourth minister in his portfolio that had no answer to the question why Brantford was the only public university campus in the province which did not have, in his own terms, a *P* for province on the back of its buildings.

The partners in The Brantford Centre gave up on the project in April 2006. The GVES had secured $250,000 in federal funding, the city had provided a building, and the city, Laurier, and Mohawk had committed capital funding. I was not sorry to spend less time meeting with the wallpaper and the pastries in the house on Nelson Street, but the failure of the project was dispiriting. The members of the working group were left feeling that the government was not ready for a new idea from Brantford. It did not seem to matter that it made good sense. Without provincial support, the partners could not, in good conscience, leave the Hydro Building empty any longer.

At city hall, the decision to end the project was met with consternation and a great deal of province-bashing. The Brantford view was summed up in a letter to *The Expositor* lamenting the failure of the Centre initiative, commending councillors John Starkey and Larry Kings for their vocal criticisms of the province. "The city cannot bear the brunt of the blame for this failure," Chris Otis wrote. "The blame rests with the province and Dalton McGuinty's government."[2]

Dave Levac was, once again, put in an impossible position by a minister of his own government. Forced to choose between a project he had lobbied hard for and his allegiance to the party, he defended the government's decision, saying that it was "the job of Wilfrid Laurier University to define its priorities and where the Brantford Centre project fits in with them, and the government has its own priorities to consider....The city and Laurier decided to build a campus. They both needed each other and they started on their own. For anyone to come and say 'we've done all this and now you have to ante up' is unfair and wrong."[3] Minister Bentley himself wrote an ingratiating letter to *The Expositor* congratulating "all who have worked so hard to develop the opportunities we now see in Brantford," arguing, once again, that the province was providing support to Brantford by funding students, and Laurier and Mohawk.[4]

From a Brantford point of view, the government's perspective was a damning one. When the province was pushed to support the Brantford project, it argued that the university and the city had started the campus, and that this made its funding their responsibility. In the process, the government made the question "Who came up with the idea?" more important than the question "Was it a good idea that should be supported?" It ignored all that Laurier Brantford had to offer: an opportunity to boost education in a city with an exceptionally low participation rate in post-secondary programs, an opportunity to turn around a collapsed downtown with heritage buildings that rivalled any in the province, innovative programming, and college transfer arrangements that furthered the province's professed goals for higher education. If the government had argued that other priorities were more important, Brantford would have felt it had at least had a hearing. Instead, the province sidestepped the issues and argued, in essence, that no one should expect it to support ideas that came from Brantford.

Lost in the debate was the fact that The Brantford Centre, like Laurier Brantford, would have been a remarkably cost-effective way to support post-secondary education. It is not easy to say what a new campus should cost, but the Ontario government set something of a benchmark in June 2002, when it established the province's first new university in forty years, the University of Ontario Institute of Technology. The building of its campus was financed with a sixty-million-dollar grant from the Superbuild fund, and a $220-million bond issue, making the total cost $280 million for a campus that was designed to accommodate six thousand students. When Brantford gave up on provincial funding for The Brantford Centre, its campus had cost less than twenty-five million dollars and accommodated two thousand students. It had received no capital funding from the province. Any way one did the numbers, Brantford was a bargain.

The failure of the Centre project sent a disheartening message from the province to the city and the university, but the idea that the Hydro Building should become a post-secondary building had by then taken root. When the proposal for The Brantford Centre died, it took on a life of its own. When Laurier and Mohawk moved on to other projects, Brantford's third post-secondary institution, Nipissing University, decided that the success of its Brantford programming merited another building. A discussion with the mayor led to the city offering it the Hydro Building on the same conditions originally offered to Laurier and Mohawk. The city approved the offer and Nipissing accepted. In this backhanded way, the years spent working on the Centre project eventually produced an outcome that

Courtesy of Kevin Klein.

Brantford's 1957 Public Utilities Commission Building in 2009, after it was renovated to become a building for Nipissing University. This was the building slated to become the Brantford Centre.

contributed the downtown building we had targeted to Brantford's growing post-secondary campus. I was disappointed that Laurier had not acquired the building we had worked so long to acquire but glad the world had found a different way to make it a part of Brantford's post-secondary endeavours.

Ironically, given the struggles with the provincial government over our plan to convert the Hydro Building into a post-secondary centre, the decision to give the building to Nipissing ultimately secured government support. The key player in the situation was the tireless Dave Levac. Someone I talked to compared him to a determined tick, which finally managed to bore its way into the brain of the ministry and the government. It happened somewhat unexpectedly, in the run-up to the provincial election in 2007, when he finally convinced the government that it should contribute capital funding to the growth of Brantford's downtown campus. At a ceremony in the Odeon Building, Chris Bentley announced two million dollars in capital funding — one million for Laurier and one million for

Nipissing. Nipissing used its million to help convert the Hydro Building. All of Brantford hoped that it was not just politics, but a breakthrough that would pave the way to more support for its experiment in post-secondary education, urban redevelopment, and the reinvention of downtown. For Brantford and Levac, the best was yet to come.

| 29 |

SILLY SEASON

Bob Rosehart loved politics. He followed it with the same intensity that fervent football fans followed the sports sections of their newspapers. But Rosehart was ambivalent about elections. He dubbed them "silly season" — an extended version of Question Period in the House of Commons, a time when politicians *try* to be indignant, searching for any possible pretext for outrage and the opportunity to slam their opponents in front of the media. When I told him that this kind of posturing — and its influence on the general public — was the reason Plato did not like democracy, he smiled and nodded in approval, but I don't think that I convinced him that he should study *The Republic*.

Rosehart was a pro at political survival. He dealt with elections by keeping his head low, trying to ensure that no university matter became a political football that someone contending for a title used to score points with the electorate. In Brantford, where all eyes were focused on the university, this was more than a theoretical possibility. It was something we worried about when the decision to give up on The Brantford Centre reignited debates about the city's funding for the post-secondary project. In an intriguing article, Michael-Allan Marion argued that the province's failure to fund the building of the campus had a positive side to it, for it allowed the city to exert a great deal of influence over its development.[1] Few commentators shared this positive point of view. In a situation in which almost everyone criticized the provincial government, the focus of debate was the question whether the city should, in the absence of funding from the province, continue to provide funds for the development of the downtown campus.

As Brantford made its way toward the 2006 municipal election, the battle lines for and against city spending on downtown projects formed and engaged each other with new intensity. According to those opposed to city spending, it was time to stop funding operations that should have been funded by the province. Even Mike Quattrociocchi, a downtown councillor, argued that "enough is enough" and the city should stop financing the growth of Laurier and its partners. In an early skirmish in the lead-up to the election, he tried to force the issue by proposing a referendum that would have asked voters whether they supported more funding for post-secondary projects. He and councillor Greg Martin proposed that the city's share of the profits from the casino — money that had been used to support the university — be redirected and used to lower taxes. In an informal poll conducted by *The Expositor*, 62 per cent of 415 respondents said that the city should not continue to assist Laurier downtown.

On March 4, Gerry Van Dongen, one of the letter writers who helped make *The Expositor* an interesting read, wrote:

> The result of *The Expositor*'s reader poll seems to indicate that a majority of Brantford citizens share the opinion expressed by some Councillors that it is time that Laurier Brantford stands on its own two feet....Nearly two-thirds of the phone-in responses share the opinion expressed by some Councillors that we, the taxpayers, should stop subsidizing Laurier with our tax dollars. So, council, please pay heed to the message conveyed to you....[2]

In the council meeting that decided on referendum questions for the election, Councillor Martin supported Quattrociocchi's motion for a referendum. The motion was opposed by councillors Ceschi-Smith, McCreary, and Kings, and by others who argued that the post-secondary project was the engine of downtown redevelopment. When it came time to vote, the referendum motion was defeated by a vote of eight to three. In a later meeting, an attempt to resurrect the idea of a post-secondary referendum suffered a similar defeat.

In many ways, the 2006 debate over post-secondary spending reflected issues that arrived in Brantford when Laurier came to town. In a letter to the editor written during the campus's second year of operation, a concerned citizen, Horst Stanzlik, wrote:

> The decay of the downtown has been going on for the past 20 or so years and to spend more money on consultants, architects and urban developers or other pet projects, is a blatant waste of taxpayers' money. In regard to the Laurier University campus, that project started out as a sinkhole for taxpayers' money and will remain as such, just like the Sanderson Centre.[3]

By 2006, Laurier Brantford had over 1,700 full-time students, over one hundred full-time employees, and eight buildings. But Stanzlik's position was still the same. In a new letter to the editor, he reiterated his position, that "Too much public and private property paid for by the taxpayers is being handed over to an institution that has proven to be a bottomless pit for taxpayers' money."[4]

In the months leading up to the election, those who opposed downtown spending claimed there was a "Bloc" of city councillors that drove downtown expenditures. The issue between the alleged bloc and those who opposed them was not a genteel disagreement. In a number of situations it led to angry denunciations and sarcastic comments. Those who had been waiting years to see a turnaround downtown were just as angry as those who accused the city of spending all its money on a love affair with the university. In his own letter to *The Expositor*,

In its early years, the struggle to establish and grow the Brantford campus precipitated much debate and vehement disagreement. The city's financial support for the building of the campus — in the absence of provincial support — became a major matter of debate at city council. In the 2006 municipal election, the sign pictured here was erected by a downtown businessman who took exception to the views of those councillors who rejected city support for the campus.

John O'Neil, who had owned and operated a down-town stereo store for thirty years, responded to the charge that a group of councillors were unfairly favouring the downtown, writing:

> In my opinion, the members of the Bloc are the heroes of downtown development. Their ideas are developed from the position that downtown Brantford has the potential to be a thriving community. Despite the criticism directed toward this group's methods of operating, the results they achieved for downtown were nothing short of terrific. The present council includes the new group I refer to as the "Blockage." They do not show any vision. They are simply negative....[5]

As the election neared, I tried to follow President Rosehart's example, telling my managers that we would stay firmly on the sidelines. This was something not easy to do when the gloves came off and we were faced with vehement criticism of the university. Every manager lived a life enmeshed in events and activities in Brantford, a reality that inevitably put one in uncomfortable situations. On one occasion I attended what I took to be an innocent official opening of a restaurant in the new city square. After drinks and chat with many well-heeled guests, the speeches turned out to be a carefully orchestrated ambush that levelled blistering criticisms at those councillors who opposed spending on the university and downtown revitalization. In my heart of hearts, I supported their perspective, if not their way of expressing it, but it was not a good place to be when I was trying to stay out of the debates. I remember, in the middle of one of the speaker's tirades, looking at the person next to me, and discovering that it was one of the councillors under attack. I lowered my eyes and left as soon as I could manage.

In the end, the 2006 election results boded well for the downtown and the university. Not everyone elected supported downtown redevelopment, but most did. The new council was one that was "friendly" to more development downtown. Looking back at the election campaign, it could be said that the issues were not as silly as those raised in earlier campaigns. No one suggested that Laurier was going to abandon Brantford. When one dug beneath the vitriolic tone of the discussion of downtown, one could discern an important debate about city spending. Those who defended spending argued, as they always had, that it was a key investment in Brantford's future. In 2002, Vern Gale, the chair of the Grand Valley Education Society, had said this in a letter to *The Expositor*, writing:

> The financial contribution, cultural revitalization, and spirit that a university campus adds to a city is well-documented — the numbers are in the millions. A reminder to all of us — money allocated and contributed to the Laurier-Mohawk's future growth is not a burden on the taxpayers, it is an investment in our community that will be repaid 10-fold.[6]

In 2005, the GVES decided to put debates about the impact of the downtown campus on a more factual footing. To this end, it commissioned an independent study of its economic impacts. The study was conducted by Adventus Research, a Guelph-based firm, and funded by Enterprise Brant, the City of Brantford, Laurier, and Mohawk. Adventus was asked to chart the economic state of the downtown before the university campus was established, the current economic situation, and the likely situation in the future. A year before the 2006 election, six years after Laurier came to Brantford, Adventus released its report. It traced the problems downtown to the 1960s, when "longstanding" economic issues were compounded by closures in the manufacturing sector and the opening of suburban retail malls. Large-scale redevelopment projects like the mall and the Massey deal were supposed to arrest the decline but they "proved unsustainable and … just added to and complicated the downtown's decline."[7]

Adventus was more positive about the future. Its survey of businesses in the community concluded that an "overwhelming majority" believed that the university and the college had improved the economic well-being of Brantford and the downtown. Ninety-five per cent believed that Laurier enhanced Brantford's reputation. The average annual economic impact of Laurier Brantford[8] during the 2006–10 time period was estimated at between twenty and twenty-seven million dollars. The annual economic impact of Mohawk[9] was estimated to be nineteen to twenty-two million. Together, the three post-secondary institutions in Brantford were expected to generate more than two hundred million dollars of activity during the following five years.

The Adventus findings prepared the way for an election campaign in which it was difficult to deny the benefits of downtown spending. To anyone who lived or worked downtown, the Adventus conclusions came as no surprise. By the time the company did its research, some twenty downtown buildings were devoted to the universities, the college, and their students. More than two thousand students, staff, and faculty were making downtown Brantford their working destination. Three hundred first-year students lived in Laurier Brantford residences. Another seven hundred students lived in private accommodation. Students and faculty shopped for groceries and supplies and restaurant meals downtown. It would have been odd if this did not generate a significant economic payoff.

In ways that were equally important, but less easily measured, the quality of life in downtown Brantford improved dramatically. For many, the most important downtown issue was safety and security. Empty streets with rundown buildings, rough bars, and intimidating patrons had been one of the key forces that pushed people away from the downtown. In 1961, in her opus magnum, *The Death and Life of Great American Cities*, Jane Jacobs argued that crime could be reduced with "eyes on the street." In Brantford, the eyes that the universities and the college brought downtown established safer streets. To further enhance security, the city improved street lighting. The university provided the police with an office in the Odeon Building. As the campus grew, Laurier established a security force to patrol the campus and adjacent streets. The service, established by Tracy Arabski, the director of campus operations, was affectionately referred to as "The Arabski Army."

Another "foot patrol" was established by Laurier students. In its early years, "Footy" was the most popular club on campus. I would hear them talking and laughing when I worked late in the office. The first time I heard them — at 2:00 a.m. — I investigated with some trepidation, wondering if someone had broken into the building. When I — carefully — went downstairs and poked my head around a corner, I found a jovial group of students sitting on the couches in the basement of the Carnegie Library, waiting to see if anyone called for the free walk-home service they provided. A few years later, Footy acquired a van from Waterloo, which it used to provide a free drive-home service to anyone who wanted it. The club, which was a special hit with criminology students, had forty or more volunteer members who were given distinctive jackets, two-way radios and a flashlight, and were trained in emergency first aid.

Once a term, Footy organized a Spirit of the Community walk, in which its members and supporters walked "in proud recognition of our involvement in the downtown community of Brantford." The walk was followed by a barbeque to raise money for the soup kitchen St. Andrews Church operated on Victoria Square, and trips for local schoolchildren. Other volunteer activities were a key component of the Brantford campus. As part of first-year orientation, students worked for Shinerama, a national fundraiser for cystic fibrosis (CF), which dispersed first-year students at locations throughout the city, where they offered to shine shoes, cars, or anything else to raise money for CF research. Project Empathy conducted an annual drive that brought attention to the plight of AIDs victims in Africa, raising funds to purchase food, clothing and medical supplies.

Every year it sent Brantford students to Botswana to witness, work, and chronicle the AIDS epidemic. I remember one of the returning students telling me how her experience had transformed her life forever. What struck her most of all was the joy of life she found among the people that she had worked

Courtesy of Wilfrid Laurier University Students' Union.

A student sign for SHINERAMA, *an annual fundraiser for cystic fibrosis. It originated in 1961, when students at Laurier, then Waterloo Lutheran University, decided to shine shoes to raise money for charity. It has now become a key component of first-year orientation at universities across the country.*

The new Millard, Rouse & Rosebrugh Building a few blocks from Laurier. Like other projects downtown, the firm's new headquarters embraced the Brantford Revival style.

with — people struggling in the most desperate circumstances.

Inspired by a Contemporary Studies course, one of Laurier's students, Tracy Bucci, organized an environmental club that became a Laurier-Mohawk club when she moved on to Mohawk College. The club worked on garbage and pollution issues in the Grand River, community parks, and walking trails.

In 2002, it initiated an annual spring clean-up that picked up garbage from the banks of the Grand River, and, from rafts, the river itself.[10] In local schools, Laurier Students for Literacy promoted reading with young children. Professor Lisa Wood's Student Online Mentorship Program (STOMP) paired Laurier students with high-risk students in grades seven and eight. Nipissing students worked in local schools, and a service-earning project directed by Darren Thomas tied courses to volunteer placements in Brantford, Six Nations, and the New Credit Reserve.

In a host of other ways too long to list, the downtown campus exerted a positive influence on life in Brantford.[11] The different ways in which the campus connected to the community promoted a more fundamental change in attitude that was manifest in Brantford's reawakening pride in its own history. The new historical consciousness was evident in joint projects undertaken in co-operation with the local historical society and museum. Visually, it expressed itself in a new, Brantford Revival style of architecture that became a hallmark of the campus's old and new buildings. The style spread downtown, to the edge of the new civic square and beyond. When the accounting firm, Millard, Rouse & Rosebrugh, decided to replace a block of older houses with a new building, they embraced this new ideal, building an office complex that epitomized the new downtown.

It is difficult to put a number on the value of pride in one's history, buildings that please the eye, more cultural events, safer streets, and more downtown restaurants. But these and many other elements too subtle and intangible to be measured by simple economic indicators were key ways in which the decision to spend money on a downtown campus enhanced the quality of life in Brantford. The Adventus Research project showed that this spending had an enormous economic impact, but its positive impacts were still deeper and more significant. In view of all the benefits, it was not surprising that the debates in the 2006 election were not able to derail Brantford's post-secondary experiment.

A POST-BRANT FORDIAN COMMUNITY

Henry Ford was a remarkable businessman. His Model T automobile revolutionized transportation. His way of doing business revolutionized American industry. "Fordism" is the economic system he devised. It included cheap production, assembly-line construction, and high wages for his workers. It is credited as the way of doing business that moved North America from an agricultural to an industrial economy.

One hundred years ago, Brantford grew rich from "Brant Fordism." It consisted of the Ford approach applied to industry in Brantford. Its most successful manufacturing endeavours were in the field of agricultural manufacturing. The businesses that made Brantford most famous — Massey-Harris, Massey Ferguson, Cockshutt Plow, White Farm, the Waterous Engine Works, Verity Plow, and others — operated Ford-type factories in Brant County. The greatest of them all, Massey Ferguson, outshone Ford itself in the production and sale of tractors.

The demise of Brantford in the 1980s was the demise of Brant Fordism. It was the closing of its factories and its lack of an alternative economy that left Brantford spiralling downward. Amidst the doom and gloom I found when I arrived in Brantford, there were some who saw things differently. When I took one of the members of the Grand Valley Education Society to lunch, he told me that he was glad to see the collapse of White Farm and Massey Ferguson. "People should stop complaining," he said bluntly. "This was a company town. There were owners and workers. No one knew how to do anything but build farm machinery. Thank god it ended. Nothing else could have forced Brantford to look for a diversified economy."

This was a trenchant insight that few shared. Even those who agreed did not know how to build a post–Brant Fordian community. In the bleakest period for the downtown, just before the university arrived, few could imagine any good coming from the collapse of Brantford's industrial society. Jay Johnson, the chair of the Downtown Business Improvement Association in 1995, remembered that nobody foresaw the changes soon to come.[1] The mayor who started it all, Chris Friel, echoed the same sentiments: "When I first took office, people felt nothing could be done, everything is bad…. We had to convince people that things could be good, that the downtown could be turned around."

Tim Philp, a popular local commentator, has credited Laurier, Nipissing, and the City of Brantford's downtown grant program as the engines of a revitalized downtown. "Brantford is booming! This is an incredible statement for anyone from Brantford who lived through the collapse of the farm machinery industry and the subsequent gradual deterioration not only of our downtown infrastructure but also of the confidence of its citizens. What a change this community has been through in the past five years."[2] The transition from a Brant Fordian to a Post–Brant Fordian community has been built on one constant that spans both. It is a shared commitment to community. In the case of the campus downtown, this has been a major driving force in its development, evident in the way that it has built a campus and the set of programs it has offered — programs with deep ties to the local community.

This does not mean that positive city-university relations are easy to accomplish. Since the Middle Ages, "town and gown" rivalries[3] have led to contention and dispute. In extreme cases, the result has been violent confrontation. In 1355, at the Battle of St. Scholastica Day, the citizens of Oxford attacked its university, killing students and professors. Most confrontations have been less extreme, but the tensions that produced battles like St. Scholastica Day have been a constant throughout the history of universities. At Laurier in Waterloo, student–city tensions came to a head in 1995 at the Ezra Street riot. The confrontation occurred when 1,500 revellers showed up to an end-of-the-year party, drank too much beer, threw bottles, and partied until the police came and arrested forty-two students. Two serious injuries occurred when a man was run over by a jeep and a woman was hit by a chunk of flying concrete.

Nothing so drastic occurred in Brantford. The closest we came to a riot was an attempt to raise money for a charity. It occurred when a group of students imbued with good intentions bought a beat-up old automobile, towed it to one of our parking lots, and sold swings of a sledgehammer. As they carried on with youthful enthusiasm, the police arrived, having received phone calls from upset residents who lived in adjacent buildings — residents who looked out their windows, saw a group of students yelling, smashing windows, and jumping up and down on a parked car. They told the police that students were rioting in the middle of downtown. Innocent of the complications that should attend the organization of such events, it had not occurred to the students that they should inform the police and the city of what they were up to.

Inevitably, there were issues that arose between the university and its neighbours. To ensure that this did not disrupt the sense of community downtown, the campus manager, Tracy Arabski, took the lead by establishing a Town and Gown Committee that brought university and city managers together. They built great camaraderie as they tackled all the day-to-day annoyances that could have set the city and the campus against each other: parking, noise, safety, building issues, student behaviour, and more. The committee worked so well that it gained a reputation beyond Brant County. It was approached by other cities and institutions trying to find ways to constructively to resolve their issues and played a key role in establishing The Town and Gown Association of Ontario, which was formally recognized by the Ontario government at a meeting in Brantford on May 12, 2006.

One of the most important ingredients that nurtured the university's relationship to the broader community was the attitudes of its students. There were some, often students who had grown up in Brantford, who did not like the "undesirables" and the "creepy unsafe people" who made downtown "a little scary."[4] When asked what they thought Laurier should do, one suggested that it should "Choose a new location — Brantford downtown is disgusting and it is sad that they would put the university here, it is embarrassing." But this was the minority view. Most students had learned to appreciate the downtown and what it had to offer:

> "I like it that the campus is spread out throughout the downtown and all the buildings look different. They don't all look the same like the University of Waterloo."
>
> "Laurier Brantford is an incredibly attractive and historically rich campus. Not only does it rival some of the nicest-looking campuses in Ontario, but also owns the nicest buildings in Brantford."
>
> "The buildings are great, keep on making Brantford more beautiful."

The most hopeful trend was an understanding that students themselves were an important part of the attempt to change Brantford — and through it, the world — for the better:

> "Downtown Brantford is a little sketchy, but the university is changing this and definitely makes up for it!"
>
> "I'm making history, and it feels excellent."

The feelings of community this evinced outside the university was very well expressed in a letter to me from the president and director of Why Not City Missions, which supported the homeless and the poor downtown:

> We were privileged to have a class from Professor Robert Feagan's course on "Community" come to the Java on Monday January 22nd, 2007.... I would just like to say that we appreciate this kind of dialogue with the students, since this is the premise of what we do here at the Mission. It's all about Community Helping Community.
>
> The biggest fear that I think many people in the downtown harbored when Laurier first moved into our city was that it would it be "us" and "them" — the Laurier Students being totally separate from the Downtown Community. However, with initiatives like this, and many others that are being promoted through the University, we have been *so* encouraged!
>
> We work with students from Laurier with our Literacy Program for children and we will soon be working with a 4th year student from

Professor Lamine Diallo's Leadership Program. We are hoping that this student will help us set up training and marketing strategies for our non-profit restaurant — The Downtown Java. This is a program that we run here at the Mission and it also serves as financial sustainability for us for the many other programs we run for Youth at Risk....

As a non-profit organization, we benefit greatly from the hours of service provided by the students from Laurier and also from Mohawk College. We just wanted to drop you a line to say that we thank you! We are *so* pleased with the work you are doing here in our Community, and we look forward to many *more* ways we can work together in the future. Together we can rebuild and make our downtown a thriving community once again.[5]

In downtown Brantford, the greatest obstacle to the development of a new post–Brant Fordian community was the province's unwillingness to support the building projects the new campus needed to evolve. After a whole life in politics, Bob Nixon told me that Brantford had no cachet in the provincial government's view of things. This made things difficult for Brantford, but there was a silver lining. It was an emphasis on fundraising that became, by necessity, an integral part of campus culture. Brantford began with a fundraising campaign. It continued to grow because private and public donations raised money for buildings, scholarships, bursaries, and endowments. Under the leadership of Sherri Bocchini, who directed the campus's fundraising efforts, the university's support for the city and the community was repaid with financial support that allowed the building of the campus.

As a campus, Laurier Brantford tried to emulate American universities that make fundraising a key component of their activities. Their supporters and graduates become integral members of their communities, and maintain their allegiance and commitment through donations that allow them to fund everything from building construction to guest lecturers, from scholarships to new programs. Even in difficult times, the large endowments at American universities — hundreds of millions of dollars at small institutions and billions of dollars at larger ones — generate annual funding that allows them to provide an education internationally regarded as the best in the world.[6] In a very conscious way, Laurier Brantford set out to build its own philanthropic tradition. Its success was evident in contributions that came from all sectors of the community.[7] On the campus itself, students, administrators, faculty, and staff participated in fundraising efforts at a higher rate than their counterparts in Waterloo.

Many philanthropic projects were purposely designed to consolidate the campus's identity and its relationship to the community. One of Brantford's most enduring legacies began with the Colborne Street bookstore that gave rise to the Stedman Department Store chain. The last manager of the store was Mary Stedman. She and her sisters, Margaret and Ruth, made philanthropy a key

The Brantford campus's associate director of development, Sherri Bocchini, in front of the campus donor board that recognizes major donations to the campus.

element of their lives in Brantford and Brant County. Mary supported the push for university education in the early days, before it became a cause that almost everyone supported. She and her sisters were generous when Laurier came to Brantford. We were looking for a way to better recognize their support when the right opportunity came with plans to establish a new university bookstore only a few blocks from the original Stedman bookstore. A donation by Ruth and Mary allowed the campus to make it a one-of-a-kind bookstore that will be named the Stedman Community Bookstore. The name celebrates not only their donation, but also the history of the downtown and the campus's connection to it. Historical effects from the last instantiation of the original Stedman bookstore are included in the donation to its Laurier descendant.[8]

Other goodwill gestures that built the Brantford campus's ties to the community came from downtown churches. They opened their doors for university functions, welcomed members of the university community into their congregations, and partnered on charitable works. When Grace Anglican, founded in 1830, approached me to discuss ways in which it might support the university's growth downtown, the result was a decision to turn the church's 1905 rectory into St. Stephen's House, a residence and chaplaincy centre for students attending Laurier and Nipissing. When a 2006 fire destroyed St. Andrew's United, the church across from the Student Centre, the congregation restored its heritage exterior but redesigned the interior, in part to make it a space that could be used by the university.

The positive partnership Laurier Brantford established with the community around it has gone a great distance in turning downtown Brantford into a post–Brant Fordian community. A progressive provincial government could have learned from the Brantford experience and turned it into a model for higher education and urban development across the province. Because a good idea is hard to stop, the absence of such leadership did not prevent the spread of the Brantford model, which was emulated by other Ontario municipalities that very quickly saw its merits. Just twenty-five minutes from Brantford, the City of Cambridge and the University of Waterloo's School of Architecture established a downtown campus, moving the school from a nondescript, architecturally unimaginative building in Waterloo to a refurbished historic silk mill situated on the banks of the Grand River. Like Brantford, Cambridge embraced its new campus, which revelled in positive community relations and a progressive partnership between the city and the school. In support of the initiative, the city contributed eight million dollars. Thirty local business leaders raised another twelve million in support.

In an attempt to revive its ailing downtown, the City of Kitchener studied Brantford and then embarked on a thirty-five-million-dollar plan to make it a place for university education. The initial project in the reinvention of its downtown moved Laurier's Faculty of Social Work from the Waterloo campus to a wonderfully restored 1909 high school. A second project was a University of Waterloo health sciences campus that includes a school of pharmacy. The Region of Waterloo contributed fifteen million dollars in additional support to bring a McMaster University medical program to the same site. The new health sciences campus was housed in new buildings located on a reclaimed industrial site downtown.

In view of Laurier's success in Brantford, the City of Orillia asked the university to consider establishing another satellite campus there. President Rosehart, Vice-President Smith, and I drove to Orillia to inspect the proposed site, a sequence of old buildings that had served as a mental institution (a use that precipitated many jokes about those among us and our fellow Laurier administrators and professors who belonged inside a mental institution).

The School of Architecture, the University of Waterloo. The campus opened in September 2004.

The buildings were scattered on a beautiful plot of beachfront land but one that was in a poor state of repair. Smith dismissed them with a disdainful look and the comment, "These are rickety old buildings. There is nothing to match the Carnegie Library." A residence building that the Ontario Provincial Police had used to train its SWAT teams was riddled with bullet holes. The president left skeptical and told the Orillia development committee that Laurier's plate was full. He suggested they contact Lakehead University in Thunder Bay. They opened the doors of an Orillia satellite campus in September 2006, at

Courtesy of Mary Basler.

Laurier held a Grand Opening for its new Hallman School of Social Work on September 6, 2006. The project turned a vacant heritage high school in downtown Kitchener into new premises for the Faculty of Social Work.

a site in downtown Orillia. Like Brantford, the campus's curriculum combined multidisciplinary studies and a concurrent education program.

In Stratford, a saga with more twists than its Shakespeare plays began with a partnership the city formed with Breakwell Education Association, a not-for-profit corporation dedicated to academic excellence and moral education. It attempted to establish the Stratford College of Liberal Arts, a college with a curriculum inspired by Baha'i principles. The college worked its way through a formal approval process conducted by Ontario's Post-Secondary Education Quality Assessment Board, and looked set to go until the minister of training, colleges and universities went against the recommendation of the Board and refused to accredit the college. The refusal drew much public criticism.[9] In the aftermath, Stratford formed an alliance with the University of Waterloo, which put together a plan for a liberal arts campus with a curriculum much like the one that informed the initial Laurier Brantford. When that plan lost its momentum, the university and the city replaced it with a plan for a campus and research centre focused on global business and digital media. Open Text, a Waterloo based software company, has pledged ten million dollars toward the initiative.

Numerous other satellite campuses are in the planning stage. Officials from the city and the University of Guelph have visited Brantford as they prepare plans for their own downtown initiative. In Burlington, McMaster University, Halton Region, and the city have raised twenty million dollars to fund the development of a satellite campus focused on business and medicine. Milton, the fastest growing community in Canada, is working with a new Laurier president, Max Blouw, to try to establish a satellite campus on a greenfield site close to the 401. The initiative began when Milton saw what was happening in Brantford and elsewhere, and sent a letter to every university in the province, promising free land to any institution willing to establish a satellite campus in Milton. When Laurier first visited and Blouw told them that the parcel of land they offered was too small to be worth the effort, they promptly located and then secured a sixty-hectare parcel of undeveloped land bordering the Niagara Escarpment.

In other provinces in Canada, other universities have embarked on projects that tie new campuses to urban renewal. In Vancouver, Simon Fraser University has established a thriving Harbour Front campus that incorporates the 1927 Spencer Building and a refurbished 1916 Bank of Montreal. For the past five years, students at the University of Calgary have been engaged in downtown initiatives that will culminate in a downtown campus. The University of Manitoba has placed the William Norrie Centre, designed to teach an inner-city program in social work, on Selkirk Avenue in Winnipeg, next door to a seedy downtown bar known for drug dealing.[10]

It will take time to glean whatever lessons can be learned from all the satellite projects that have followed in the wake of Laurier's experiment in Brantford. Urban redevelopment through campus development is an idea whose time has come. Much may be accomplished in those cases where campuses are, like the one at Brantford, designed as vehicles for downtown revitalization. No one should imagine that downtown campuses are a panacea for all the problems that have attended the decline of the

North American downtown. But one cannot look at the results in Brantford and ignore the possibility that similar initiatives elsewhere could make a major contribution to the revitalization of the North American downtown.

A FUTURE LIKE THE PAST

The arrival of a university did bring downtown Brantford back to life. Streets that were deserted a decade ago are alive again, connecting students, staff, faculty, and residents to the campus and the developments that support it. The new focus on higher education has combined well with the downtown's more traditional activities: municipal government, artistic and cultural events, the courts, social programming, active churches, and journalism. For the first time in many years, everyone envisages a positive future for Brantford's historic core. A once-defunct downtown is springing back to life.

The ancient philosopher Heraclitus is famous for his dictum that "Everything is in flux." The change that he embraced has been described as a never-ending cycle of birth and death and birth. In Brantford, the cycle was manifest in the birth and death, and the ultimate rebirth, of downtown Brantford. To celebrate the transition this made possible, the Brantford Arts Block, an organization dedicated to art and culture downtown, organized a funeral for the old downtown. On June 7, 2008, a group of dignitaries followed a coffin pulled by bicycles. With music in the background, the procession wound its way down an art-festooned Colborne Street to formal ceremonies in the new Harmony Square.

Formal eulogies remembered the old downtown and the events that gave rise to it. Before Six Nations, the Grand River Valley was the hunting ground of the Mississauga. In 1784, in recognition of Joseph Thayendanegea Brant's attacks on the Americans in the War of Independence, England gave the land

The Reverend Barry Pridham of Sydenham United Church prepares for the funeral for the downtown, in front of the painted casket symbolizing its remains. Photo by Heather King.

Courtesy of the Brantford Arts Block.

to Six Nations. In 1805, John Stalts erected the first log cabin on the hill beside today's Lorne Bridge. Legitimately or illegitimately, a series of land transactions led to a growing settlement. Grand River Ferry was a place to cross the river at the juncture of the road that became Colborne Street. Travellers to Hamilton and Buffalo and London and Detroit stopped for rest and whisky, and agriculture flourished in the surrounding area. In 1826 or 1827, the village was named Brant's Ford, after the ford that Brant made famous. The names Biggar Town and Lewisville were advocated by Mr. Biggar and

J.S. Hamilton was a successful Brantford businessman who was a member of the first city council in 1878. In 1888, he became the first president of the Pelee Island Wine and Vineyards Company, which amalgamated with J.S. Hamilton and Company in 1919.

Courtesy of Pelee Island Winery.

Mr. Lewis, but rejected. As Brant's Ford became Brantford, the downtown flourished, spreading along the sides of Colborne Street. At the bottom of Colborne Hill, the Grand River Navigation Company built a canal to connect Brantford industry to other settlements, but the advent of railways quickly rendered it obsolete.

By the end of the nineteenth century, Brantford was booming. In the heart of its downtown, its success was evident in parks, buildings, stores, and well-to-do homes. A flair for industry and business made it one of the most important exporting cities in the country. Brash and self-assured, Brantford described itself as The Greatest and Best Known Manufacturing City in Canada.[1] Over the course of a century, the city and the downtown were a key location for the activities of an impressive group of businesses and manufacturers. They included, among many others: A.G. Spalding, Barber-Ellis, the Brantford Box Company, the Waterous Engine Works, J.O. Wisner, the Verity Plow Company, Cockshutt Plow, A. Harris & Son, Massey-Harris, Massey Ferguson, Goold, Shapley and Muir Company, the Goold Bicycle Company, White Farm, S.C. Johnson and Son Ltd., Schultz Bros., and Stedman Stores.[2]

For most of the twentieth century, the city remained prosperous and the downtown healthy, though its growth did not match that of its competitors. Increasingly, the local economy focused on agricultural manufacturing.

In the 1980s the Brantford economy collapsed. The fall of White Farm, Massey Ferguson, and their suppliers left Brantford reeling. At the centre of the city, the financial problems and the rise of the suburbs undermined the downtown, which degenerated into a frail and feeble image of its former self. Mega-projects designed to resuscitate the core of the city failed. The building of Massey House, an Eaton's mall, and the Icomm Centre could not curtail the downward spiral. There were no public funerals to mark the transition, but the downtown was, for all intents and purposes, dead. The businesses and residents that could find a way to leave fled a rising sea of boarded-up, dilapidated buildings. Those that remained were marginalized in an increasingly bleak and desperate setting.

The death of Brantford's downtown was not marked until 2008 because no one cared enough to provide a decent funeral. A proper burial was arranged only after a new downtown was born. Like a person wanting to commemorate his parents, it wanted to mark the passing of the old — all the more so given that the transition to the new downtown had not been an easy one. The newly re-emerging downtown Brantford faced skepticism every step along the way. Many turned a blind eye to the problems festering downtown. Others rejected key initiatives as a waste of money. Those who supported change frequently disagreed with one another, pushing the downtown in different directions. Despite the obstacles, things began to change. The Sanderson Centre was refurbished and re-opened as an inspiring theatre. A controversial, but highly successful, charity casino opened. In 1999, after other attempts to bring post-secondary downtown failed, Laurier opened the doors of a tiny university campus.

Initially, the campus faltered, but then found its stride. It established partnerships with Mohawk College and Nipissing University, which followed it downtown. Innovative programming, dedicated

Courtesy of Brant Museum and Archives, 9984612.

In Brantford, Emily Howard Stowe became the first woman principal of a public school in Upper Canada. After family illnesses sparked an interest in herbal and homeopathic remedies, she went on to become the first woman to practise medicine in Canada, and the second licensed woman physician in 1880. She was a prominent early suffragist, considered by some to be the mother of the movement in Canada.

staff and faculty, and the support of the community allowed the campus to grow much more quickly than anyone thought possible. In one decade, the results were impressive: enrollment grew from forty to more than two thousand full-time students; the number of full-time employees rose from five to more than a hundred; the campus footprint expanded from one to fourteen buildings; over twenty million dollars was raised to support the project. The gains were consolidated with student-housing projects, commercial developments, and cultural activities that reinforced the new focus on higher education. Against the odds, the downtown found a way to reinvent itself.

The most significant feature of the new downtown was not its new streetscapes, but a rejuvenated confidence; a feeling that the downtown was headed in a direction that would make it what it was historically — a place that mattered. Unlike earlier attempts to rehabilitate the old downtown, this new approach allowed it to leave its mark on its new offspring — an offspring that embraced and revived the history of downtown Brantford while it embarked on a new and very different future. The face of the old downtown was still evident in buildings that included a 1902 Carnegie library, a former Dominion-Grocery-Store-turned-Toronto-Dominion-Bank, an abandoned 1947 Odeon theatre, an 1870 mansion built by one of Brantford's founding families, an 1880 home, Brantford's first post office and customs house, and, in its later stages, a 1986 office building. Only a few years ago, many of the buildings sat vacant. In the worst cases, they were jarring eyesores in an extreme state of disrepair. When they had to be demolished, key projects replaced them with a revival style of architecture that consciously embraced Brantford's downtown past.

GRATEFUL RECOGNITION
OF THE INVENTOR OF
THE TELEPHONE

ALEXANDER GRAHAM BELL

Courtesy of Kevin Klein.

Laurier students (Kaitlin Reaume, Zachary Mealia, and Amanda Flanagan) pose at the large, Lincoln-like statue of Alexander Graham Bell that commemorates Brantford's most famous thinker at the entrance to the Bell Building downtown.

More deeply, the new downtown's emphasis on higher education and culture has some affinities with Brantford's intellectual past, which included important authors, thinkers, and artists known around the world. They included Alexander Graham Bell, Emily Howard Stowe, the poet Pauline Johnson, Sara Jeannette Duncan, Thomas B. Costain, James Hillier, Debra Brown, and Lawren Harris. Underneath Brantford's success as a manufacturing centre lay a spirit of experiment and inventiveness that finds an intellectual analogue in its status as a new home for post-secondary education. The passing of the old downtown has been remembered in a funeral, but its spirit of thinking and pushing beyond the commonplace lies beneath the surface of the new downtown that has replaced it. There has been a funeral but not without an heir.

It is difficult to predict what will happen to downtown Brantford and its post-secondary campus in the future. When Laurier came downtown, many doubted it would stay. During its first five years in Brantford, it leased the Carnegie Building for one dollar a year. The city would not give the building to Laurier because it worried that the university might sell it, take the proceeds, and run back to Waterloo. Doubts of this kind persisted long after the university had made an irreversible decision to stay. It took years, but such concerns were eventually extinguished. The university now owns the Carnegie Building. No one believes that Laurier Brantford will head back to Waterloo. Everyone expects it to expand.

In a very different way, the campus's future trajectory remains a matter of debate. Many in Brantford have their hearts set on an independent university.

President Rosehart sometimes called the Brantford campus "my Quebec." Like Quebec, Brantford has a zealous pride of place. It is difficult to say what reigniting it will lead to. It is not hard to find prominent Brantfordians who envisage an Alexander Graham Bell University that would combine the city's post-secondary operations within a downtown institution named after Brantford's most famous thinker. Such a future may or may not come to be. The history of universities in Ontario includes many cases where universities split like amoebae. In 2008, Algoma University separated from Laurentian and became a separate institution. Laurier was once a college of its rival, the University of Western Ontario, and the University of Waterloo separated from Laurier. Nipissing was once part of Laurentian. Whatever happens in Brantford, the most important question is not one of separation, but of how the campuses downtown can build on their successes and flourish in a way that furthers the interests of the different communities they embrace — communities that include not only their faculty, students, and their downtown neighbours, but the province, the nation, and ultimately the world.

| EPILOGUE |

Brantford's downtown continues to evolve. At Laurier, President Rosehart has retired. Reflecting on what happened in Brantford, he compares it to a romantic relationship. "The city was spurned by other universities. Laurier was ripe for a new relationship. They came together and produced an offspring, Contemporary Studies, which captured the imagination of the academic community." Both Laurier and Brantford managed their aspects of the project well. "Laurier did a great job making itself an integral part of the community." Brantford made a wise and courageous choice when it decided to reinvest its share of casino profits in post-secondary education. "Without the city's capital funding, Laurier Brantford would have failed. Every time I received it, I was told not to come back for more, but I always did, and the city always gave me more!" The crowning idea that glued the campus together was the Heritage Block, which successfully tied the new Brantford to the old.

A new Laurier president, Max Blouw, strongly supports Brantford growth. His decisions have been supported by federal and provincial governments, which have recognized Brantford as a city that deserves post-secondary spending. In the wake of the 2008 financial crisis, both levels of government agreed to allocate a portion of their multi-billion-dollar stimulus spending to Laurier Brantford, providing twenty-six million dollars for a new research and academic centre. The city is contributing $2.4 million to the project. With the help of the municipal, the provincial, and the federal governments, the university has committed fifty-two million dollars to new capital projects in downtown Brantford.

The scope of the campus's current construction projects was unimaginable ten years earlier. Its evolution will continue with new offices and classrooms, the campus's first significant research space, food services, residences; and a campus bookstore. Gifts from the Ruth and Mary Stedman will make The Stedman Community Bookstore an expansive space designed to integrate sales to the university and the community. The campus's new buildings will be designed in a style that complements the heritage style the university has already established. Other projects will refurbish old Brantford buildings in the style that has come to characterize downtown Brantford. The new buildings will be the most energy-efficient in Brantford, incorporating Laurier's first LEED (Leadership in Energy and Environmental Design) project.

In a gesture that symbolizes the transformation of the downtown, the university has bought Moody's — a sleazy strip bar that was the epitome of seedy downtown Brantford when the university arrived. Dean Read's first office on the second floor of a former Royal Bank overlooked the bar. It was an awkward office with windows that provided a plain view of naked strippers walking around the club. As the university took root and the downtown began to move forward, the strip bar remained — an awkward blemish on a recuperating downtown. The city eventually bought the building as a way to usher the club out of the downtown. The city sold it to Laurier. In the aftermath, some have suggested that the university should preserve the poles the dancers used in the club, as a gesture that would preserve the downtown's heritage.

Another project will renovate a 1907 Bank of Commerce building constructed in the classic revival style. A building that represents the heyday of Brantford's rise as an industrial economy, it features three additions from other periods. The restoration will preserve many of the key architectural elements of the building. The bank's location will strengthen the university's presence on Market Street, the street that connects the north and the south sides of the campus. The building will house a co-op program that would assign Laurier students to work placements in the community.

Other plans are in the making. Mohawk College is expanding its downtown operations. A new president would like to move the entire Brantford campus from Elgin Street to a location in the city core. This would bring hundreds more faculty and staff and

Dalhousie St. showing Bank of Commerce, Brantford, Canada.

Courtesy of the Brantford Heritage Inventory.

Two of the university's new projects will reclaim historically significant buildings. One began as the Woodbine Hotel in 1877. It was operating as a strip bar before the university acquired it. The other is the 1907 Bank of Commerce pictured here. The bank is part of a joined complex of four distinct buildings that were used by the Canadian Imperial Bank of Commerce for a century. The exterior of the original building remains almost unaltered.

thousands more students downtown. To promote post-secondary expansion, the city plans to expropriate forty properties on Colborne Street — all the buildings that stretch from the university's Grand River Hall to the riverfront. The properties will be a land bank available to post-secondary institutions that want to expand downtown. A joint YMCA/Laurier/Nipissing recreation centre has been proposed for this stretch of properties.

As the growth and development of the Brantford campus continues to feed the renewal of downtown, there will be challenges. Downtown post-secondary operations have grown dramatically for a decade. Continued growth will create internal issues that will have to be resolved as the university and its partners adjust to larger and more complex operations. New academic programs will have to be developed to fill the new post-secondary space that is planned for Brantford. They will have to be instituted in the middle of a global financial crisis that is creating serious problems for university budgets in Ontario. As it has in the past, the university, its partners, and the city will have to find creative ways to steer around these obstacles. They will need to do so in the context of a continuing debate and discussion of the ideal size and the role of the downtown campus.

The City of Brantford will need to decide the right mix of activities downtown. Any skepticism the city had about the role of the university evaporated thousands of students ago. In the midst of the successes so far, it will need to find ways to reinforce the gains it has made at the same time that it broadens downtown activities so that they extend beyond post-secondary ones. The old downtown collapsed because the city was built around one industry — agricultural manufacturing — which ultimately failed. Higher education is inherently adaptable, but a downtown which is wholly devoted to student housing and post-secondary development raises its own issues.

If Brantford wants a balanced downtown, it will need to find ways to include other kinds of residential development. It will need to integrate post-secondary activities with other cultural, business, and government pursuits, not push other possibilities away. Ten years ago, Brantford had the foresight to begin a major reinvention of its old downtown. If it is to continue to flourish, it needs to consolidate its gains as it engages a process of continual reinventing.

| APPENDIX A |

Proposal to Wilfrid Laurier University
(Excerpt)

Proposal to
Wilfrid Laurier University

To Locate a University
in the
City of Brantford

May 1998

Brant University Committee
and
The City of Brantford

EXECUTIVE SUMMARY

This proposal to Wilfrid Laurier University demonstrates the community's ongoing desire, dedication and strong commitment to establish a university in Brantford.

The proposal contains significant contributions of financial resources, human resources, and community partnerships to attract Wilfrid Laurier University to locate a campus in Brantford including:

(A)   Use of a renovated Carnegie Library building on historic Victoria Square.

(B)   Renovations to the Carnegie building to suit the University's needs. Renovations to be complete by August 1999. The value of these renovations is estimated at $910,000.

(C)   Reservation of space for a period of three years in the Provincial Court House for use by Wilfrid Laurier.

(D)   Renovations to the Court House building to meet code requirements for disabled access and washrooms for 100 seat and 50 seat lecture theatres. The value of these renovations is estimated at $225,000.

(E)   Subsidized operating costs for the Carnegie Building consisting of utility costs to a value of $25,000 for a period of 3 years.

The value of the above commitments totals $1,210,000.

In addition, and as part of the ongoing efforts to ensure Wilfrid Laurier is part of the community for the long term, the following commitments are being made:

(A)   Seed money of $2 million to go towards the completion of Phase Two has been identified and committed by the City.

(B)   Identification of, negotiations with, and procurement of other locations and funding, suitable for expansion purposes, will be undertaken in cooperation with Wilfrid Laurier University.

(C)   Ongoing capital fundraising for the University will be undertaken by the Brant University Committee and the Grand Valley Education Society. A professional fundraiser has already been retained for this purpose.

(D)   Ongoing Student bursary and scholarship fundraising will be undertaken by the Brant University Committee and the Grand Valley Education Society. A professional fundraiser has already been retained for this purpose.

(E)   Ongoing liaison, linkage and negotiations with community partners including: the Brantford Public Library, the Sanderson Centre for the Performing Arts, the YMCA and other recreational facilities, the two district Boards of Education, daycare, housing and other social agencies etc. operating within the community, will be undertaken to use existing community assets and services and to make the community a partner in the university.

(F)   Marketing and promotion of the University will be included in all community promotional materials produced.

(G)   Liaison and cooperation with City departments such as Engineering, Parks and Recreation, Economic Development etc. will be forged.

In return for these substantial contributions, commitments will be sought from Wilfrid Laurier University to accomplish the following objectives:

(A)   Establish a presence in the community by March, 1999.

(B)   Offer a distinctive full University degree program, by September 1, 1999, such that students would be able to obtain a University degree without leaving the community.

(C)   Set up the operations of the Brantford campus as a Federated independent college, with autonomy and independent decision making capabilities, within 10 years.

(D)   Seek community input into and give 12 months notice of any changes or reductions to curriculum or programs to be offered in Brantford.

(E)   Commit to making an annual report to the Community on the University.

(F)   Ensure active community involvement and participation in the community.

The purpose of this proposal is to present a package and vision to encourage and assist Wilfrid Laurier University to locate a campus in Brantford. The proposal is also meant to convey the extensive support, commitment, cooperation and endorsement from the community for Laurier.

It is hoped that from this proposal, an immediate process for dialogue and discussion will be set in motion, to ensure a University in Brantford becomes not just a dream but a reality.

| APPENDIX B |

Agreement Between the City of Brantford and Wilfrid Laurier University, Articles I and XV

THIS INDENTURE made this 10 day of January, 1999

IN PURSUANCE OF THIS SHORT FORMS OF LEASES ACT

BETWEEN:

THE CORPORATION OF THE CITY OF BRANTFORD
Hereinafter called the "City" or the "Landlord"

OF THE FIRST PART;

-and-

WILFRID LAURIER UNIVERSITY
(hereinafter called the "University" or the "Tenant")

OF THE SECOND PART;

WHEREAS the City and the University are entering into this Agreement for the purpose of providing premises in the City of Brantford where the University can establish a "degree granting program" in the City of Brantford and with the intention of establishing at some time in the future a permanent campus in Brantford;

AND WHEREAS the parties have agreed upon the terms under which the City will provide such premises as hereinafter set forth:

ARTICLE I
Demise and Term

Sections 1.01 Premises

WITNESSETH that in consideration of the rents, covenants and agreements hereinafter respectively reserved and contained and in consideration of the Tenant establishing and continuing a "university degree granting program" in the City of Brantford, the Landlord doth hereby demise and lease unto the Tenant, that certain parcel or tract of land and premises situate, lying and being in the City of Brantford, known as the "Carnegie Building", located at 73 George Street in the said City of Brantford and described as more particular set out in Schedule "A" to this lease.

Section 1.02 Term

TO HAVE AND TO HOLD the demised premises, for and during the term of five (5) years commencing on the first day of May, 1999 and to end on the 30th of April, 2004. Provided however that, unless terminated pursuant to the terms of this Lease, and provided that the University continues to provide the "minimum university program" in the City of Brantford this lease shall be automatically renewed for further 5 year terms upon the expiry of any term.

Section 1.03 Definition of University Degree Granting Program

In this lease the phrase "University Degree Granting Program" mean the General Bachelor of Arts (B.A.) program (and/or any similar University level degree offered by the University and approved by the City.)

Section 1.04 Definition of the "minimum university program"

In this lease the phrase "minimum university program" means that the University will provide the University Degree Granting Program to a sufficient number of full-time students annual in the City of Brantford (commencing in September 1999) to make the program viable. For the purpose of this lease the program is considered viable when sufficient students are registered that a reasonable operator of a similar university program in a similar facility would consider that the program should be continued.

ARTICLE XV
Special Provisions

15.01 Tenant's Renovations

The Tenant shall carry out such renovations and repairs, including any necessary capital repairs as defined in this lease, as are necessary to make the demised premises suitable for use as a University in accordance with Article IX of this Lease at its sole expense.

15.02 Landlord's Loan

15.02.1   In order to facilitate the improvements to the demised premises which are to be carried out by the Tenant as referred to in Section 15.01 the Landlord shall provide the University with a load (without interest) in the amount of nine hundred and ten thousand dollars ($910,000) in accordance with the following provisions:

    a)   The loan monies shall be used only for improvements to and renovations made to the Carnegie Building or for tenant's fixtures and equipment to be used in the demised premises;

    b)   The loan monies shall be advanced upon receipt of invoices or other evidence of expenditures or expenses incurred in accordance with this section;

    c)   All of the said monies shall be advanced on or before the 30th day of September, 1999 and the City shall have no obligation to advance any further monies subsequent to that date.

15.02.2   The University acknowledges its indebtedness to the City and covenants and agrees to repay the loan to the City upon the following terms:

    a)   The said loan shall be repayable upon the expiry or other termination of this lease;

    b)   The University will discharge the loan by providing the "minimum university program" as defined in this Lease over a period of 5 years commencing in September of 1999;

    c)   Each year that the "minimum university program" in provided for at least the period from September to April shall reduce the outstanding loan by the sum of one hundred and eighty-two thousand dollars ($182,000.00);

    d)   For the purposes of this section the provision of the "minimum university program" by the University at premises within the City of Brantford other than at the demised premises, (in the event that an alternative or permanent campus is provided in the City of Brantford) shall also count towards the reduction of the loan and shall not require the repayment of the said loan.

15.03 Contribution towards Operating Costs

In addition to the Landlord's Loan, the Landlord agrees to make a grant to the University in the amount of twenty-five thousand dollars ($25,000.00) towards the operating costs of the demised premises in each of the calendar years 2000, 2001 and 2002 provided that this Lease is in full force and effect and the Tenant is not in default of its obligations pursuant to this Lease. The said payments shall be made on or before the 5th day of January in each of the said calendar years.

15.04 Alternative Campus Established

In the event that the University find that the Carnegie Building does not satisfy the requirements of the University in order to satisfactorily offer the "minimum university program" in the City and the University moves the Brantford Campus to another location within the City, the City of Brantford will pay to the University the amount of any capital investment made by the University in the Carnegie Building, to assist the University in re-establishing its Brantford Campus at a different location within the City, provided:

a)   the monies used by the University to make such capital investment were not donated or raised within the County of Brant, or

b)   the improvements are not transferable to the new location, and

c)   that prior to making such capital investment in the Carnegie Building, the University obtained the approval of the City of Brantford in writing that this paragraph would apply with respect to such investment, and

d)   the monies paid to the University are re-invested in the Brantford Campus of the said University.

15.05 Establishment of Permanent Campus

The City of Brantford will commit the sum of two million dollars ($2,000,000.00) towards the establishment of a permanent campus or towards the capital cost of the expansion of the University's activities in the City of Brantford. For the purpose of this Section the said funding will be available for any capital project which expands

252 REINVENTING BRANTFORD

the Brantford Campus of the University beyond the Carnegie Building and provides for an annual attendance of a minimum of 400 or more fulltime students in Brantford.

15.06 Use of Sanderson Centre

Subject to its availability, the City is prepare to enter into mutually satisfactory arrangements with the University for the use of the Sanderson Centre for the Performing Arts for University purposes.

| APPENDIX C |

Proclamation by the Brantford Town Crier on the Commencement of the Laurier Brantford Campus Campaign

OYEZ! OYEZ! OYEZ!

Your Worship, honoured dignitaries, good Brantfordians, welcome visitors from near and far: Be it known that the need for a degree-granting institution which would allow the bright young minds of Brantford to achieve their highest academic goals whilst remaining at home, is now met with a unique partnership.

The City of Brantford has donated the historic Carnegie Building and some funding in order that the venerable Wilfrid Laurier University may provide educational programmes of the first order within Brantford.

But, funding for equipment and student assistance are still necessary. And so, the Grand Valley Education Society, whose mandate is to enhance post-secondary education in our community, has

picked up the torch to raise two million dollars.

Now therefore, it is my pleasureful duty to

Proclaim underway the Laurier Brantford Campus Campaign.

May your generosity light a beacon of knowledge that will forever shine in Brantford.

Cried this 29th day of April, 1999.

God save the Queen.

David V. McKee, Town Crier, Brantford

| APPENDIX D |

Expositor Editorial on the Official Opening of the Brantford Campus, October 2, 1999

THE BEST IS YET TO COME

In the life of a community, with all of its twists, turn, ups and down, it is rare when you can point to one event and say: "This changed history."

One of those rare events took place on Friday with the official opening of the Brantford Campus of Wilfrid Laurier University.

The opening of Laurier in the old Carnegie Library building plugs two holes — one real, one psychological.

The real one was the absence of an easily accessible university that students could attend while living at home. While most high-school grads are eager to leave their hometown to attend university, if only of the novelty of the experience, not everyone is in a position to do so. Some students don't have the money, some can't because of family commitments, and some won't, simply because they already like where they are.

The opening of Laurier plugs that hole.

The second hole is the psychological one. Brantford has a long and illustrious history; over the years it was an economic powerhouse, it's name known across the continent for its manufactured ware; it has sent premiers to Queen's Park and top-ranking cabinet ministers off to Ottawa.

But, somehow, Brantford never quite has the cache of a Kingston, Kitchener-Waterloo or London. They were college towns, where the province's best were educated before they packed up and went out to conquer the world. Brantford ... well, it was a place where you packed your lunch bucket before going out onto the factory floor.

The addition of Laurier to the Brantford community plugs that psychological hole, too. Though there may only be a few score students in the delightful old library — only a tenth of the number of students who might take one first-year course at a major school — it is enough that they are there, attending class, at a university, in Brantford. We have arrived.

Even bigger than the impact Laurier has on the city today is the rich promise it offers for the future. The 50-plus students of today could become 500-plus in five years. It could be 1,000–2,000 a decade from now. That's thousands of people each year, contributing to the energy of the city, helping it to reach its potential as they reach their own.

The next few years could be a magical and inspiring time in the history of Brantford. And it all started on a sunny, crisp fall day in October.

| NOTES |

Foreword

1. Storm Cunningham, "The Healing Economy," in *The World and I* (September/October 2005), 70. See also Storm Cunningham, *The Restoration Economy* (San Francisco: Berrett-Koehler Publishers, 2002).

2. See Storm Cunningham, *reWealth!* (New York: McGraw-Hill, 2008).

Introduction

1. Eric Lloyd, "Brantford Bids Final Farewell to the Old Downtown," Brantford.com, June 12, 2008, *www.brantford.com/index.cfm?page=home&section=News&id=436* (accessed May 15, 2009).

2. Pierre Filion, Heidi Hoernig, Trudi Bunting, and Gary Sands, "The Successful Few," in *Journal of the American Planning Association*, Vol. 70, No. 3 (Summer 2004), 328.

3. Robert M. Fogelson, *Downtown: Its Rise and Fall, 1880–1950*, (New Haven, CT: Yale University Press, 2001), 5.

4. *Ibid.*

Chapter 1: Brant's Ford

1. Bell described Brantford as "the birthplace of the telephone," though the idea and the plans for creating the device were made in Brantford and the first telephone built in Boston. As Bell himself put it: "the Brantford telephone was made in Boston." See F. Douglas Reville, *History of the County of Brant*, (Brantford, ON: Hurley Printing, 1982), 320. Reprint of the 1920 edition.

2. Life in Brantford was the setting for Sara Jeanette Duncan's widely acclaimed 1904 novel, *The Imperialist*, which remains a must-read for anyone interested in Canadian literature. When the *Literary Review of Canada* made a listing of Canada's 100 Most Important Books, Vol. 16, No. 1 (January/February 2006), they ranked *The Imperialist* as number 10. Thomas Costain began his career as a sports reporter on the *Brantford Courier*, became the editor of *Maclean's* magazine and *The Saturday Evening Post*, and wrote a series

of bestselling novels that were turned into Hollywood movies.

3. Contemporary Brantfordians of note include the comedian Phil Hartman, the poet Pauline "Tekahionwake" Johnson, actors Jay Silverheels and Graham Greene, Robbie Robertson, lead singer of The Band; and Debra Brown, whose choreography has been featured in the Cirque du Soleil, New York Opera, Madonna, and the Olympic games.

4. See John Robertson, *History of the Brantford Congregational Church, 1820 to 1920: With Some Account of the Story of the Puritans ... the Migration of the Family of Mr. John Aston Wilkes to Canada ...* (Renfrew, ON: Renfrew Mercury Printing, 1920), 28. The book is available on the Our Roots: Canada's Local Histories Online, *www.ourroots.ca/f/toc.aspx?id=2761*.

5. For a very detailed account of Brant and his life, see William L. Stone, *Life of Joseph Brant-Thayendanegea: Including the Border Wars of the American Revolution, and Sketches of the Indian Campaigns of Generals Harmar, St. Clair, and Wayne, and Other Matters Connected with the Indian Relations of the United States and Great Britain, From the Peace of 1783 to the Indian Peace of 1795.* Vols. 1 and 2. (New York: Alexander V. Blake, 1838). A complete digital version of the book is available on Google Books, *books.google.ca/books?id=vbsRAAAAYAAJ&dq=joseph+brant&printsec*, or on the website of the Brantford Public Library (BPL), *brantford.library.on.ca/genealogy/pdfs/jbrant1.pdf* and *brantford.library.on.ca/genealogy/pdfs/jbrant2.pdf*. For

a recent account of Brant, see James Paxton, *Joseph Brant and His World: 18th Century Mohawk Warrior and Statesman.* (Toronto: James Lorimer & Company Ltd., 2008).

6. Alan Taylor. *The Divided Ground: Indians, Settlers, and the Northern Borderland of the American Revolution* (New York: Knopf, 2006), which discusses the details of what happens.

7. C.M. Johnston, *Brant County: A History 1784–1945* (Toronto: Oxford University Press, 1967), 5–7. Published under the auspices of the Ontario Historical Society.

8. (Author not identified) *The History of the County of Brant, Ontario* (Toronto: Warner, Beers, & Co., 1883), 263. A complete digital version of the book is available on the BPL website, *www.brantford.library.on.ca/genealogy/digital.php*.

9. Reville, 71–72.

10. For historical accounts of what happened, see Stone, Vol. 1, Chapter 13, 396–404; and Reville, 45–47. For the official Six Nations view of the land disputes see *www.sixnations.ca/LandsResources/ClaimSummaries.htm*. The aboriginal perspective on current events is well-presented by *Turtle Island News, www.turtleisland.org/news/news-sixnations.htm*.

11. Reville, 97.

12. Reville, 98, quoting "the late J.J. Hawkins" from "a paper read before the local Historical Society, some years ago, on the "Early Days in Brantford." Reville and Hawkins both emphasize that things were turbulent "for whites."

13. Reville, 97–99.

14. *The Industrial Recorder of Canada,* Vol. 1, Special Number (Brantford, 1901). A digital version of this edition of the paper is available on the BPL website, *www.brantford.library. on.ca/genealogy/pdfs/industrial.pdf.*

15. Thirteen between 1860 and 1997, according to the list kept by the public library, available on the BPL website, *www.brantford.library. on.ca/genealogy/royalvisits.php.*

Chapter 2: The Worst Downtown in Canada

1. In a personal interview with Mayor Mike Hancock, conducted on May 9, 2006.

2. *Hansard* (January 27, 1994), 467.

3. A style defined by its use of "rough, heavy reinforced concrete" and "chunky angular solids" "to reflect the harshness and the confusions of modern life," Archepedia Encyclopedia of Architecture, *www.archepedia.com*, accessed September 15, 2006.

4. Available at *www3.sympatico.ca/john.winter/ 1970s.htm*, accessed September 16, 2006.

5. Rod McQueen, *The Eatons: The Rise and Fall of Canada's Royal Family* (Toronto: Stoddart Publishing, 1998), 257.

6. Pierre Filion and Karen Hammond, "The Failure of Shopping Malls as a Tool of Downtown Revitalization in Mid-Size Urban Areas," in *Plan*, Vol. 46, No. 2 (Winter 2006).

7. From "The Internet Movie Database," *www. imdb.com/title/tt0384537*, accessed May 16, 2008.

8. The Grand River Navigation Company was created in 1832. Five dams, five locks, and two canals were built to connect communities along the river. The company was, in a number of ways, a disaster, and ceased operations in 1861. A significant portion of the financing came from Six Nations. The financing was arranged through the government without the proper formal consent of the Natives. For more information on the company, see Bruce Emerson Hill, *The Grand River Navigation Company* (Brantford, ON: Brant Historical Publications, 1994).

Chapter 3: In Andrew Carnegie's Footsteps

1. Opinions on Andrew Carnegie are mixed. In his account of Carnegie's donation to Brantford, C.M. Johnston writes that "The relieved ratepayer of Brantford was only dimly aware that he was indebted as well to those unnamed thousands who had toiled to make Pittsburgh's grimy industrial revolution such a profitable success for enterprisers of Carnegie's ilk." See *Brant County: A History, 1784–1945*, 88.

2. Joseph Frazier Wall, *Andrew Carnegie* (New York: Oxford University Press, 1970). For more on Andrew Carnegie, see Peter Krass, *Carnegie* (Hoboken, NJ: John Wiley and Sons, Inc, 2002).

3. The monument was dismantled in the 1960s, then reconstructed and rededicated in 1988.

4. Andrew Carnegie, *Autobiography of Andrew Carnegie*, John Charles Van Dyke, ed. (New York: Houghton Mifflin Company, 1920). The entire autobiography is available on the web at *www.wordowner.com/carnegie*, accessed May 16, 2008.

5. Johnston, 88.

6. "A Library Built to Last," *The Expositor*, December 16, 2002.

7. Gary Muir, "Public Library Born in Controversy," *The Expositor*, October 8, 1980, 41.

8. "Vast Sums Are Being Expended For New Buildings in City of Brantford This Year," *The Expositor*, July 5, 1904.

9. "Library Now Open: Large Crowds Inspected New Building Last Night," *The Expositor*, July 5, 1904.

10. John Merriman, "Public Library Suffers from Success," *Brant News*, June 6, 1979, 6.

11. David Judd, "Let's Move the Museum to the Library," *The Expositor*, June 24, 1989.

12. Gary Muir, "Carnegie Building May Get Reprieve from 'Death Row,'" *Brant News*, November 28, 1995, 9.

Chapter 4: A New Direction

1. Walter J.J. Szmigielski (assisted by Kathleen Pickard, supervised by Jack Herron), "An Historical Investigation of Trends in Post-Secondary Education in Brant County, 1784–1933," prepared for the Council on Continuing Education for Brantford and Brant County, May 1979.

2. *Sixteenth Annual Calendar of the Brantford Young Ladies' College*, Session 1890–91 (Brantford, ON: The Expositor Book and Job Printing House, 1890), 6. The calendar is available as a genealogical document at *brantford.library.on.ca/genealogy/pdfs/ladiescollege1890.pdf*, accessed on May 16, 2008.

3. Other members of the council included Scott Flicks, Terry Finley, Jack Herron, and Joan Avison.

4. The lecture series ran until 1999. It was named after one of Brantford's most prominent twentieth-century politicians, W. Ross Macdonald (1891–1976). He served as Brantford's member of Parliament, and became speaker of the House of Commons, Canada's solicitor general, and the lieutenant governor of Ontario. He served as the Chancellor of Wilfrid Laurier University (then Waterloo Lutheran University) from 1964–72.

5. Luciano Calenti, a pharmaceutical executive, tried to organize a university that would emphasize science programs and applied research.

6. As a manager in the Treasury, Trick was not directly responsible for universities and colleges, so Nixon arranged for Rick Donaldson to represent the Ministry of Colleges and Universities in the discussions.

7. Caroline Freibauer, "Moving Mohawk," *The Expositor*, October 4, 1997, A11. Freibauer says that the initial proposals were for a campus in downtown Brantford. This was contradicted by the members of the committee I spoke to. I have not been able to resolve the different accounts.

8. From a speech given by John Starkey on October 7, 1994.

9. *John Starkey for Mayor*, Election Pamphlet, October 1994.

10. Freibauer, *The Expositor*, A11.

11. Planworks, "The Right Time," 2, Draft of the *Brant Community Strategic Plan*, 1996.

12. *Brant Community Strategic Plan*, April 1997, 10. In keeping with developments discussed below, it recommends a "private" university.

Chapter 5: Chasing "UBC"

1. The Brant Community Futures Development Corporation, a federally funded non-profit agency that worked on the development of the Brant economy, renamed a less cumbersome Enterprise Brant. The corporation played a central role in the establishment of a university in Brantford.
2. City College Project Group, *University College of the Grand Valley: Business Plan (Draft)*, 4, presented to Brant Community Futures Development Corporation, November 1996.
3. The proposed curriculum was an interdisciplinary liberal arts amalgam designed to include a freshman year with courses in five core areas, and a unique university preparation course that would incorporate written communication, public speaking, research skills, computer literacy, thinking skills, and an introduction to the arts.
4. *Ibid.*, 34.
5. The committee eventually included many of the local figures who played a key role in bringing a university to Brantford: Doug Brown, Colleen Miller, Vyrt Sisson, John Wilson, Cindy Swanson, Len Park, Vern Gale, Sue Vincent, Ron Eddy, Karen Williamson, and others.
6. John Starkey, "Brantford Needs a University," In My Opinion, *The Expositor*, September 11, 1997, A3.

7. *Ibid.*
8. "School of Hard Knocks," *The Expositor*, October 2, 1997, A6.

Chapter 6: Three Ways

1. Freibauer, *The Expositor*, A11.
2. The meeting took place November 5, 1997.
3. The delegation included Bob Rosehart, Terry Copp, Rowland Smith, and Arthur Stephen.
4. Freibauer, *The Expositor*, A11.

Chapter 7: Leaning Toward Laurier

1. Susan Gamble, "WLU Still Interested in City," *The Expositor*, March 3, 1998, A1.
2. *Ibid.*
3. Elizabeth Meen, "University Plans Rolling Along," *The Expositor*, March 5, 1998, A5.
4. City of Brantford, Grand Valley Education Society, *Proposal to Wilfrid Laurier University to Locate a University in Brantford*, May 1998, 14 (Section 10.0, "Benchmarks to be Achieved").
5. *Ibid.*, 7 (Section 5.0, "The Vision: Phase II.")
6. Ross Marowits, "Council's Infighting Spoils Moment," *The Expositor*, May 19, 1998, 12.
7. Susan Gamble, "Looks Good for University," *The Expositor*, May 16, 1998, A1.

Chapter 8: A Timely Move

1. "Canada's Universities Look for Cash," *Economist*, September 17, 1998, 46.
2. Jennifer Lewington, "University Plan Excites Brantford," *Globe and Mail*, June 29, 1998.
3. Susan Gamble, "WLU Prefers Icomm Campus," *The Expositor*, September 15, 1998.

4.   City of Brantford–Wilfrid Laurier University "Memorandum of Agreement," October 26, 1998.
5.   Grand Valley Education Society/Wilfrid Laurier University "Memorandum of Agreement," November 10, 1998, Clause 3.
6.   *Ibid.*, Clause 6.
7.   Letters to the Editor, *The Expositor*, November 18, 1998.
8.   Chris Friel, quoted in Laurier's "Brantford Development Update, Winter '98."

Chapter 9: The Liberal Arts
1.   In place of a concentrated liberal arts approach, Canadian universities have tended to offer a broad array of specialized undergraduate, graduate, and professional programs. Within this mix, some universities found room for a liberal arts program (the Bachelor of Humanities at Carleton, the foundation year at King's College, and the Liberal Arts College at Concordia), but the great bulk of teaching has been assigned to specialized disciplines not integrated into a common liberal arts curriculum.
2.   Its members were Professor Copp, who had already played a key role pushing the university toward Brantford, Jane Rutherford, Peter Erb, Bob Sharpe, and myself.
3.   From an article by Susan Harada, "The McLachlin Group," in *The Walrus*, Vol. 6, No. 4 (May 2009), 20.
4.   The address was available on the website of the Association of Universities and Colleges of Canada for more than five years. A version of the address was published in *University Affairs*, April 2000.
5.   Legislative Assembly of Ontario, *Hansard*, October 21, 1999.
6.   This is the first point enumerated in the Brantford campus mission statement.

Chapter 10: A Grand Opening
1.   Especially active members of the GVES included John Wilson, Vern Gale, Paul Halyk, Doug Brown, David Chambers, Vyrt Sisson, John McGregor, Stuart Parkinson, Seig Holle, Cindy Swanson, Cathy Czikk, Sue Vincent, Pat Zorge, Karen Williamson, and Ron Eddy.
2.   The team consisted of Carolynn Wyckoff, Tracy Arabski, Holly Cox, Angela Madden, Professor Leslie O'Dell, Professor Peter Farrugia, and Professor Gary Warrick.
3.   From the GVES board meeting minutes, February 15, 2000.
4.   There was a remarkable amount of work to do. In addition to overseeing the building preparation, preparing all aspects of university operations, and liaising with the community, the university was discussing the possible co-production of a play with the Sanderson Centre; negotiating a partnership with the Brantford Public Library; and make arrangements with the YM/YWCA to provide students with access to recreational facilities.
5.   Susan Gamble, "Laurier Offers Cash to 'Pioneers': $500 Scholarship Awaits Students Enrolling at City Campus" *The Expositor*, March 18, 1999.
6.   "Laurier Enrolment Climbing," *The Expositor*, June 17, 1999.

7. "University Boom a Boon to Brantford, WLU Expert Says," *The Expositor*, March 18, 1999.

8. The situation was ignored and in some way misrepresented in the media. When the *Kitchener-Waterloo Record* reported that 140 students were enrolled, e.g., it conflated full-time and part-time students (the full-time equivalent enrollment was sixty to eighty), and ignored the fact that many of these 140 were seniors who were not paying tuition (see "WLU's Brantford Campus Welcomes 140 Students," *Record*, October 2, 1999).

9. "Colleen Miller Makes It Happen," *The Expositor*, January 22, 1999, 1.

10. Elizabeth Meen, "Campus 'The Birth of a Vision': Laurier Brantford Predicted to be Development of the Century," *The Expositor*, October 2, 1999, A6.

Chapter 11: The Wow and the Ow Factor

1. Elizabeth Meen, "Campus 'The Birth of a Vision': Laurier Brantford Predicted to be Development of the Century" *The Expositor*, October 2, 1999, 6.

2. *The Cord Weekly*, Vol. 40, No. 8 (October 6, 1999), 1.

3. "The Best Is Yet to Come," *The Expositor*, October 2, 1999.

4. GVES "Workplan" for the period April 1, 2000 to December 31, 2001.

5. "Brantford Fights Back," *Hamilton Spectator*, April 6, 2000.

6. Cheryl Bauslaugh, "Gypsy Production Derailed," *The Expositor*, November 20, 1999.

7. *The Cord Weekly*, March 22, 2000, 5.

8. Sometimes the university's supporters did not themselves appreciate the nuances of the university's point of view. In announcing the Brantford curriculum, *The Expositor* ran the headline "WLU Campus to Focus on Job Skills," and quoted John McGregor, who emphasized (in a manner that exaggerated, perhaps wishfully) the "business, communication, and information technology" aspects of the curriculum (Elizabeth Meen, "WLU Campus to Focus on Job Skills," *The Expositor*, November 3, 1998).

9. Michael Todd, "Wake Up Call: The Future of Liberal Arts in a Fast-Forward World," *Profiles: The York University Magazine for Alumni and Friends*, November 1998. Available at *www.yorku.ca/ycom/profiles/past/nov98/current/cover/cover2.htm*, accessed June 1, 2008. 10. Statement of the Ontario University Chancellors on the "Importance of University Education and the Value of the Liberal Arts," *York University Gazette Online*, Vol. 30, No. 23, March 8, 2000. Available at *www.yorku.ca/ycom/gazette/past/archive/2000/030800/issue.htm#10*, accessed June 3, 2008. 11. "School's In," in *Brantford Development Update*, Wilfrid Laurier University, Winter 1998.

Chapter 12: The Trouble with Brantford

1. Joe Rapai, letter to President Rosehart, October 27, 1999.

2. Cheryl Parker, "Laurier Should Have Teachers' College," *The Expositor*, March 29, 2000.

3. Jarrett Churchill, "Teachers' College Out at Laurier," *The Expositor*, March 29, 2000.

4. Memo from Brendan Ryan to the GVES Board of Directors, "Re: Update," April 17, 2000.
5. *Ibid.*

Chapter 13: Two Challenges
1. Dr. Stephen Haller.
2. For an account of the approach we took to curriculum, see Leo Groarke and Rowland Smith, "The Brantford Experiment: A Core Without A Core," in *Reforming Liberal Education and the Core After the Twentieth Century: Selected Papers from the Eighth Annual Conference of the Association for Core Texts and Courses*, J. Scott Lee, Darcy Wudel, Ronald J. Weber, eds. (Washington: University Press of America, 2006).

Chapter 14: Taking Up Residence
1. Reville, *History of the County of Brant*, 167.
2. Ron DeRuyter, "Campeau Will Build Office Tower in Core with MG as Major Tenant," *The Expositor*, July 3, 1985.
3. Dave Neumann, quoted in "City's Image Being Reshaped," *The Expositor*, April 17, 1986.
4. Michael Jiggens, "Massey House Now Underway," *Brant News*, April 23, 1986.
5. Remarks by R.F. Nixon in Hansard, June 1, 1988.
6. Supreme Court of the United States, *Varity Corp. v. Howe et al.* (94–1471), 516 U.S. 489, March 19, 1996.
7. Advertisement in *The Expositor*, October 11, 1952.
8. MMMC architects, with Reid and Deleye, and Vicano Construction.

9. "Insiders, Outsiders," *The Expositor*, November 8, 2000.

Chapter 15: The Mohawk Connection
1. See M.L. Skolnik, "Articulation Between CAATs and Universities in Ontario: Issues, Problems and Prospects," in G. Jones ed. *Higher Education Group Annual*, Vol.1 (1990), 32–48.
2. The other two were the University of Guelph-Humber and The York-Seneca Institute for Science, Technology and Education.
3. Wendy Stanyon, "College University Collaboration: An Ontario Perspective," in *College Quarterly*, Vol. 6, No. 1 (2003). Available at *www.senecac.on.ca/quarterly/2003-vol06-num01-fall/stanyon.html*. Behind the scenes, the leadership of the COU was fundamentally opposed to collaboration. One of the key figures told me they had decided that they could best thwart it by talking a great deal about it and the ways in which it might operate, instead of actually pursuing it. Within the college system, the result has, in some cases, been college collaborations with universities outside the province, often in the United States.
4. For two studies of the Laurier Brantford experience, see Timothy Gawley and Rosemary McGowan, "Learning the Ropes: A Case Study of the Academic and Social Experiences of College Transfer Students within a Developing University-College Articulation Framework" and "The University Side of the College Transfer Experience: Insights from University Staff," in *College Quarterly*, Vol. 9, No. 3 (Summer 2006).

5.   About 20,000 students. See the website of The Ontario Federation of Teaching Parents, *www.ontariohomeschool.org/FAQ.html#howmany*.

6.   Ontario Hansard, April 26, 2001, 1420. Available at *www.ontla.on.ca/hansard/house_debates/37_parl/session2/ L005.htm#P602_136954*.

7.   Ontario Ministry of Education, "Policy/Program Memorandum No. 131," released June 17, 2002. Available at *www.edu.gov.on.ca/extra/eng/ppm/131.html*.

8.   See "From Kitchen Table to University Campus; Secondary Schools Welcome Graduates of Home Schooling," *Ottawa Citizen*, October 23, 2007, A1.

Chapter 16: Courting Nipissing

1.   Within a few years of the establishment of a Brantford education program, some faculty on the Waterloo campus complained that the university built a teacher-training program at Brantford rather than Waterloo. It was ironic that this was done precisely because their campus had rejected the idea when the president had first proposed it. Ironically, this "Brantford envy" gave Rosehart the impetus he needed to acquire Laurier's own Faculty of Education, which was accomplished in 2007.

2.   For details of the calculations, see the Nipissing University website, *www.nipissingu.ca/100/history.html*.

   Nipissing summarizes the history as follows:

   The original North Bay Normal School opened its doors in September 1909, after the Ontario government, concerned about the quality of rural education, built four normal schools to increase the supply of qualified teachers in the province. Identical buildings, featuring an Italian Renaissance design, were built in Hamilton, Stratford, Peterborough and North Bay. In 1953, the normal school was renamed the North Bay Teachers College. On September 1, 1973, Nipissing University College and the North Bay Teachers' College were integrated, with the teacher's college becoming the Faculty of Education, and relocated to brand new facilities at the Education Centre, also the new home of St. Joseph's School of Nursing, and Cambrian College (the precursor to Canadore College). Nipissing University, received its charter as an independent degree granting university on December 10, 1992.

   A major research on the North Bay Normal School is currently underway. Available at *www.nipissingu.ca/ICSOH/currentprojects_NBNS.html*.

3.   "To the Head of the Class," *The Expositor*, January 16, 2002.

4.   Edmund Cockshutt was known for philanthropy and his love of the arts. When Brantford needed a treatment centre for

tuberculosis and opened the Brant Sanatorium in 1913, Edmund provided substantial funding and donated two hectares of land. He helped found and/or support social organizations such as the Social Service League and the YMCA. But his most enduring legacy came following his death in 1956 at the age of 95, when he donated his home and gardens to the city for an arts centre, known today as the Glenhurst Art Gallery.

5.   Alexander Temporale & Associates Ltd., "Victoria Park Square Study" (1991) *Brantford Heritage Inventory*, quoted in the 58 Market Street entry, *mail.brantford.ca/inventory.nsf*.

6.   Richard Beales, "TD Canada Trust Gives Empty Building to Laurier Brantford," *The Expositor*, December 1, 2001.

7.   Temporale et al., "Victoria Park Study."

Chapter 17: Working with Vicano

1.   Patchen Barss, "A New Model in the Liberal Arts," *University Affairs*, Vol. 43, (May 2002), 20–23.

2.   "Holstein Breeders' Association Secures Old Post Office from City for $28,000," *The Expositor*, March 9, 1920.

3.   "Old Brantford Post Office Gets New Life," *Toronto Star*, February 28, 2004, M14.

Chapter 18: Building Community

1.   Laurier Brantford, "A Strategic Plan for Laurier Brantford," October 30, 2002, 9.

2.   Information on journalism applications is available from the Ontario University Application Centre (OUAC), which tracks all university applications in the province, *www.ouac.on.ca/news/uapp/underappstats.html*.

3.   Patricia Treble, "Crunching the Crime Numbers," *Maclean's*, Vol. 121, No. 11 (March 12, 2008). Available at *www.macleans.ca/article.jsp?content=20080312_162114_5536*.

4.   Robert C. Allen, "The Employability of University Graduates in the Humanities, Social Sciences, and Education: Recent Statistical Evidence," Discussion Paper No. 98-15, 6. Department of Economics, University of British Columbia (August 1998). Available at *www.econ.ubc.ca/dp9815.pdf*.

Chapter 19: The Odeon

1.   "Letter to the Editor," *The Expositor*, January 14, 2000.

2.   "Curtain Rises Friday on City's Newest and Most Modern Theatre," *The Expositor*, December 16, 1948.

3.   *Ibid.*

Chapter 20: A Change of Status

1.   "Arrogant, noble, principled, devout, courageous, and legendary, a warrior and a sell-out — in such contradictory terms did the Six Nations of Grand River use to describe Joseph Brant or Thayendanegea, as he was called by the Mohawks" by Tom Hill, "Brant: A Six Nations Perspective" in Valerie Greenfield and Tom Hill, *Portraits of Thayendanegea, Joseph Brant*. (Burlington: Burlington Cultural Centre, 1993), 33.

2.   Michael-Allan Marion, "On the Record:

City Needs to Know Laurier's Plans," *The Expositor*, December 29, 2003.

Chapter 21: Finding a Middle Way

1. Dave Harrison, "Downtown Building Destruction Opposed," *Brant News*, November 22, 1978.
2. "Developer-Lawyer Defends Proposals," *Brant News*, November 22, 1978.
3. I am grateful to John Quinn for comments and research on these origins. See Paul Dilse, "John Turner and English Architectural Influence in Southern Ontario," in *SSAC-SEAC Journal*, Vol. 10, No. 3 (September 1985), 3–7 (Society for the Study of Architecture in Canada), and Warner, Beers, & Co., 507. The latter is available at *brantford.library.on.ca/genealogy/pdfs/warners1883.pdf*, accessed August 31, 2009.
4. Warner, Beers, & Co., 507.
5. Michael-Allan Marion, "Laurier Proposes Five-Storey Building for Classes, Students," *The Expositor*, December 9, 2003.

Chapter 22: The Wilkes House

1. On John Liberty Wilkes, see Arthur H. Cash, *John Wilkes: The Scandalous Father of Civil Liberty*. (New Haven: Yale University Press, 2006).
2. Warner, Beers, & Co., 263.
3. Reville, 100.
4. Warner, Beers & Co., 338.
5. John Robertson, *History of the Brantford Congregational Church, 1820 to 1920*.
6. *Brantford Telegram*, Christmas Edition, 1888, 21; available on the BPL website, *brantford.*

library.on.ca/genealogy/pdfs/1888telegram.pdf.
7. Reville, 313.
8. "The Petition of Henry Moyle, Esquire of the Township of Brantford, in the County of Brant," 1st Session, 4th Parliament, 1853. CIHM/ICMH Microfiche series, No. 22419.
9. Many thanks to Liz Rhodes for providing this photograph.
10. I erroneously made this suggestion at a public meeting, before I checked with the Bell Homestead and discovered the mistake. Though I have repeatedly tried to correct the misidentification, it has acquired a life of its own, and threatens to become an integral part of the lore of the Wilkes House.
11. Thanks to Wayne Hunter for pointing this out to me.

Chapter 23: A Temple and a Clubhouse

1. For information on the history and activities of the Odd Fellows, see the website of The Sovereign Grand Lodge of the Independent Order of Odd Fellows, *www.ioof.org*.
2. For an early account of the various lodges and societies in Brantford, see Warner, Beers, & Co., 300–07.
3. John Merriman, "New Hall for City Oddfellows," *Brant News*, May 18, 1984, 36.
4. The first addition was the second floor in 1877, the second was a new conservatory and east verandah in 1906, the third was the Odd Fellows Ballroom, erected in 1932.
5. Brantford Heritage Inventory, entry on 119–121 Dalhousie, *mail.brantford.ca/inventory.nsf*.
6. City of Brantford, "Community Development

Committee Minutes," Wednesday, May 22, 2002, 4:30 p.m. Available at Brantford City Hall.

Chapter 24: The Wilkes House Reborn
1. Terry Pender, "Heritage Comes at a Cost; Those Hoping to Preserve Older Buildings Could Hinder Push to Revitalize Downtown," *The Record* (Kitchener-Waterloo), June 23, 2005.
2. The dance team earned silver at the American Dance Awards' University Cup in 2005.

Chapter 25: The BPL — A Brantford Icon
1. Erica Olsen, "Why You Should Fall to Your Knees and Worship a Librarian," *Librarian Avengers*, July 13, 2005, available at *librarianavengers.org/worship-2*.
2. *Ibid*. She adds: "And they will kick the crap out of anyone who says otherwise."
3. See Pamela Haley, "The Scarlet 'P': Public Librarians in the World of Academe," *COLAJ: Canadian Online Library and Archives Journal*, Vol. 1, No. 1 (2006). Available at *library.queensu.ca/ojs/index.php/colaj/article/viewFile/559/736*, accessed June 15, 2009.
4. For an account of a collaboration that illustrates the inherent tensions but also the possibilities, see the account of the Dr. Martin Luther King Jr. Library, a joint project of the San José public libraries and the library of San José University city: Anne Jordan, "Double Booking: A City and a University Sharing a Library? It's Not Easy, but San Jose Is Doing It," *Governing*, *18* (11), 44–49 (November 2005). Available at *www.governing.com/archive/archive/2005/aug/library.txt*, accessed August 31, 2009.
5. For details of the collaboration between the BPL and WLU, see Virginia Gilham, Wendy Newman, Sophie Bury, Angela Madden, "Wilfrid Laurier University and the Brantford Public Library: A Unique Exercise in Joint Service Provision," Canadian Library Association, *Feliciter 49*, No. 6 (2003).
6. Claudelle Boudreau, "Library Renovation Adds Greatly to Core's Revitalization," *The Expositor*, June 26, 2006.
7. News Release: "Summer Construction: New Back Entrance, Information Commons on the Third Floor and Expanded Service for Main Library," Brantford Public Library, May 12, 2006, *www.brantford.library.on.ca/about*.

Chapter 26: A University Precinct
1. The programming didn't change when the Y (initially a YMCA) went from being a YM/YWCA to back being a YMCA. Rather, the association aligned itself with the YMCA because it wanted to offer programs for girls and boys, men and women at a time when the YWCA decided to focus very specifically on women and girls.
2. The project was carried out with MMMC, Inc. as architects and Vicano Construction as contractors.
3. "General Implementation Plan for Downtown," 13, Policy Planning, Heritage & Special Projects Department, City of Brantford, January 2002.

4. Email from John Starkey, April 20, 2006.

Chapter 27: A New Square

1. "Restoring Our Pride," *The Expositor*, August 9, 2003.
2. Michael-Allan Marion, "Rebuilding the Temple," *The Expositor*, September 4, 2004.
3. Starkey published his charges on a website, *http://starkey.on.ca/*, which he later took down. The David Sharpe article, "Marriages of Convenience," dated Friday, December 2, 2005, is available at *brantford-news-politics. blogspot.com*.
4. "Police Investigate City Grants," John Starkey press release, September 22, 2006.

Chapter 28: The Brantford Centre

1. The Brantford Centre for Postsecondary Education, "Enabling University-College-Community Collaboration: A Response Paper to the Higher Expectations for Higher Education Discussion Paper," Brantford: November 15, 2004.
2. Chris Otis, "Blame McGuinty Gov't," *The Expositor*, April 21, 2006, A5.

    Councillor Starkey had remarked that "What upsets me is the utter failure of the province to support the growth of post-secondary education in this community." See Michael-Allan Marion, "Downtown Education Project Shelved: Province Blamed for Lack of Funding Commitment," *The Expositor*, April 20, 2006, A1.
3. The quote is from the Marion article referred to in note 2, page A1.

4. Christopher Bentley, "Province Does Help Finance City Campus," *The Expositor*, April 28, 2006, A17.

Chapter 29: Silly Season

1. Michael-Allan Marion, "A Keystone of Core's Renewal," *The Expositor*, April 24, 2006, A9.
2. Gerry Van Dongen, "Give Casino Money to Taxpayers," *The Expositor*, March 4, 2006, A11.
3. Horst Stanzlik, "Lots of Questions about Downtown Plan," *The Expositor*, December 18, 2001.
4. Horst Stanzlik, "How Much Has City Given?" *The Expositor*, April 24, 2006.
5. John O'Neill, "A Threat to Colborne Street Projects," *The Expositor*, March 6, 2006, A11.
6. Vern Gale, "Investment Will Pay Back 10-fold," *The Expositor*, January 20, 2002, A7.
7. Adventus Research Inc., "Economic Impact & Benchmarking Analysis of Laurier Brantford & Mohawk College On the City of Brantford, Brant County & Other Local Regions," Final Report, August 11, 2005.
8. Figures for Nipissing were included in the Laurier calculations because Nipissing students also attended Laurier.
9. This included the Mohawk downtown and the Elgin Street campuses.
10. The event began at Brant's Crossing Park, the location where Joseph Brant crossed the river so many years ago. In recognition of its work, the Grand River Conservation Authority

presented the environmental club with a Watershed Honour Roll Award in 2005.

11. An Indigenous Studies program explored First Nations history and culture. The Criminology program initiated research with judges and lawyers. The Leadership program was linked to government, businesses, and local social service agencies. The university provided businesses and residents with opportunities to participate in courses and public lectures, to rent rooms for meetings and events, and the benefit of improved library services for themselves and their children. Members of the university community volunteered and contributed to an ever-expanding and continually evolving list of community organizations: the Brantford Heritage Committee, the Sanderson Centre Board, the YM/YWCA Board, the Board of Y Homes, the Brant Cultural Network, the Glenhyrst Gallery Board, Brant Museum and Archives, the Downtown Business Improvement Association, the Willet and Brant General Hospitals, and the local Farmers' Market.

Chapter 30: A Post–Brant Fordian Community

1. The Johnson and Friel quotes are from: Vincent Ball, "Reformed Downtown Has Its Draws," *Focus on Brant*, *The Expositor*, June 27, 2005.

2. Tim Philp, "Hard to Believe, but Brantford is Booming," *The Expositor*, May 29, 2006, A9.

3. The "town and gown" label was so called because medieval students wore clerical gowns.

4. These quotes are from the Brantford campus's student satisfaction survey — a survey of first and fourth year students — in 2005.

5. Letter to Leo Groarke, from Charlie and Sue Kopczyk, dated February 9, 2007.

6. A handful of Canadian universities have significant philanthropic traditions, but most turned to philanthropy only when public funding began to decline. In 2008, Harvard's twenty-four-billion-dollar endowment was more than twice the accumulated total of all university endowments in Canada, which were valued at less than ten billion dollars. Laurier, with endowments of a paltry twenty million dollars, did not traditionally define itself as an institution built around philanthropy.

7. Some of the most significant donors included the City of Brantford, the County of Brant, the Grand Valley Education Society, many Brantford individuals, locally based companies (S.C. Johnson Canada, Proctor & Gamble, Westcast Industries, Calbeck Investments, Gates Canada, Kuriyama Canada, Davis Fuels, and Millard, Rouse & Rosebrugh) and community organizations (the Brantford Bisons, the Brant Foresters, the Rotary Clubs of Brantford, and the Perpetual Success Foundation).

8. Another example is the Art and Caroline Read Community Lounge, which celebrates the leadership of Art Read, the campus' first dean. It has converted a Carnegie computer lab that had begun its life as the library reading room back into a lounge with historically appropriate chairs and wainscoting, and a refurbished fireplace.

9. See "Post Secondary Accreditation Called Arbitrary," *National Post*, November 6, 2007.

10. These and other projects are discussed in John Lorinc, "Heeding the City's Call," in *University Affairs*, Vol. 47, No. 4 (April 2006), *www.universityaffairs.ca/heeding-the-citys-call.aspx*, accessed August 31, 2009.

Chapter 31: A Future Like the Past

1. See "Greater Brantford Number," *The Expositor*, October 1, 1909, available from the BPL website, *brantford.library.on.ca/genealogy/pdfs/1909expositor.pdf*.

2. For a list of Brant County industries, see the BPL website, *brantford.library.on.ca/genealogy/industries.php*.

| BIBLIOGRAPHY |

Books

Carnegie, Andrew. *Autobiography of Andrew Carnegie*, edited by John Charles Van Dyke. New York: Houghton Mifflin Company, 1920. *www.wordowner.com/carnegie*.

Cash, Arthur H. *John Wilkes: The Scandalous Father of Civil Liberty*. New Haven, CT: Yale University Press, 2006.

Duncan, Sara Jeannette. *The Imperialist*. Ottawa: Tecumseh Press, 1996.

Fogelson, Robert M. *Downtown: Its Rise and Fall, 1880–1950*. New Haven, CT: Yale University Press, 2001.

Groarke, Leo and Rowland Smith. "The Brantford Experiment: A Core Without A Core." In *Reforming Liberal Education And the Core After the Twentieth Century: Selected Papers from the Eighth Annual Conference of the Association for Core Texts And Course*, edited by J. Scott Lee, Darcy Wudel, and Ronald J. Weber. Washington: University Press of America, 2006.

Hill, Bruce Emerson. *The Grand River Navigation Company*. Brantford: Brant Historical Publications, 1994.

Hill, Tom. "Brant: A Six Nations Perspective." In Valerie Greenfield and Tom Hill, *Portraits of Thayendanegea, Joseph Brant*. Burlington: Burlington Cultural Centre, 1993.

The History of the County of Brant, Ontario. Toronto: Warner, Beers, & Co., 1883.

Johnston, C.M. *Brant County: A History 1784– 1945*. Toronto: Oxford University Press, 1967.

McQueen, Rod. *The Eatons: The Rise and Fall of Canada's Royal Family*. Toronto: Stoddart Publishing, 1998.

Muir, Gary. *Images of a City: Brantford 1895–1950*. Brantford: Tupuna Press, 2005.

Paxton, James. *Joseph Brant and His World: 18th Century Mohawk Warrior and Statesman*. Toronto: James Lorimer & Company Ltd., 2008.

Reville, F. Douglas. *History of the County of Brant*, 2 vols. Brantford: Brant Historical Society, 1920; Hurley Printing, 1982 (reprint of the 1920 edition).

Robertson, John. *History of the Brantford Congregational Church 1820–1920*. Renfrew, ON: Renfrew Mercury Printing, 1920. *www.ourroots.ca/page.aspx?id=574071&qryID=b70d93ab-2344-4ba6-971f-eb1ee4359dff*.

Stone, William L. *Life of Joseph Brant-Thayendanegea: Including the Border Wars of the American Revolution, and Sketches of the Indian Campaigns of Generals Harmar, St. Clair, and Wayne, and Other Matters Connected with the Indian Relations of the United States and Great Britain, From the Peace of 1783 to the Indian Peace of 1795*, 2 vols. New York: Alexander V. Blake, 1838.

Wall, Joseph Frazier. *Andrew Carnegie*. New York: Oxford University Press, 1970.

Journals

Barss, Patchen. "A New Model in the Liberal Arts." *University Affairs* 43, No. 5 (May 2002), 20–23.

Bentley, David M. "Humanities for Humanity's Sake." *University Affairs* 41, No. 4 (April 2000). *www.uwo.ca/english/canadianpoetry/artsnew.htm*.

"Canada's 100 Most Important Books." *Literary Review of Canada* 16, No. 1 (January/February 2006), 1–6.

Dilse, Paul. "John Turner and English Architectural Influence in Southern Ontario." *SSAC-SEAC Journal* 10, No. 3 (September 1985), 3–7.

Filion, Pierre and Karen Hammond. "The Failure of Shopping Malls as a Tool of Downtown Revitalization in Mid-size Urban Areas." *Plan* 46, No. 2 (Winter 2006), 49–52.

Filion, Pierre, Heidi Hoernig, Trudi Bunting, and Gary Sands. "The Successful Few." *Journal of the American Planning Association* 70, No. 3 (Summer 2004), 328–43.

Gawley, Timothy and Rosemary McGowan. "Learning the Ropes: A Case Study of the Academic and Social Experiences of College Transfer Students Within a Developing University-College Articulation Framework." *College Quarterly* 9, No. 3 (Summer 2006), *www.senecac.on.ca/quarterly/2006-vol09-num03-summer/index.html*.

Gawley, Timothy and Rosemary McGowan. "The University Side of the College Transfer Experience: Insights from University Staff." *College Quarterly* 9, No. 3 (Summer 2006). *www.senecac.on.ca/quarterly/2006-vol09-num03-summer/index.html*.

Gilham, Virginia, Wendy Newman, Sophie Bury, and Angela Madden. "Wilfrid Laurier University and the Brantford Public Library: A Unique Exercise in Joint Service Provision." *Feliciter* 49, No. 6 (2003), 298–301.

Haley, Pamela. "The Scarlet 'P': Public Librarians in the World of Academe." *COLAJ: Canadian Online Library and Archives Journal* 1, No. 1 (2006). *library.queensu.ca/ojs/index.php/colaj/article/viewFile/559/736*.

Jordan, Anne. "Double Booking: A City and a University Sharing a Library? It's Not Easy, but San Jose Is Doing It." *Governing* 18, No. 11 (November 2005), 44–49. *www.governing.com/archive/archive/2005/aug/library.txt*.

Lorinc, John. "Heeding the City's Call." *University Affairs* 47, No. 5 (May 2006). *www.university-affairs.ca/heeding-the-citys-call.aspx*.

Skolnik, M.L. "Articulation between CAATs and

Universities in Ontario: Issues, Problems and Prospects." In *Higher Education Group Annual* 1, edited by G. Jones. (1990), 32–48.

Stanyon, Wendy. "College University Collaboration: An Ontario Perspective." *College Quarterly*, 6, No. 1 (2003). *www.senecac.on.ca/quarterly/2003-vol06-num01-fall/stanyon.html*.

Newspapers

Ball, Vincent. "Reformed Downtown Has Its Draws." *The Expositor*, June 27, 2005.

Bauslaugh, Cheryl. "Gypsy Production Derailed." *The Expositor*, November 20, 1999.

Beales, Richard. "TD Canada Trust Gives Empty Building to Laurier Brantford." *The Expositor*, December 1, 2001.

Bentley, Christopher. "Province Does Help Finance City Campus." *The Expositor*, April 28, 2006.

"The Best Is Yet to Come." *The Expositor*, October 2, 1999.

Blumenson, John. "Old Brantford Post Office Gets New Life." *Toronto Star*, February 28, 2004.

Boudreau, Claudelle. "Library Renovation Adds Greatly to Core's Revitalization." *The Expositor*, June 26, 2006.

"Canada's Universities Look for Cash." *Economist*, September 17, 1998.

Christmas Edition, 1888, *Brantford Telegram*. *brant-ford.library.on.ca/genealogy/pdfs/1888telegram.pdf*.

Churchill, Jarrett. "Teachers' College Out At Laurier." *The Expositor*, March 29, 2000.

"City's Image Being Reshaped." *The Expositor*,

April 17, 1986.

"Colleen Miller Makes It Happen." *The Expositor*, January 22, 1999.

"Curtain Rises Friday on City's Newest and Most Modern Theatre." *The Expositor*, December 16, 1948.

DeRuyter, Ron. "Campeau Will Build Office Tower in Core with MG as Major Tenant." *The Expositor*, July 3, 1985.

"Developer-Lawyer Defends Proposals." *Brant News*, November 22, 1978.

Freibauer, Caroline. "Moving Mohawk." *The Expositor*, October 4, 1997.

"From Kitchen Table to University Campus; Secondary Schools Welcome Graduates of Home Schooling." *Ottawa Citizen*, October 23, 2007.

Gale, Vern. "Investment Will Pay Back 10-fold." *The Expositor*, January 20, 2002.

Gamble, Susan. "WLU Still Interested in City." *The Expositor*, March 3, 1998.

Gamble, Susan. "WLU Prefers Icomm Campus." *The Expositor*, September 15, 1998.

Gamble, Susan. "Laurier Offers Cash to 'Pioneers': $500 Scholarship Awaits Students Enrolling at City Campus." *The Expositor*, March 18, 1999.

"Greater Brantford Number." *The Expositor*, October 1, 1909.

Harrison, Dave. "Downtown Building Destruction Opposed." *Brant News*, November 22, 1978.

"Holstein Breeders' Association Secures Old Post Office from City for $28,000." *The Expositor*, March 9, 1920.

"Insiders, Outsiders." *The Expositor*, November 8, 2000.

Jiggens, Michael. "Massey House Now Underway."

Brant News, April 23, 1986.

Judd, David. "Let's Move the Museum to the Library." *The Expositor*, June 24, 1989.

"Laurier Enrolment Climbing." *The Expositor*, June 17, 1999.

Lewington, Jennifer. "University Plan Excites Brantford." *Globe and Mail*, June 29, 1998.

"A Library Built to Last." *The Expositor*, December 16, 2002.

"Library Now Open: Large Crowds Inspected New Building Last Night." *The Expositor*, July 5, 1904.

Marion, Michael-Allan. "Laurier Proposes Five-Storey Building for Classes, Students." *The Expositor*, December 9, 2003.

Marion, Michael-Allan. "On the Record: City Needs to Know Laurier's Plans." *The Expositor*, December 29, 2003.

Marion, Michael-Allan. "Rebuilding the Temple." *The Expositor*, September 4, 2004.

Marion, Michael-Allan. "Downtown Education Project Shelved: Province Blamed for Lack of Funding Commitment." *The Expositor*, April 20, 2006.

Marion, Michael-Allan. "A Keystone of Core's Renewal." *The Expositor*, April 24, 2006.

Meen, Elizabeth. "University Plans Rolling Along." *The Expositor*, March 5, 1998.

Meen, Elizabeth. "WLU Campus to Focus on Job Skills." *The Expositor*, November 3, 1998.

Meen, Elizabeth. "Campus 'The Birth of a Vision': Laurier Brantford Predicted To Be Development of the Century." *The Expositor*, October 2, 1999.

Merriman, John. "Public Library Suffers from Success." *Brant News*, June 6, 1979.

Merriman, John. "New Hall for City Oddfellows." *Brant News*, May 18, 1984.

Muir, Gary. "Public Library Born in Controversy." *The Expositor*, October 8, 1980.

Muir, Gary. "Carnegie Building May Get Reprieve from 'Death Row.'" *Brant News*, November 28, 1995.

O'Neill, John. "A Threat to Colborne Street Projects." *The Expositor*, March 6, 2006.

Otis, Chris. "Blame McGuinty Gov't." *The Expositor*, April 21, 2006.

Parker, Cheryl. "Laurier Should Have Teachers' College." *The Expositor*, March 29, 2000.

Pender, Terry. "Heritage Comes at a Cost: Those Hoping to Preserve Older Buildings Could Hinder Push to Revitalize Downtown." *The Record*, June 23, 2005.

Philp, Tim. "Hard to Believe, but Brantford Is Booming." *The Expositor*, May 29, 2006.

"Post Secondary Accreditation Called Arbitrary." *National Post*, November 6, 2007.

"Restoring Our Pride." *The Expositor*, August 9, 2003.

"School of Hard Knocks." *The Expositor*, October 2, 1997.

Special Number, Brantford, 1901. *Industrial Recorder of Canada*, 1.

Stanzlik, Horst. "Lots of Questions about Downtown Plan." *The Expositor*, December 18, 2001.

Stanzlik, Horst. "How Much Has City Given?" *The Expositor*, April 24, 2006.

Starkey, John. "Brantford Needs a University." *The Expositor*, September 11, 1997.

"Statement of the Ontario University Chancellors on the Importance of University Education and the Value of the Liberal Arts." *York University Gazetteer Online*, March 8, 2000. *www.yorku.ca/ycom/gazette/past/archive/2000/030800/issue.htm#10.*

"To the Head of the Class." *The Expositor*, January 16, 2002.

Todd, Michael. "Wake Up Call: The Future of Liberal Arts in a Fast-forward World." *Profiles: The York University Magazine for Alumni and Friends*, November 1998. *www.yorku.ca/ycom/profiles/past/nov98/current/cover/cover2.htm.*

Treble, Patricia. "Crunching the Crime Numbers." *Maclean's*, March 12, 2008. *www.macleans.ca/article.jsp?content=20080312_162114_5536.*

"University Boom a Boon to Brantford, WLU Expert Says." *The Expositor*, March 18, 1999.

Van Dongen, Gerry. "Give Casino Money to Taxpayers." *The Expositor*, March 4, 2006.

"Vast Sums Are Being Expended for New Buildings in City of Brantford This Year." *The Expositor*, July 5, 1904.

"WLU's Brantford Campus Welcomes 140 Students." *Record*, October 2, 1999.

Reports

Adventus Research Inc. "Economic Impact & Benchmarking Analysis of Laurier Brantford & Mohawk College On the City of Brantford, Brant County & Other Local Regions." Final Report. Guelph: August 11, 2005.

Alexander Temporale & Associates Ltd. "Victoria Park Square Study." Compiled for the City of Brantford, 1991.

Allen, Robert C. "The Employability of University Graduates in the Humanities, Social Sciences, and Education: Recent Statistical Evidence." Discussion Paper 98-15. Vancouver: Department of Economics, University of British Columbia, 1998, *www.econ.ubc.ca/dp9815.pdf.*

The Brantford Centre for Postsecondary Education. "Enabling University-College-Community Collaboration: A Response to the Higher Expectations for Higher Education Discussion Paper." Brantford: November 15, 2004.

Brantford Young Ladies College. *Sixteenth Annual Calendar of the Brantford Young Ladies College.* Brantford: The Expositor Book and Job Printing House, 1890. *66.207.114.162/genealogy/pdfs/LadiesCollege1890.pdf.*

City of Brantford. "General Implementation Plan for Downtown." Policy Planning, Heritage & Special Projects Department, January 2002.

Laurier Brantford. *A Strategic Plan for Laurier Brantford.* Brantford, 2002.

Moyle, Henry. *The Petition of Henry Moyle, Esquire of the Township of Brantford, in the County of Brant*, 1st Session, 4th Parliament, 1853. Ottawa: Canadian Institute for Historical Microreproductions, 1984 (CIHM/ICMH Microfiche series; no.22419).

Szmigielski, Walter J.J. "An Historical Investigation of Trends in Post-Secondary Education in Brant County 1784–1933." (Assisted by Kathleen Pickard, supervised by Jack Herron). Council on Continuing Education for Brantford and Brant County, May 1979.

United States Supreme Court. *Varity Corp. v. Howe et al.* (94–1471), 516 U.S. 489 (March 19, 1996).

Websites

Brantford Heritage Inventory. *mail.brantford.ca/ inventory.nsf*.

Brantford Public Library. Digital Archives. http:// brantford.library.on.ca/genealogy/digital.php.

Lloyd, Eric. "Brantford Bids Final Farewell to the Old Downtown." June 12, 2008. *www.brantford.com*.

Mohawk College. *www.mohawkcollege.ca*.

Nipissing University. *www.nipissingu.ca*.

Olsen, Erica. "Why You Should Fall To Your Knees and Worship a Librarian." *Librarian Avengers*, July 13, 2005. *librarianavengers.org*.

The Ontario Federation of Teaching Parents. *www. ontariohomeschool.org*.

Six Nations Lands and Resources. "Six Nations Land Claim Summaries (Basis & Allegations)." *www. sixnations.ca/LandsResources/ClaimSummaries. htm*.

Legislative Assembly of Ontario Hansard. *www.ontla. on.ca/web/house-proceedings/house_current.do*.

Ontario Ministry of Training, Universities and Colleges. *www.edu.gov.on.ca*.

The Internet Movie Database. *www.imdb.com*.

The Sovereign Grand Lodge of the Independent Order of Odd Fellows. *www.ioof.org*.

Wilfrid Laurier University. *www.wlu.ca*.

Winter, John. "Memorable Moments in Ontario Retailing." *www3.sympatico.ca/john.winter/home.htm*.

| INDEX |

| ABOUT THE AUTHOR |

LEO GROARKE, Principal of the Brantford campus of Wilfrid Laurier University, has been the senior administrator of the campus since 2000. He has studied at the University of Calgary, Simon Fraser University, the University of Helsinki, and the University of Western Ontario, and received a Ph.D. in Philosophy from Western in 1982. He has published many articles on the history of ideas, the theory of argument, social issues, peace and conflict, visual argument, and the role of higher education in contemporary society. His previous books include *Greek Scepticism* (McGill-Queen's), *Good Reasoning Matters!* (Oxford, with Christopher Tindale), and *The Ethics of the New Economy* (WLU Press).

Courtesy of Wilfrid Laurier University.

OF RELATED INTEREST

BELLEVILLE: A Popular History
Gerry Boyce

978-1-55002-863-8 / $18.99

Belleville, on the shores of the Bay of Quinte, traces its beginnings to the arrival of the United Empire Loyalists. For thirty years the centre of the present city was reserved for the Mississauga First Nation but the new town quickly became an important lumbering, farming, and manufacturing centre. This is a personal history of Belleville, based on Gerry Boyce's half-century of research.

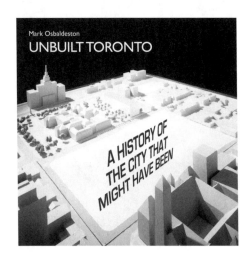

UNBUILT TORONTO: A History of the City that Might Have Been
Mark Osbaldeston

978-1-55002-835-5 / $26.99

Unbuilt Toronto explores never-realized building projects in and around Toronto, from the city's founding to the twenty-first century, delving into unfulfilled and largely forgotten visions for grand public buildings, landmark skyscrapers, highways, subways, and arts and recreation venues. Featuring 147 photographs and illustrations, many never before published, *Unbuilt Toronto* casts a different light on a city you thought you knew.

Available at your favourite bookseller.

DUNDURN
www.dundurn.com

Tell us your story!
What did you think of this book?

Join the conversation at
www.definingcanada.ca/tell-your-story
by telling us what you think.